• MASTERING THE BASICS •

Desserts

MURDOCH BOOKS

• MASTERING THE BASICS •

Desserts

Basics to Brilliance
Techniques, Tips and Trusted Recipes

MURDOCH BOOKS

Contents

Introduction 7
Basics 9

Custards and Batters 37
Fruit Desserts 61
Cold Desserts 85
Hot Puddings 123
Dessert Cakes and Cheesecakes 141

Conversion charts 154
Index 156

Introduction

Desserts provide the perfect 'full stop' to a meal, whether you're after a soul-warming pudding, the refreshing tang of a frozen dessert or the sheer indulgence of a rich chocolate concoction. *Mastering the Basics: Desserts* has a sweet ending to complement any main course, from creamy, vanilla-scented baked custard to melt-in-the-mouth peach pie, classic Italian tiramisu to cooling mango sorbet, comforting steamed golden-syrup pudding with lashings of pouring custard to an impressive hazelnut and chocolate meringue torte. Backed up by a comprehensive 'Basics' chapter with useful information about ingredients and equipment, as well as fundamental techniques for dessert making, this collection of over 60 recipes, all accompanied by step-by-step photography, provides the perfect sweet finish for every occasion.

Basics

Common ingredients

Butter is the most commonly used fat when making desserts. It adds flavour, shortness/tenderness and colour. When it is beaten, air is incorporated which, in turn, helps leaven baked goods as they cook. It can also be rubbed into flour or melted and mixed with other ingredients. Unsalted butter is sweeter than salted and gives you more control over the amount of salt in your desserts — you can then add as much as you want. If you are creaming butter, make sure it is softened by standing at room temperature for 30–60 minutes (depending on the room temperature) before using. If rubbing into dry ingredients, make sure it is well chilled.

Cocoa powder is simply the unsweetened ground powder made from grinding the cocoa solids when the cocoa butter (the fat) is removed from cocoa beans. Make sure you sift it before using to remove any lumps. Sweetened cocoa powder is sold as drinking chocolate. Dutch cocoa is considered the best quality cocoa powder, having a rich and intense flavour and a dark colour.

Cream is used extensively in dessert making. The fat content of cream determines how rich it is and also its whipping characteristics — the higher the fat content, the easier it will be to whip and the thicker it will be when whipped (low-fat cream won't whip at all). Double (thick/heavy) cream has a 48 per cent butter fat content and is the thickest type of cream. Pouring cream, also known as whipping or single cream, has a fat content of 35 per cent. Thickened cream, also known as whipping cream, is pouring cream with gelatine added to thicken it slightly and make it more stable. It is ideal for whipping. Sour cream adds a pleasant acidity, as well as richness, to dishes.

Eggs enrich, give structure, bind, lighten, tenderise and add flavour to desserts. Store them, pointed end down, in their original carton in the refrigerator. Always bring eggs to room temperature before using — if you're short on time, you can put them in a bowl of lukewarm water for 10 minutes. All of the recipes in this book use 59/60 g (2¼ oz) eggs.

Flour is used extensively in dessert making and provides the basic structure for the majority of baked desserts. Self-raising flour is simply plain (all-purpose) flour with baking powder added. You can make your own by adding 2 teaspoons baking powder to every 150 g (5½ oz/1 cup) plain flour. Sift them together several times before using.

Gelatine is used in many chilled desserts to help them hold their shape. It is a tasteless ingredient and is available in both powdered and leaf (sheet) form. See pages 138–39 for more information about gelatine.

Mastering the Basics: Desserts

Honey and golden syrup are used to sweeten desserts. Honey should be selected to suit the type of dessert, such as a delicate floral honey to sweeten a panna cotta. Golden syrup is invaluable in rich hot puddings, tarts and sweet sauces.

Milk forms the basis for many desserts, such as ice creams and baked and stirred custards. Always use full-fat milk unless otherwise specified in the recipe. Buttermilk, a cultured milk, adds a subtle acidity to baked desserts and batters such as pancakes.

Oil is mostly used in dessert making to deep-fry or pan-fry. The oils used generally have a mild flavour, such as sunflower, vegetable and light and regular olive oils.

Sugar adds sweetness, flavour, moisture and tenderness. There are several types of sugars and the most widely used in dessert making is white — granulated, caster (superfine) or icing (confectioners'). Granulated is the most commonly available, but caster sugar, with its fine grains that dissolve quickly, is a better choice for most desserts. Icing sugar is powdered white sugar and is available as pure icing sugar or icing sugar mixture, which has a little cornflour (cornstarch) added to prevent it forming lumps. Brown sugar, sometimes called light or soft brown sugar, is fine, granulated sugar with molasses added to enrich the flavour. Dark brown sugar has even more molasses added. If you want to substitute brown sugar for white, or vice versa, measure out the same weight (grams or ounces), rather than volume (cups).

Vanilla is used in various forms. Natural vanilla extract and vanilla essence are concentrated flavours derived from vanilla beans. Buy pure essence or extract and avoid those labelled with 'artificial' or 'imitation' as they don't contain any real vanilla. Thick vanilla bean paste is also available and offers a convenient way of adding vanilla seeds to desserts. If using vanilla beans, wash and dry the pod thoroughly after use and place it in a container of sugar to subtly flavour it.

Basics 11

Equipment

Measuring

Careful, accurate measuring, whether by weight or volume, is essential for success when making desserts, especially for those that are going to be baked. Always use one set of measurements when preparing a recipe — metric (ml) or imperial (fl oz) by weighing, or measuring by volume (cups).

Measuring cups are used to measure dry or non-liquid ingredients. They are generally available in plastic or metal and in sets of 60 ml (2 fl oz/¼ cup), 80 ml (2½ fl oz/⅓ cup), 125 ml (4 fl oz/½ cup) and 250 ml (9 fl oz/1 cup) measures. Spoon the ingredient into the cup until heaped, then, without compressing it, run a flat-bladed knife across the top to level. All cup measures in this book are level, not heaped.

Measuring jugs are used to measure liquids. Look for a glass or see-through jug with clear markings and a good spout. A small, heatproof jug is particularly helpful when dissolving gelatine.

Measuring spoons are used to measure small amounts of both dry and liquid ingredients. They are available in sets that generally include a ¼ teaspoon, ½ teaspoon, 1 teaspoon and 1 tablespoon. One teaspoon equals 5 ml in volume. Tablespoons, however, can come in either 15 ml (½ fl oz/3 teaspoon) or 20 ml (½ fl oz/4 teaspoon) volumes. This book uses 20 ml tablespoons. Check your tablespoon volume and if you are using a 15 ml tablespoon, add an extra teaspoon for every tablespoon of the ingredient specified in the recipe. This is particularly important for ingredients such as baking powder and bicarbonate of soda (baking soda). All tablespoon and teaspoon measures in this book are level — use a flat-bladed knife to level ingredients, as for cup measures.

Scales, electronic versions in particular, are the most accurate way of measuring dry ingredients, such as flour or sugar, and non-liquid, soft ingredients, such as yoghurt or jam. Electronic scales are now affordable and are an invaluable addition to your kitchen. Most give metric and imperial weights, and let you switch between the two. They may also let you 'zero' the reading so you can measure several ingredients in the same bowl one after another, which is handy for one-bowl mixes.

Mixing

Bowls are fundamental to dessert making and it is important to have a good selection of sizes. Stainless-steel bowls are versatile and durable and are good conductors of heat and cold. Ceramic and glass bowls are sturdy and are also suitable for heating and melting ingredients. Plastic bowls aren't a good choice for mixing as they absorb flavours and become greasy over time.

Electric mixers offer an easy, efficient way to cream butter and sugar, whisk egg whites and combine batters.

Hand-held electric beaters have detachable beaters and sometimes whisk attachments, and a range of speeds. They are relatively inexpensive, store easily and can be used to whisk or beat mixtures. They are also needed if whisking or beating a mixture over a saucepan of simmering water. However, they aren't suitable for heavy-duty mixing, such as for bread doughs, and are not as efficient as the stand versions.

Electric stand mixers are mounted on a stand, as the name suggests, with a bowl that fits into the stand. They usually have a range of attachments such as a beating paddle, whisk and dough hook. They have a range of speeds, like hand-held beaters, but their motors are more powerful and therefore able to cope with larger and thicker mixtures.

Food processors are invaluable when dessert making, from finely chopping or grinding nuts to mixing batters and making pastry.

Again, buy the best quality food processor you can afford, and ensure it has a large bowl. A separate **mini food processor** that will efficiently cope with small quantities of nuts and spices is also a good investment.

Ice-cream machines are worthwhile kitchen appliances if you are going to regularly make ice cream, sorbet or gelato. There are three main types of ice-cream machines available: free-standing electric machines that have an inbuilt stirring and freezing mechanism (the most expensive of the options and generally with the largest capacity); free-standing churns that have a removable bowl surrounded by a chemical refrigerant that is frozen before using; and stand mixer ice-cream attachments with a bowl (also surrounded by a chemical refrigerant). All of them have a paddle that automatically stirs and aerates the mixture while also

Mastering the Basics: Desserts

scraping the sides of the bowl, preventing ice crystals forming and keeping the mixture smooth while it freezes.

Saucepans, frying pans and crepe pans are used for everything from pan-frying fruit to deep-frying fritters, cooking crepes and pancakes, making caramel, cooking stirred custard, syrups and sauces, and poaching fruit. Have a selection of different sizes for a variety of uses. A heavy frying pan with a heatproof handle is perfect for making tarte tatin as it can be used on the stovetop and in the oven.

Bakers' friends

Baking beads are small re-usable ceramic or metal weights that are used when blind baking pastry. You can use dried beans or uncooked rice instead, but proper weights are handy.

Cake testers are thin metal or bamboo skewers. Metal ones are available from kitchenware stores and some supermarkets and are the best option as they won't leave large holes. The skewer is inserted into the centre of a cake and if it's cooked, it will be clean when withdrawn (unless otherwise stated in the recipe). Some recipes, such as rich chocolate dessert cakes, specify that crumbs will cling to the skewer.

Kitchen blowtorch This is a must if you are passionate about your crème brûlée and creating a perfectly crisp caramel topping with ease. They are relatively inexpensive and can be bought from speciality kitchenware stores.

Large metal spoons are useful for folding dry ingredients into a mixture or folding in whisked egg whites without losing the incorporated air.

Oven thermometers are important kitchen gadgets. Not all ovens are calibrated and are likely to be at least a couple of degrees out. 'Hot spots' are also common. A thermometer will allow you to check if your oven is accurate and adjust the temperature if necessary. Move the thermometer around in the oven when set at the same temperature and note the reading to check if you have any 'hot spots'. There is no need to remove it from your oven between oven uses.

Palette knives can be bought in various sizes and degrees of flexibility. They have a thin flat blade with a rounded end that makes them useful for loosening cakes and puddings from tins and for spreading icing (frosting) and fillings.

Pastry brushes have natural, nylon or silicone bristles and are used to glaze tarts with sugary mixtures, wash down the side of a saucepan to dissolve sugar crystals when making caramel, brush butter onto filo pastry and grease cake tins. Make sure you wash and dry them thoroughly before storing. Avoid cheaper brushes as they tend to shed their bristles.

Rolling pins should be straight, solid and long enough to roll out a full quantity of pastry or dough without marking the surface with the ends. A good size is about 45 cm (17¾ inches) long and 5 cm (2 inches) in diameter. Wood is preferable to ceramic or marble, as it can hold a fine layer of flour on its surface that will help prevent the pastry or dough sticking. The best ones are made of hard wood with a close grain and very smooth finish. Clean it by wiping with a damp cloth — never immerse a wooden rolling pin in water.

Sieves are used to sift flour to help incorporate air, to combine ingredients evenly, such as flour and unsweetened cocoa powder or baking powder, and to dust flour onto a work surface before rolling out pastry.

Spatulas are used for folding and combining mixtures and scraping mixtures from bowls, blenders and food processors. They can be made of silicone, rubber or plastic. Silicone and rubber ones are more flexible, however rubber ones tend to absorb colours and flavours more readily.

Whisks are used to incorporate air into a mixture, remove lumps and combine liquid mixtures, such as eggs and melted chocolate. They come in all shapes and sizes — a large and small wire balloon whisk will usually cover all required tasks.

Wooden spoons are used to mix, beat and stir. They are particularly good for mixtures being heated in a saucepan, such as sauces and sugar syrups, and 'heavier' mixtures that require stirring or beating.

Cutting and grating

Graters come in many different shapes and sizes, from the traditional box grater to rasp-shaped Microplanes. They have various perforations of different sizes designed for specific uses, from finely grating citrus zest and nutmeg to coarsely grating chocolate. Look for a grater with a variety of perforations or have a couple on hand for different tasks.

Knives An all-purpose cook's knife is handy for chopping ingredients such as chocolate, nuts and dried fruits. A paring knife can be used to trim pastry, cut fruit and make small incisions. A long serrated knife is best for cutting cakes into even layers and slices.

Bakeware

Baking trays Choose the largest trays that will fit in your oven and make sure they are solid so they don't buckle. Have two or more trays so you can cook a few batches at once.

Cake tins come in various sizes, shapes and finishes. They are not only used for baking cakes, but are also effective when freezing frozen desserts and moulding chilled desserts. It is important to use the size and shape specified in the recipe.

All the cake tins in this book have been measured at the base. If a cake tin is marked with a diameter measurement, always measure it to ensure it's correct (there are spring-form tins available, for example, that are incorrectly marked).

Charlotte moulds are special bucket-shaped metal moulds with gently sloping sides and small handles that help make unmoulding easy. Although they are used specifically for making the classic dessert of the same name, you can also use them for baked puddings and soufflés.

Dariole moulds and ramekins are mostly available in metal or ceramic form and are used to make individual frozen, chilled and baked desserts. Flexible plastic dariole moulds are great for chilled desserts as they make unmoulding easier.

Muffin tins are mainly used in dessert making for individual puddings. They generally come in three sizes — Texas or large (250 ml/9 fl oz/1 cup), medium (80 ml/2½ fl oz/⅓ cup) and mini (20 ml/¾ fl oz/1 tablespoon).

Ovenproof dishes are used to cook oven-baked puddings in, and also to make a water bath for delicate desserts that need gentle cooking (roasting pans can also be used for this).

Pie and tart (flan) tins come in a range of shapes, sizes, depths and finishes. They often don't need greasing before using as the pastry's high butter content prevents it sticking. Tart tins with removable bases ('loose-based') are often used as they allow tarts to be removed easily. Like all cake tins, pie and tart tins should be cleaned in

14   Mastering the Basics: Desserts

hot soapy water and dried thoroughly (preferably in a low oven) before storing.

Pudding basins are generally used for steamed puddings and are available in ceramic or earthenware form, as well as metal. Metal basins often come with a handy lid that clips into place, while the ceramic or earthernware basins need to be sealed tightly with foil before steaming your pudding.

Spring-form tins have a removable base that is released when a sprung latch on the side is opened. You will need to use a spring-form tin when making delicate cakes, such as flourless ones, or cheesecakes that can't be upturned onto a wire rack. Make sure the latch is strong so the base and side fit snugly together — this will prevent any leaking. Turning the base upside down before locking it in place will create a base without a lip, which will make removing the cake easier.

Ovens

Not all ovens cook in the same way so it is important to get to know your oven and make your own adjustments to recipes if necessary. Even when an oven is accurately calibrated its temperature may be slightly out. Use a good-quality oven thermometer to monitor the temperature regularly and make sure the seals are in good order to prevent heat escaping.

Fan-forced or convection ovens, which use a fan to circulate the heat, cook at a higher temperature and more quickly than conventional ovens. The recipes in this book have been tested in conventional ovens — if cooking in a fan-forced oven, reduce the oven temperature by 20°C (68°F) and check regularly towards the end of cooking as the time may need to be reduced by 10–20 per cent.

When baking in a conventional oven place cakes, baked desserts and puddings in the centre of the oven. If you have two cakes or multiple desserts in the oven at once, make sure there is plenty of room between them to allow the heat to circulate evenly.

Basics 15

Pâte sucrée and sweet shortcrust pastry

A very high butter content and the addition of egg yolk gives pâte sucrée and sweet shortcrust pastry their characteristic melt-in-the-mouth texture and rich flavour. These pastries aren't difficult to master, but there are a few basic rules to note when making them. The pastry should be kept as cool as possible at every stage of the process — if it becomes too warm at any point, the finished result will be heavy and greasy. The pastry will also become difficult to work with if it becomes too warm. As with all pastries, care must be taken not to overwork it when mixing and rolling out or it may shrink and toughen during cooking. Always rest the finished pastry in the refrigerator before rolling it out and again when it is in the tin(s) before baking. This assists in preventing shrinkage and toughening of the pastry.

1 Rub in the butter using your fingertips, with your palms facing upwards so you can lift and aerate the flour mixture.

2 Use a flat-bladed knife to gradually incorporate the liquid ingredients into the dry ingredients until a coarse dough forms.

3 Knead the dough lightly, just a few times, until it is smooth.

4 Shape the dough into a disc and wrap in plastic wrap.

Pâte sucrée

PREPARATION TIME 10 minutes
(+ 30–45 minutes chilling)

MAKES enough to line a shallow 24 cm (9½ inch) fluted tart (flan) tin or four 8 cm (3¼ inch) fluted tart tins

....

250 g (9 oz/1⅔ cups) plain (all-purpose) flour
½ teaspoon salt
110 g (3¾ oz/½ cup) caster (superfine) sugar
150 g (5½ oz) unsalted butter, cut into 1.5 cm (⅝ inch) cubes and left at room temperature for 10 minutes
3 egg yolks, lightly whisked

1 Sift the flour and salt together into a large bowl. Stir in the sugar. With your palms facing upwards, use your fingertips to rub in the butter, lifting the flour mixture up as you rub to aerate it, until the mixture resembles fine breadcrumbs *(pic 1)*.

2 Make a well in the centre of the dry ingredients. Add the egg yolks and use your fingertips to gradually incorporate until a coarse dough forms.

3 Turn the dough out onto a lightly floured, cool work surface. Quickly and lightly knead the dough to distribute the butter and eggs evenly, until it is smooth *(pic 3)*.

4 Shape the dough into a disc and then wrap in plastic wrap *(pic 4)*. Refrigerate for 30–45 minutes to rest before rolling out and using as desired.

VARIATION

Chocolate pâte sucrée: Reduce the flour to 225 g (8 oz/1½ cups). Sift 30 g (1 oz/¼ cup) unsweetened cocoa powder with the flour and salt.

Sweet shortcrust pastry

PREPARATION TIME 10 minutes
(+ 30 minutes chilling)

MAKES enough to line a shallow 24 cm (9½ inch) fluted tart (flan) tin, four 8 cm (3¼ inch) fluted tart tins or 24 patty pan holes

....

225 g (8 oz/1½ cups) plain (all-purpose) flour
30 g (1 oz/¼ cup) icing (confectioners') sugar
½ teaspoon salt
125 g (4½ oz) chilled unsalted butter, cubed
1 egg, lightly whisked
Chilled water (optional)

1 Sift the flour, icing sugar and salt together into a large bowl. With your palms facing upwards, use your fingertips to rub in the butter, lifting the flour mixture up as you rub to aerate it, until the mixture resembles fine breadcrumbs *(pic 1)*.

2 Make a well in the centre. Add the egg and use a flat-bladed knife to gradually incorporate until a coarse dough forms, adding a little water if necessary *(pic 2)*.

3 Press the dough together — it should be soft, but not sticky. Turn it out onto a lightly floured, cool work surface and lightly knead a few times, until the dough is smooth *(pic 3)*.

4 Shape the dough into a disc and then wrap in plastic wrap *(pic 4)*. Place in the refrigerator for 30 minutes to rest before rolling out and using as desired.

VARIATIONS

Almond shortcrust pastry: Replace 75 g (2¾ oz/½ cup) of the flour with 50 g (1¾ oz/½ cup) almond meal and reduce the butter to 100 g (3½ oz).

Brown sugar shortcrust pastry: Replace the icing sugar with 60 g (2¼ oz/⅓ cup, lightly packed) brown sugar.

TIP Both pastries can be made up to 3 days in advance and stored, wrapped in plastic wrap, in the refrigerator. Set aside at room temperature to soften slightly before rolling out. Uncooked pastry can be frozen, wrapped well in plastic wrap and then sealed in a freezer bag, for up to 4 weeks. Place it in the refrigerator to thaw completely, rather than leaving it out at room temperature.

Making sweet shortcrust pastry in a food processor

PREPARATION TIME 10 minutes
(+ 30 minutes chilling)

MAKES enough to line a shallow 24 cm (9½ inch) fluted tart (flan) tin or four 8 cm (3¼ inch) fluted tart (flan) tins

....

225 g (8 oz/1½ cups) plain (all-purpose) flour
30 g (1 oz/¼ cup) icing (confectioners') sugar
½ teaspoon salt
125 g (4½ oz) chilled unsalted butter, cubed
1 egg, lightly whisked
Chilled water (optional)

1 Put the flour, icing sugar, salt and butter in a food processor and process until the mixture resembles coarse breadcrumbs *(pic 1)*.

2 Add the egg and use the pulse button to process briefly until the dough just starts to cling together, adding a little water if necessary *(pic 2)*.

3 Press the dough together — it should be soft, but not sticky. Turn it out onto a lightly floured, cool work surface and lightly knead a few times, just until the dough is smooth.

4 Shape the dough into a disc and then wrap in plastic wrap. Place in the refrigerator for 30 minutes to rest before rolling out and using as desired.

Rolling out pastry

1 Remove the pastry from the refrigerator and, if necessary, set aside at room temperature for 20–30 minutes or until it is slightly pliable so it can be rolled out easily. Lightly flour a rolling pin and work surface (preferably a cool one, such as a slab of marble, to prevent the pastry becoming too warm). Always roll from the centre of the pastry out to the edges and in the same direction, turning the pastry regularly to ensure it is rolled evenly and doesn't stick to the work surface. Roll until the pastry is the desired thickness, usually 3–5 mm (⅛–¼ inch) *(pic 1)*.

2 It is not necessary to grease a tart (flan) tin when baking sweet shortcrust pastry, even if it's not a non-stick one, as the high butter content in the pastry will prevent it sticking. The easiest way to transfer the rolled dough to the tin is to carefully, and loosely, roll it around the rolling pin and lift it over the tin, then carefully unroll it *(pic 2)*. If you are using small individual tins, cut a suitable-sized portion of the dough before rolling it around the rolling pin.

3 Use your fingers to carefully press the pastry into the base and side of the tin, making sure it is pressed right into the base edge *(pic 3)*.

4 Use the rolling pin to roll over the top of the tin to trim the excess pastry *(pic 4)*. Alternatively, use a small sharp knife to cut outwards along the edge of the tart to trim any excess pastry.

Mastering the Basics: Desserts

1 Process the flour, icing sugar, salt and butter until the mixture resembles coarse breadcrumbs.

2 Add the egg and use the pulse button to process briefly until the dough just starts to cling together.

1 Always roll from the centre of the pastry out to the edges and in the same direction. Turn the pastry often to ensure it's rolled evenly.

2 Carefully and loosely roll the pastry around the rolling pin and lift it over the tin, then carefully unroll it.

3 Use your fingers to carefully press the pastry into the base and side of the tin, making sure it's pressed right into the base edge.

4 Roll the rolling pin over the top of the tin to trim the excess pastry.

Basics

Blind baking

Some pastry shells need to be partially or completely cooked before the filling is added. This is to make them crisp and prevent them becoming soggy once the filling is added. The technique used for this is called 'blind baking'. The uncooked pastry shell is covered with a piece of non-stick baking paper and then filled with ceramic or metal baking beads, dried beans or uncooked rice. The weight of the beads prevents the base from puffing and the sides from slumping during cooking. Whether the pastry is partially or completely cooked will depend on the filling that is being added. Moist fillings that will be baked in the pastry shell (such as baked custard-based fillings or frangipane) require the pastry to be partially cooked. Fillings that won't be baked (such as pastry cream) need to go into pastry shells that have been completely cooked and cooled.

1 Chill the prepared pastry shell until firm — this helps prevent shrinkage during baking. Place the pastry-lined tin on a baking tray. Preheat the oven to 220°C (425°F/Gas 7) or as specified.

2 Take a square of baking paper large enough to cover the base and side of the shell generously. Fold it in half twice, so you end up with a small square. Fold the square in half diagonally to make a triangle, then again to make a thin triangle with a tail. Cut the tail off, then open it out — you should have an octagon about 5 cm (2 inches) larger than the diameter of the tin. Place it inside the pastry shell to cover, pressing it gently into the edge of the tin *(pic 1)*.

3 Fill the pastry shell three-quarters full with baking beads, dried beans or uncooked rice to weigh the pastry down, making sure they reach right to the sides *(pic 2)*.

4 Bake the pastry shell for 10 minutes. Reduce the oven temperature to 190°C (375°F/Gas 5), or as instructed in the recipe, and bake for a further 5 minutes or until the pastry is partially cooked and pale gold. Lift out the paper and weights *(pic 3)*. Use as directed.

5 If cooking the shell completely, return it to the oven and cook for a further 8–12 minutes or until golden and cooked through *(pic 4)*. Set aside on a wire rack until cooled before removing from the tin and filling.

1 Open out the paper octagon and place it inside the pastry shell to cover, pressing it gently into the edge of the tin.

2 Fill the pastry shell three-quarters full with baking beads.

3 Remove the beads from the pastry shell by lifting out the paper.

4 If cooking the shell completely, it needs to be golden and cooked through. Cool it completely in the tin before filling.

Basics 21

Creams, sauces and custard

Chantilly cream

MAKES 500 ml (17 fl oz/2 cups)

300 ml (10½ fl oz) thickened (whipping) cream
2 tablespoons pure icing (confectioners') sugar, sifted
1 vanilla bean, split lengthways and seeds scraped, or 1 teaspoon natural vanilla extract

1 Combine the cream, icing sugar and vanilla seeds or extract in a medium bowl and use a balloon whisk to whisk until soft peaks form. Serve immediately.

VARIATIONS

Orange cream: Add 2 teaspoons orange liqueur (such as Cointreau) to the cream before whisking.

Rosewater cream: Replace the vanilla with ½ teaspoon rosewater.

Chocolate cream: Replace the vanilla with 2 tablespoons sifted unsweetened cocoa powder.

Butterscotch sauce

MAKES 420 ml (14½ fl oz/1⅔ cups)

75 g (2¾ oz) butter
185 g (6½ oz/1 cup, lightly packed) light brown sugar
185 ml (6 fl oz/¾ cup) pouring (whipping) cream

1 Combine the butter, sugar and cream in a small saucepan. Stir over low heat until the sugar dissolves. Bring to the boil, then reduce the heat and simmer for 2 minutes. Serve warm.

Dark chocolate sauce

MAKES 300 ml (10½ fl oz)

150 g (5½ oz) dark chocolate, chopped
30 g (1 oz) chopped butter
185 ml (6 fl oz/¾ cup) pouring (whipping) cream

1 Combine the chocolate, butter and cream in a small heatproof bowl over a saucepan of simmering water (make sure the base of the bowl doesn't touch the water). Stir until the chocolate and butter melt, and the sauce is smooth and well combined. Serve warm.

Chocolate fudge sauce

MAKES about 500 ml (17 fl oz/2 cups)

200 g (7 oz) dark chocolate, chopped
50 g (1¾ oz) butter
185 ml (6 fl oz/¾ cup) pouring (whipping) cream
1 tablespoon golden syrup

1 Combine the chocolate, butter, cream and golden syrup in a small saucepan. Stir over low heat until the chocolate and butter melt, and the sauce is smooth and well combined. Serve hot or warm.

TIP The butterscotch sauce, dark chocolate sauce and chocolate fudge sauce will each keep, in an airtight container in the refrigerator, for up to 4 days. Reheat gently to serve.

Pouring custard

MAKES 330 ml (11¼ fl oz/1⅓ cups)

3 egg yolks
2 tablespoons caster (superfine) sugar
375 ml (13 fl oz/1½ cups) milk
1 vanilla bean, split lengthways and seeds scraped

1 Use a balloon whisk to whisk together the egg yolks and sugar in a medium bowl until well combined.

2 Place the milk and vanilla bean and seeds in a small saucepan over high heat and bring to scalding point (small bubbles will appear around the edge). Stir if a skin starts to form. Remove the vanilla bean, then pour into the egg mixture, stirring with the balloon whisk until well combined.

3 Clean the saucepan and return the custard to the pan. Stir constantly with a wooden spoon over the lowest possible heat, making sure you stir through the middle of the pan and around the edge, where the custard is hottest, so it will cook evenly. Keep the custard below simmering point to prevent it curdling. The custard is ready when it forms a coating on the back of a spoon that you can draw a line through with your finger and which holds its shape.

4 When it is ready, pour the custard quickly through a sieve into a bowl or plunge the base of the pan into chilled water to stop the cooking process. If chilling the custard, lay a piece of baking paper or plastic wrap directly over the surface to prevent a skin forming. If keeping the custard warm, put it in a bowl over a saucepan of hot water. If storing, cover with plastic wrap and refrigerate for up to 2 days.

VARIATION

Rich brandy sauce: Increase the egg yolks to 4 and increase the caster sugar to 110 g (3¾ oz/½ cup). Replace the milk with 500 ml (17 fl oz/2 cups) pouring (whipping) cream and omit the vanilla bean. Stir over low heat for 5–6 minutes, until slightly thickened. Stir 60 ml (2 fl oz/¼ cup) brandy through the sauce before serving. Makes 810 ml (28 fl oz/3¼ cups).

> **TIP** You can replace the vanilla seeds in the custard with 2 teaspoons natural vanilla extract, stirred through the finished custard.
> If the custard curdles a little, remove it from the heat, add a teaspoon of chilled water and beat well. This will prevent further curdling, however it will not make a completely smooth custard.

Crème pâtissiére (pastry cream)

MAKES 660 g (1 lb 7 oz/2⅔ cups)

- 1 vanilla bean, split lengthways and seeds scraped
- 250 ml (9 fl oz/1 cup) milk
- 250 ml (9 fl oz/1 cup) pouring (whipping) cream
- 4 egg yolks
- 150 g (5½ oz/⅔ cup) caster (superfine) sugar
- 2 tablespoons plain (all-purpose) flour
- 1 tablespoon cornflour (cornstarch)

1 Put the vanilla seeds, milk and cream in a medium heavy-based saucepan over medium heat and bring just to a simmer. Remove from the heat.

2 Use an electric mixer to whisk the egg yolks and sugar in a mixing bowl until thick and pale. Sift together the flour and cornflour, then stir into the yolk mixture until smooth and well combined. Pour about half the hot milk mixture onto the yolk mixture and stir until smooth, then stir in the remaining milk. Clean the pan. Return the mixture to the cleaned pan.

3 Stirring constantly with a balloon whisk to prevent lumps, bring the mixture slowly to the boil over medium heat. Reduce the heat and simmer, whisking often, for 2 minutes; the mixture will be thick and smooth. Remove from the heat. Transfer to a glass or metal bowl and place a cartouche (a round of non-stick baking paper) on the surface to prevent a skin forming. Cool to room temperature. Whisk with a balloon whisk until smooth before using as desired. The crème pâtissiére can be refrigerated in an airtight container for up to 2 days.

Basics

Secrets to a successful meringue

Here are the 10 commandments that will ensure your meringues are crisp, light and snowy white every time.

1 Moisture is meringue's greatest enemy. Cool, dry days are best for making meringues, not humid and/or rainy ones. Moisture in the air will prevent them drying completely and can make them 'weep' during or after cooking.

2 Egg whites at room temperature are best for making meringue as they are able to hold more air than cold ones. However, eggs are easier to separate if cold so it is a good idea to separate them straight from the refrigerator, then leave them at room temperature for 30 minutes or so before using.

3 Separate eggs one at a time into a small ramekin and then transfer to the mixing bowl. This way, if a yolk breaks into the white you only lose that one egg, rather than ruining all the whites you've already separated.

4 Always ensure your equipment is totally clean and dry when whisking egg whites. Even a speck of fat, such as egg yolk, or a drop of moisture in the bowl or on the whisk attachment will inhibit the ability of the egg whites to hold air and therefore produce good volume.

5 A pinch of salt or cream of tartar added to the egg whites before beginning to whisk will help stabilise them.

6 When starting to whisk the egg whites, do it slowly on low or medium speed until soft peaks form.

7 Add the sugar a spoonful at a time and then whisk until combined. The sugar should be added gradually, but there is no need to whisk for an extended amount of time after each addition. It doesn't need to be completely dissolved before the next spoonful is added.

8 Once all the sugar has been added, increase the speed to high and whisk for 2–3 minutes, until all the sugar has dissolved and the mixture is very thick and glossy. A long trailing peak will form when the whisk is lifted. The best way to test if the sugar has dissolved is to rub a little of the mixture between your thumb and finger.

9 Don't overwork the mixture. Once the sugar has dissolved and the mixture is thick and glossy, stop whisking. If the mixture is whisked too much, the meringue will collapse during cooking and beads of sugar will form on the surface.

10 Often the oven is preheated at a slightly higher temperature and then reduced once the meringue goes in. The initial higher temperature will set the outside of the meringue and then the lower temperature will dry the mixture out without colouring it.

Basics 25

Caramel

Caramel is used as the foundation of numerous desserts, from rich caramel sauces to brittle nut pralines and for dressing fruit in a crunchy, sweet coating. Follow our step-by-step recipe below for perfect results every time.

Making caramel

1 Combine sugar and water (usually in a 4:1 ratio) in a small saucepan and stir over medium heat until the sugar dissolves. Don't allow it to boil before the sugar is completely dissolved or it will crystallise.

2 Wash down the side of the pan with a pastry brush dipped in water. This will remove any sugar crystals that have formed there. If you leave them, they may cause the mixture to crystallise later.

3 Increase the heat slightly and bring to the boil. Boil the syrup without stirring, as stirring at this stage can also cause the mixture to crystallise.

4 Boil the mixture, washing down the side of the pan occasionally to prevent sugar crystals forming, until it starts to turn a caramel colour. Continue to cook, swirling the pan once or twice, until the caramel is evenly coloured.

5 Watch the syrup closely as it will change colour quickly at this stage. When it's ready it should be a rich caramel colour — the darker the colour, the more intense the caramel flavour will be.

6 When the caramel reaches the desired colour immediately remove the pan from the heat and place it in a sink or large bowl of cold water to stop the cooking process. Allow the bubbles on the surface to subside and then use immediately, as directed.

Making praline

Praline is usually made with the same quantity of nuts (such as almonds or hazelnuts) and sugar. Toasted nuts will give a better final flavour than raw nuts. Praline is usually ground to fine crumbs in a food processor, but it can also be used roughly chopped or broken into shards.

1 Brush a baking tray with a little oil to grease or line with non-stick baking paper. Place the nuts in a single layer on the tray, loosely together.

2 Make the caramel as directed on the opposite page. When the bubbles subside, pour the caramel over the nuts to cover. Set aside until the caramel cools and sets, then break the praline into small pieces.

3 Place the praline pieces in a food processor (working in small batches is best) and use the pulse button to process briefly until the mixture reaches the desired consistency. Use as directed.

Caramel-coated fruits

This is a simple, yet effective, way to dress up berries, cherries, grapes or sliced fruits, to use as a decoration for your desserts. They also make a lovely sweet treat for kids.

1 Make a light caramel as directed on the opposite page. Hold onto the stems of the fruits if possible (this works well for fruits such as grapes), or secure them to a skewer or a fork to make dipping easy. Dip the fruits, one at a time, in the caramel. Allow any excess caramel to drain off and then transfer to a lightly greased wire rack to cool and set.

TIP Take care when making caramel as the concentrated sugar mixture reaches very high temperatures and can cause intense burns. Handle the pan and its contents with care, and never leave the pan unattended or within reach of children.

Nuts

Toasting nuts

Many dessert recipes using nuts require them to be toasted before using — it enhances their flavour and makes them slightly crunchier. Some nuts can be bought 'dry roasted', but it is easy to toast almonds, hazelnuts, macadamias, pecans, pistachios or pine nuts yourself.

1 Preheat the oven to 180°C (350°F/ Gas 4). Spread the raw nuts over a baking tray and cook for 6–10 minutes, shaking the tray occasionally to toast them evenly, until they are aromatic and lightly golden. Coconut can also be toasted this way.

Skinning hazelnuts

After toasting hazelnuts, you will need to remove their papery skins to make them more palatable.

1 Immediately wrap the warm hazelnuts, straight after they have been toasted, in a clean tea towel (dish towel). Rub with the palms of your hands to remove as much of the skin as possible. Open the tea towel and remove any remaining loosened skins with your fingernails.

Making nut meal

Almond meal and hazelnut meal can be bought ready-made, but it takes very little time to grind up a batch of nut meal at home.

1 Place raw or toasted nuts in the bowl of a food processor. If grinding a small quantity, it is best to use a small processor for efficiency. Use the pulse button to briefly process the nuts until they resemble fine, even breadcrumbs. Be careful not to overprocess — the natural oils in the nuts will be released during grinding and if processed for too long the nut meal will turn into a nut butter.

Chocolate decorations

Chocolate curls

TIP Milk chocolate has a higher content of fat solids and is less brittle than dark chocolate, so it is better suited to making curls. Dark chocolate tends to flake when making curls, but it is perfect for making chocolate scrolls and shards (see below).

1 Wrap a strip of non-stick baking paper around a block of chocolate as a barrier between your hands and the chocolate to help prevent it melting while you hold it.

2 Use a vegetable peeler to shave curls from the chocolate (the wider the blade, the larger the curls will be). Catch them on a plate or non-stick baking paper and refrigerate until required. Alternatively, do this directly over the dessert just before serving.

Chocolate scrolls and shards

1 Pour melted chocolate onto a flat, hard surface, such as a baking tray or marble benchtop, then use a palette knife to quickly spread it as evenly as possible until it is about the thickness of thick cardboard. If the chocolate is too thick, it won't roll. Leave the chocolate until almost set.

2 Holding a large sharp knife with both hands, blade facing away from you and on a 45 degree angle, gently and slowly push it along the chocolate to form thin scrolls. You can also use a metal pastry scraper. If the chocolate is warm and hasn't set enough, it will simply stick to the knife or scraper.

3 As the chocolate cools and hardens, shards will form instead of scrolls. If the chocolate hardens too much before you are finished, dip the knife in hot water and then dry it thoroughly before using.

Basics **29**

Preparing mangoes

Peeling mangoes

METHOD 1

METHOD 2

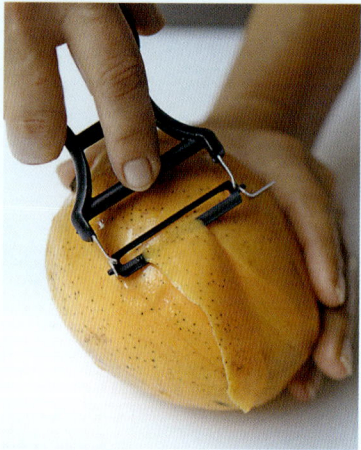

1 Cut a shallow cross in the mango, extending from the base to the stem end.

2 Place one end of the mango on the prongs of a fork. Grip the skin between your thumb and the flat of a knife and gently peel it away down the length of the mango. Repeat with the remaining sections of skin.

1 Use a vegetable peeler (a 'Y' peeler is best) to remove the skin from the mango.

Slicing mangoes

1 Trim the base of the peeled mango slightly and stand it upright. Use a sharp knife to cut the cheeks from either side of the mango and cut or slice as desired. (You can hold the mango with a corn-on-the-cob holder or fork to prevent it slipping.)

2 Place the mango cheeks on a board, cut side down, and cut into thin slices.

3 Either fan the mango slices or curl them together to decorate.

Dicing mango flesh

1 Use a small sharp knife to cut the unpeeled mango, starting at the stem end and slicing downwards on either side of the stone, as close to it as possible. These sides of flesh are often referred to as cheeks.

2 Use the knife to score the cheek flesh in a lattice pattern, cutting through the flesh but not the skin.

3 Holding the cheek in your hands with the flesh facing upwards, use your fingers to push the skin inside out so the cubes of flesh are pushed outwards.

TIP It is hard to cut the flesh remaining on the stone into neat slices. Remove it from the stone, chop and reserve for another use, such as a purée.

If you are scoring the mango cheeks for grilling or pan-frying (see page 74) or turning them outwards to serve as part of a fruit platter, follow steps 1–3 only.

4 Cut the narrow strips of flesh away from the stone, then slice off the skin and cut the flesh into cubes. Take the mango cheeks and cut the cubes of flesh from the skin. Remove the remaining flesh from the stone by cutting around it.

Basics

Preparing and storing stone fruit and berries

Peeling stone fruit is much like peeling tomatoes. Do not leave the fruit in the hot water for any longer than a minute, as it will begin to cook and soften. Plunging the fruit into iced water afterwards will prevent the flesh becoming soft and mushy, and will also help lift the skin from the fruit.

Peeling stone fruit

1 Firm, ripe fruit are the best for peeling. Use a small sharp knife to cut a shallow cross in the base of each piece of fruit and then place in a heatproof bowl.

2 Add enough boiling water to the bowl to cover the fruit, then stand for 1 minute.

3 Drain and place the fruit in a bowl of iced water for 1 minute. The skin will loosen as the fruit stands in the water.

TIP The terms 'clingstone' and 'freestone' are used to describe whether or not the stones cling to the fruit's flesh. Freestone varieties are the best choice when you would like to cut neat slices. If you are unsure, ask your greengrocer for advice on what is available.

4 Peel away the skin, from the cross towards the stem end.

32   Mastering the Basics: Desserts

Frosted fruits

Fruits such as blueberries, small strawberries, redcurrants and raspberries make great decorations for desserts when frosted or dipped in caramel (see page 27).

TIP Frosted fruits will keep in an airtight container in the refrigerator for up to 1 day.

1 Lightly whisk an egg white. Use a fork to dip the fruit, one at a time, in the egg white, then allow any excess to drain away.

2 Roll the fruit in a plate of caster (superfine) sugar to lightly coat and then transfer to a wire rack to dry.

Storing berries

All berries are highly perishable and are best eaten as soon as possible. If you need to store them however, this is the best way to do it.

1 Pick over the berries and discard any that have deteriorated. Place the remaining berries in a single layer on a tray or plate lined with a double layer of paper towels. Cover loosely with plastic wrap and keep in the refrigerator. Berries should not be washed before storing, as water will hasten their deterioration. If necessary, you can rinse them very briefly and then drain on paper towels just before using.

Freezing berries

Berries such as strawberries, raspberries, blackberries, blueberries, mulberries, red, black or white currants, boysenberries and logan berries all freeze well.

1 Spread the fresh berries in a single layer on a freezerproof tray and place in the freezer, uncovered, until frozen. Transfer to an airtight container or freezer bag and return to the freezer. The berries will keep for up to 12 months. Use frozen, as directed, or thaw by spreading in a single layer on a tray lined with several layers of paper towel and refrigerating overnight or until thawed.

Basics 33

Citrus

Making candied citrus zest

An attractive and tasty way to decorate desserts, candied citrus zest can be made using orange, lemon and lime zest. It takes just over an hour to make and all you need is zest, sugar and water.

1 Wash the fruit well, then use a vegetable peeler to remove the zest in long strips.

2 Use a small sharp knife to remove any white pith from the zest.

3 The zest can be left in wide strips or shredded finely lengthways with the knife (try to keep the strips an even thickness).

4 Add the zest to a saucepan of simmering water and cook for 2 minutes — this will remove any residual bitterness. Remove using a slotted spoon and drain well.

5 Combine equal amounts of sugar and water in a small saucepan and stir over low heat until the sugar dissolves. Bring to a simmer, add the citrus zest and simmer for 10 minutes or until the mixture is syrupy and the zest is translucent.

6 Use a fork to remove the zest from the syrup and place on a wire rack. Set aside at room temperature for about 1 hour to drain and dry slightly. Use as desired. Candied citrus zest will keep in an airtight container in a cool, dry place for up to 2 days.

Segmenting citrus

Citrus fruits are sometimes segmented when used in fruit salads and citrus desserts. This is an easy technique to master, and the results are impressive.

1 Use a small sharp knife to remove the skin and pith from the fruit.

2 Cut down the side of a fruit segment, cutting as close to the membrane that divides the segments as possible.

3 Cut down the other side of the segment and remove it. Repeat with the remaining segments until they are all removed.

Removing zest from citrus fruit

Citrus zest can be removed in a number of ways, depending on how it is to be used in a recipe. Take care to only remove the very top layer of zest so you don't include any bitter white pith.

Fine-toothed perforations on box graters and Microplanes will produce very fine, almost powder-like, pieces. To prevent zest getting stuck between the holes, cover the grater with non-stick baking paper before grating.

Fine shredding perforations on box graters and Microplanes are usually used for hard cheeses but will effectively shred citrus zest.

A zesting tool will remove citrus zest in long thin strips, which make great decorations.

Basics **35**

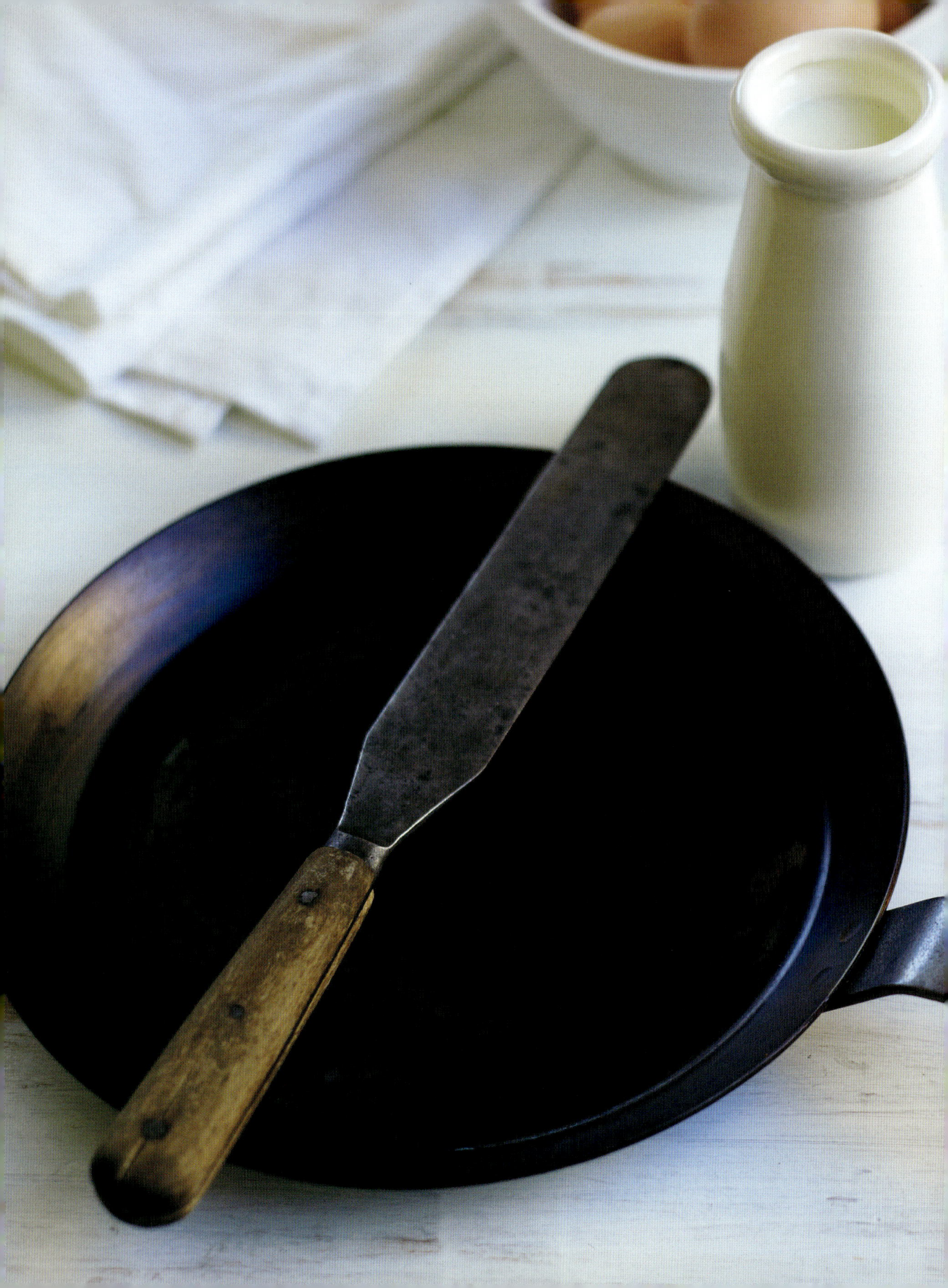

Custards
and Batters

Vanilla baked custard with drunken muscatels

Just one mouthful of this rich and velvety baked custard will transport you back to the family meals of your childhood, though the drunken muscatels anchor it firmly in the grown-up present. Simply omit them or replace with fresh fruit to give your kids a baked custard to remember.

SERVES 6–8 **PREPARATION TIME** 15 minutes (+ 2 hours chilling) **COOKING TIME** 40–45 minutes

750 ml (26 fl oz/3 cups) milk
250 ml (9 fl oz/1 cup) pouring (whipping) cream
1 vanilla bean, split lengthways and seeds scraped
6 eggs, at room temperature
110 g (3¾ oz/½ cup) caster (superfine) sugar

DRUNKEN MUSCATELS
100 g (3½ oz) muscatel raisins
125 ml (4 fl oz/½ cup) Pedro Ximenez or Marsala

1 Preheat the oven to 160°C (315°F/Gas 2–3). Grease a shallow 18 x 25 cm (7 x 10 inch), 1.5 litre (52 fl oz/6 cups) capacity ovenproof dish and place in a large roasting pan.

2 Combine the milk, cream and vanilla seeds in a medium saucepan and bring almost to the boil.

3 Use a balloon whisk to whisk the eggs and sugar in a large bowl until combined. Whisk in the hot milk mixture until combined. Strain into the prepared dish *(pic 1)*. Add enough boiling water to the roasting pan to come halfway up the sides of the dish. Bake for 35–40 minutes or until the custard is set on top but still slightly wobbly in the centre when the dish is lightly shaken. Remove from the oven and set aside to cool *(pic 2)*. Cover and refrigerate for 2 hours or until chilled.

4 Meanwhile, to make the drunken muscatels, combine the muscatels, Pedro Ximenez or Marsala and 2 tablespoons water in a small saucepan. Bring to a simmer over low heat *(pic 3)*. Remove from the heat and set aside for 2 hours to macerate.

5 Serve the baked custard topped with the drunken muscatels and their liquid.

VARIATIONS

Chocolate baked custard: Omit the vanilla seeds and melt 100 g (3½ oz) dark chocolate, chopped, in the hot milk and cream mixture.

Coffee baked custard: Omit the vanilla seeds and replace 80 ml (2½ fl oz/⅓ cup) of the milk with freshly brewed, strong espresso coffee.

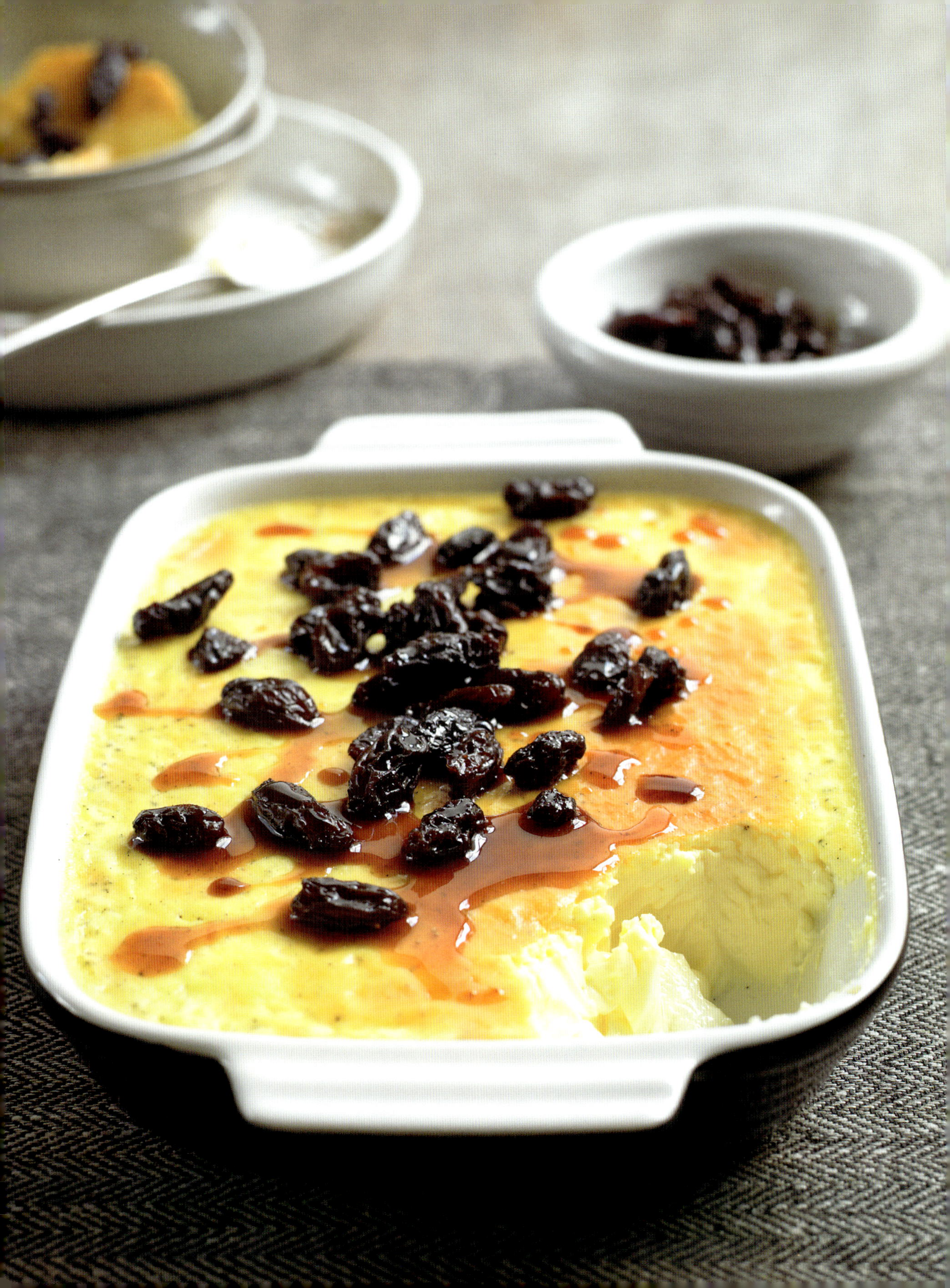

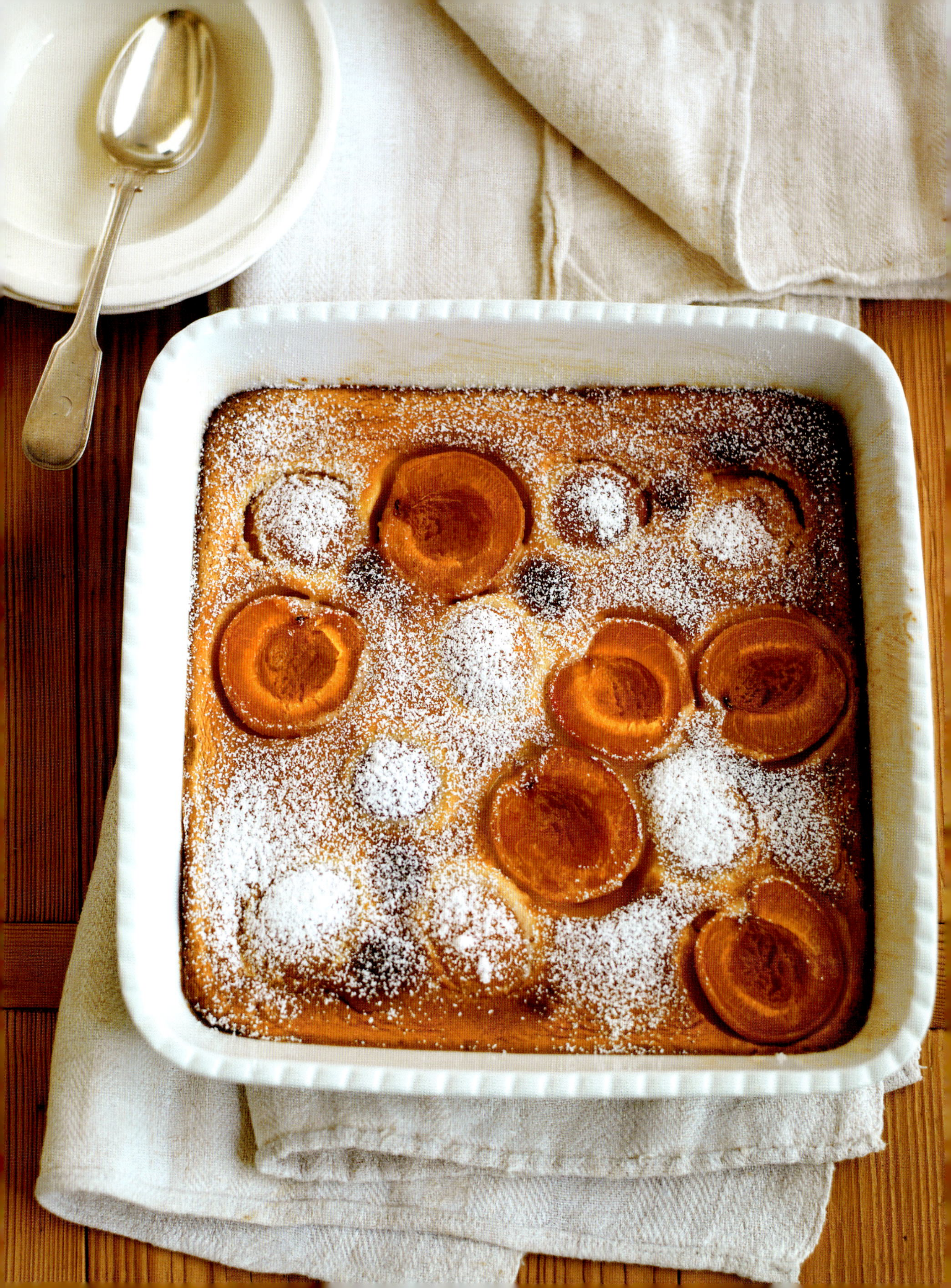

Apricot clafoutis

Hailing from the Limousin region of France, this traditional dessert is a fabulous way to make use of fresh seasonal fruit. Apricots, cherries, peaches, plums and other stone fruit all pair beautifully with the luscious baked custard-like batter. This recipe has almond meal added to the batter for extra richness.

SERVES 8–10   **PREPARATION TIME** 10 minutes   **COOKING TIME** 25–35 minutes

400 g (14 oz) ripe apricots, halved and stoned
1½ teaspoons icing (confectioners') sugar, plus extra, to dust
125 g (4½ oz/1¼ cups) almond meal
220 g (7¾ oz/1 cup) caster (superfine) sugar
2 tablespoons plain (all-purpose) flour
500 ml (17 fl oz/2 cups) pouring (whipping) cream
4 eggs, at room temperature
6 egg yolks, at room temperature

1 Preheat the oven to 180°C (350°F/Gas 4). Grease a square 24 cm (9½ inch), 2 litre (70 fl oz/ 8 cups) ovenproof dish with butter. Place the apricots in the dish, some cut-side up and others cut-side down *(pic 1)*. Sift the icing sugar over the fruit.

2 Put the almond meal, caster sugar and flour in the bowl of a food processor and process for 5 seconds. Add the cream, eggs and egg yolks and process until smooth *(pic 2)*. Transfer to a jug.

3 Pour the batter over and around the apricots in the dish *(pic 3)*.

4 Bake the clafoutis for 25–35 minutes or until puffed, golden and just set in the centre, checking after 20 minutes.

5 Serve immediately, dusted with the extra icing sugar.

TIP This clafoutis can also be made using 400 g (14 oz) cherries, pitted. The cooking time will be the same.

Custards and Batters

Apple crepes

SERVES 4   **PREPARATION TIME** 20 minutes (+ 2 hours standing)   **COOKING TIME** 30 minutes

Thick (double/heavy) cream (optional), to serve

CREPES
150 g (5½ oz/1 cup) plain (all-purpose) flour, sifted
2½ teaspoons caster (superfine) sugar
Pinch of salt
2 eggs, at room temperature, lightly whisked
250 ml (9 fl oz/1 cup) milk
15 g (½ oz) butter, melted and cooled
20 g (¾ oz) unsalted butter, extra

APPLE FILLING
4 jonathan or golden delicious apples
80 g (2¾ oz) unsalted butter, chopped
80 ml (2½ fl oz/⅓ cup) brandy
110 g (3¾ oz/⅔ cup, firmly packed) light brown sugar

1 To make the crepes, put the flour, sugar and salt in a medium bowl and make a well in the centre. Use a balloon whisk to whisk together the eggs, milk and 60 ml (2 fl oz/¼ cup) water. Pour into the well and stir with the whisk to gradually incorporate the flour until a smooth batter forms. Add the melted butter and stir until just combined. Cover with plastic wrap and stand at room temperature for 2 hours. The batter should be the consistency of pouring cream after resting. If it is too thick, whisk in a little more water. Transfer to a jug.

2 Preheat the oven to 120°C (235°F/Gas ½). Line a large baking tray with non-stick baking paper. Heat a 22 cm (8½ inch) diameter (base measurement) crepe pan or non-stick frying pan over low heat. Grease the pan with a small amount of the extra butter. Pour in 60 ml (2 fl oz/¼ cup) of the batter and tilt the pan to spread the mixture evenly over the base of the pan *(pic 1)*. Cook for 1 minute. When there are tiny bubbles on the surface and light golden underneath you should be able to loosen the crepe by shaking the pan *(pic 2)*. Use a large palette knife or egg slice to flip the crepe and cook for a further 1 minute. Transfer to the lined tray. Repeat with the remaining extra butter and batter to make 7–8 more crepes, layering them with non-stick baking paper. Cover the crepes loosely with foil and keep warm in the oven.

4 To make the apple filling, cut the apples into quarters and remove the core. Slice each quarter into wedges about 1 cm (½ inch) thick. Melt half the butter in a large non-stick frying pan over medium heat. Add half the apples and turn to coat with the butter. Cook for 2 minutes or until the apples begin to soften. Add half the brandy, then sprinkle over half the brown sugar. Stir to coat and cook for 1 minute more or until the apples are just tender. Transfer to an ovenproof dish, cover with foil and keep warm in the oven.

5 Lay a crepe out flat and spoon one-eighth of the apple filling onto one-quarter of the crepe *(pic 3)*. Fold into quarters to enclose the filling. Repeat with the remaining crepes and filling. Arrange on serving plates and drizzle with any remaining sauce from the pan. Serve with cream, if desired.

TIP Don't use too much butter to grease the pan, as it can make the crepes too dark and greasy. Just add the butter, then wipe it around the pan with paper towel (use tongs to hold the paper towel so you don't burn yourself).
The apple filling is cooked in two batches so that the apples are not crowded in the pan and do not overcook.

Mastering the Basics: Desserts

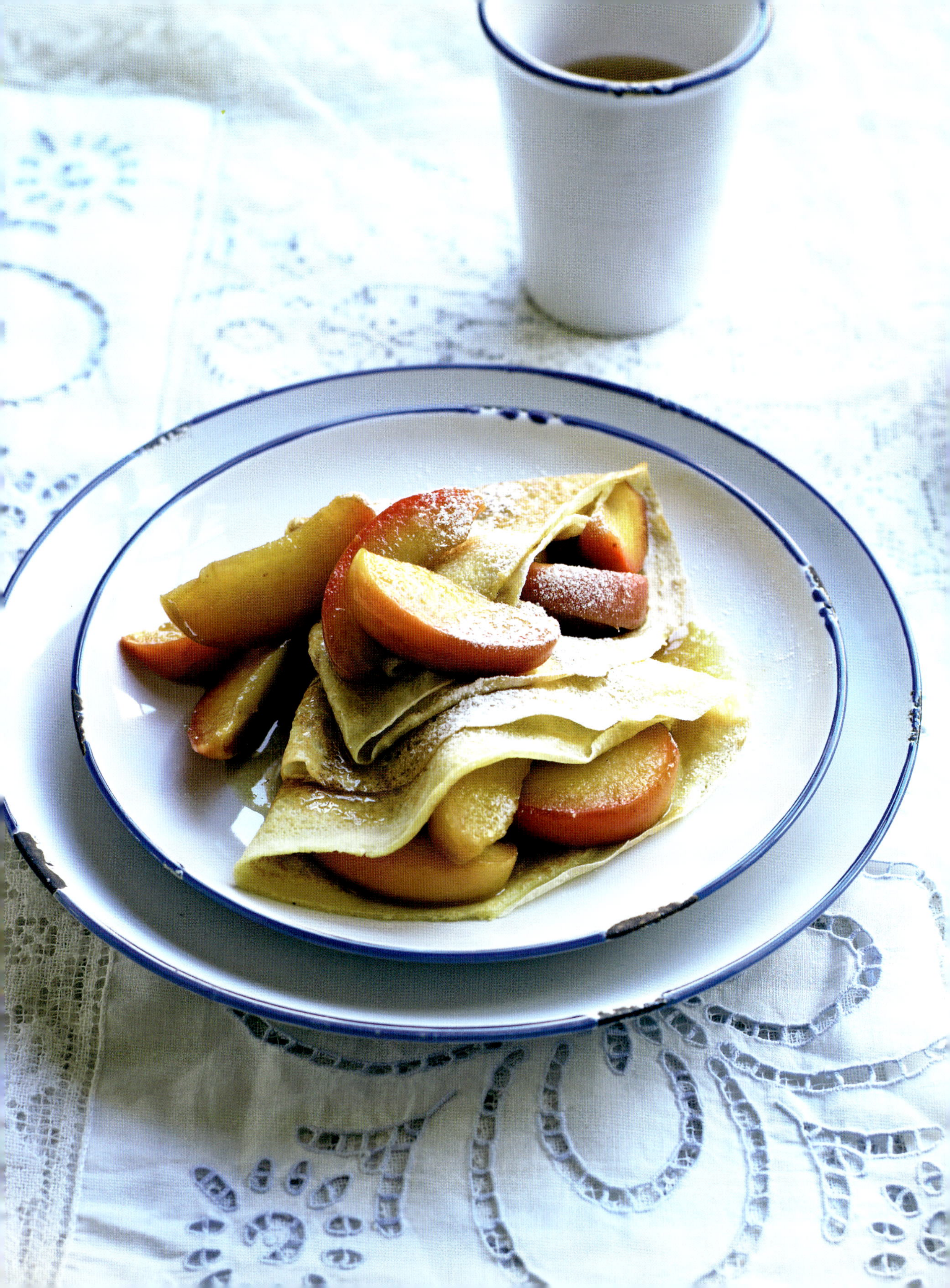

Crepe secrets

Take these tips to heart if you want to produce perfectly cooked crepes with a fine lattice of browning every time.

1 Use a balloon whisk when incorporating the milk and eggs into the sifted dry ingredients — the whisk will be more efficient and gentle in mixing the ingredients together than a wooden spoon. Add the whisked egg and milk in a steady stream and gradually incorporate the flour by stirring with the whisk. Only stir until the ingredients have been combined and a smooth batter forms — over-stirring will cause the crepes to be tough and slightly 'rubbery'.

2 Always stand the batter at room temperature for the recommended time (usually 1–2 hours). Standing the batter allows the starch grains in the flour to soften and expand, resulting in lighter crepes. The batter will thicken slightly while standing and should be the consistency of pouring cream when ready for cooking — if it is too thick, stir in a little more milk or water just before cooking.

3 The best pan to use for making crepes is a heavy-based crepe pan. New crepe pans will need seasoning before using for the first time. To do this, thoroughly wash and dry the pan then add about 5 mm (¼ inch) of vegetable oil to the pan and heat over low heat until the oil starts to smoke. Remove the pan from the heat and set aside to cool completely. Pour out the oil and then wipe the pan with paper towel. The pan is now ready to use. If it's well seasoned, you will need very little butter for greasing the pan when making crepes. If a crepe sticks, rub the pan with a little salt on paper towel to remove any cooked-on batter. Don't ever wash the pan, as then you will need to season it again. Simply wipe it out with a little oil on some paper towel before storing. Non-stick crepe pans are also available — they don't need seasoning and can be washed in hot soapy water.

Mastering the Basics: Desserts

4 Always use butter for greasing the crepe pan before cooking. Oil and margarine can be used but won't give your crepes the characteristic lacy golden pattern and rich flavour that butter will. Heat the pan over medium heat and then either brush the base of the pan evenly with a little butter, or add a knob of butter, swirl the pan to coat lightly, then tip out any excess and wipe over lightly with paper towel. Only grease the pan with more butter when it is needed (when the crepes start to stick). Using too much butter will make the crepes greasy and too dark.

5 When the pan is hot enough (a light haze will form about the pan) quickly add enough batter to just cover the base of the pan (usually about 60 ml/2 fl oz/¼ cup) — it should sizzle immediately if the pan is at the right temperature. Immediately tilt the pan using a rolling action to spread the batter evenly over the base (if there is too much batter in the pan it can be poured back into the jug or mixing bowl).

6 Only cook the crepes until small bubbles form on the surface, the underside looks lacy and the edges begin to curl up slightly.

7 To turn the crepe, loosen the edge with a palette knife and then use your fingers to lift the edge of the crepe and flip it over. Alternatively, use an egg flip to turn the crepe or give a quick flip of the wrist to toss it. Cook the crepe until the other side is cooked — the second side will take less time than the first.

8 Slide the crepe onto a plate and repeat with the remaining batter, stirring the batter and greasing the pan if necessary. To keep the crepes warm, stack them on top of each other as they are cooked (this will keep them moist) with non-stick baking paper between each if you wish, then cover with foil and place in an oven preheated to 120°C (235°F/Gas ½).

Custards and Batters

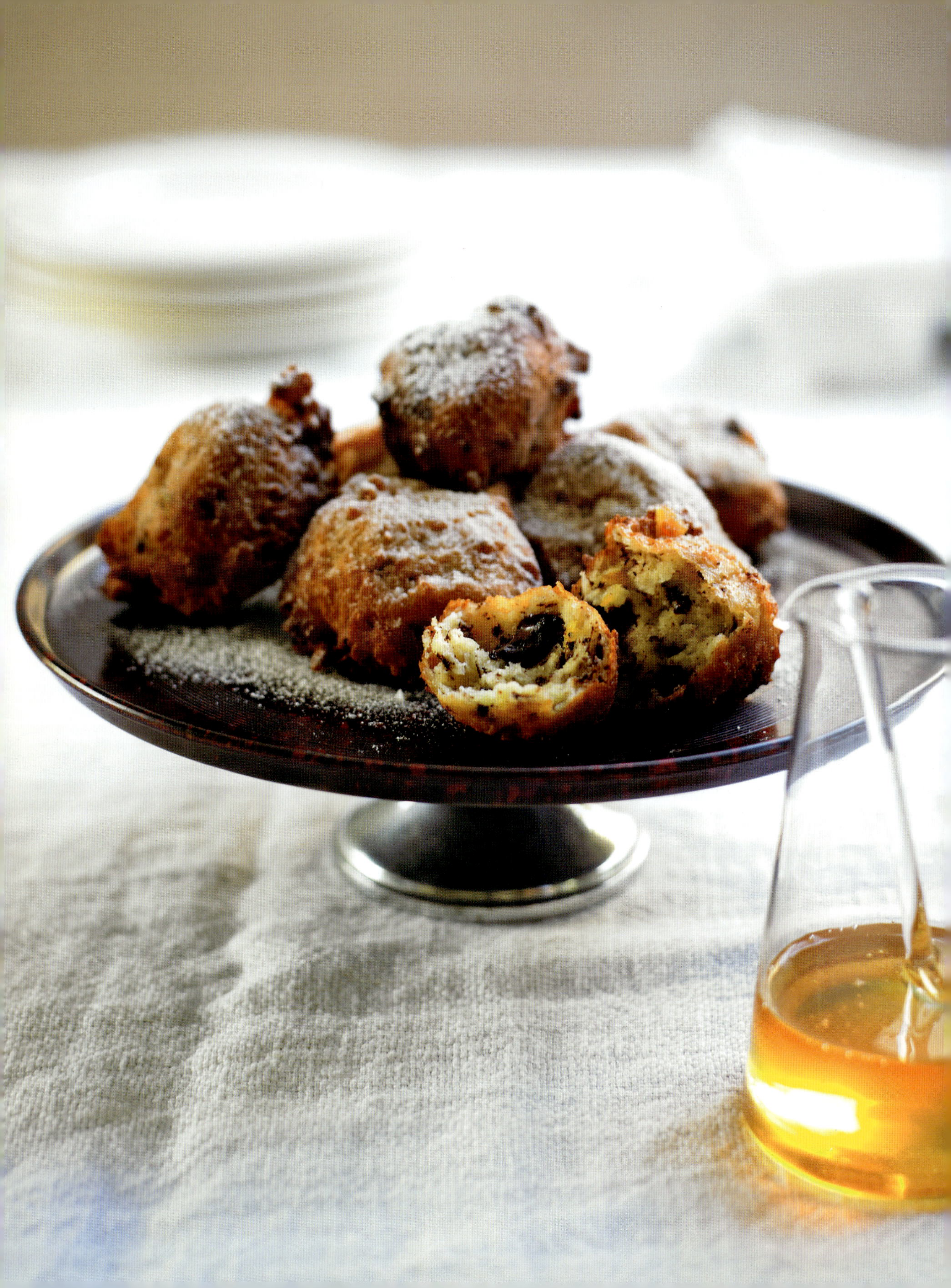

Ricotta fritters

This Italian dessert uses the classic combination of chocolate and orange, which is always a winner. The fritters are very light in texture, yet rich in flavour, and they're particularly more-ish.

SERVES 6 (makes about 18) **PREPARATION TIME** 20 minutes (+ 15 minutes standing) **COOKING TIME** 15–18 minutes

460 g (1 lb ¼ oz/2 cups) firm, fresh ricotta cheese
55 g (2 oz/¼ cup) caster (superfine) sugar
3 eggs, lightly whisked
1 teaspoon natural vanilla extract
50 g (1¾ oz) glacé orange, chopped (see tip)
75 g (2¾ oz) dark chocolate, chopped
125 g (4½ oz) self-raising flour, sifted
Vegetable oil, for deep-frying
Icing (confectioners') sugar and/or full-flavoured honey, to serve

1 Combine the ricotta, caster sugar, eggs and vanilla in the bowl of a food processor and process until the mixture is smooth, scraping down the side of the bowl occasionally. Add the glacé orange and chocolate *(pic 1)* and use the pulse button to process briefly to combine. Add the flour and process until just combined. Transfer to a bowl, cover with plastic wrap and set aside at room temperature for 15 minutes (if the weather is warm, put the batter in the refrigerator).

2 Heat enough oil for deep-frying in a medium saucepan (it should be 7–8 cm/2¾–3¼ inches deep) over medium–low heat until it reaches 170°C (325°F) on a sugar thermometer, or until a cube of bread dropped into the oil turns golden brown in 20 seconds. Line a tray with several layers of paper towel.

3 Slide slightly heaped tablespoons of batter into the hot oil *(pic 2)*. You should be able to cook about 8 fritters at a time, but make sure you don't overcrowd the pan. Cook the fritters, carefully turning them once, for 5–6 minutes or until golden and cooked through *(pic 3)*.

4 Use a slotted spoon to transfer the fritters to the lined tray to drain. Cook the remaining batter in batches, reheating the oil between each batch.

5 Serve immediately, dusted with icing sugar and with honey to drizzle over.

TIP Glacé orange is available from selected delicatessens, gourmet food stores and health food stores.

Custards and Batters

Crepe cake with berries

A clever and sophisticated way to serve crepes, this show-stopping cake is rich and decadent due to the layers of crème pâtissiére and sweet vanilla syrup drizzled over before serving. It's perfect to make for a party as it must be prepared beforehand so there's time to chill it and firm up the layers.

SERVES 10　**PREPARATION TIME** 25 minutes (+ overnight chilling)　**COOKING TIME** 40–45 minutes

940 g (2 lb 1 oz/3¾ cups) crème pâtissiére (see page 23) (see tip)
16 cooked crepes (see page 42) (see tip), at room temperature
250 g (9 oz) strawberries, hulled, large berries halved
125 g (4½ oz) blueberries
125 g (4½ oz/1 cup) raspberries
Icing (confectioners') sugar, to dust

VANILLA SYRUP
110 g (3¾ oz/½ cup) caster (superfine) sugar
½ vanilla bean, split lengthways and seeds scraped
3 wide strips lemon zest

1 Place the crème pâtissiére in a bowl and use a balloon whisk to stir until smooth and spreadable. Place a crepe in the centre of a large, flat serving platter. Use a palette knife to spread with 60 g (2¼ oz/¼ cup) of the crème pâtissiére. Top with another crepe and repeat, spreading each crepe layer with 60 g (2¼ oz/¼ cup) of crème pâtissiére *(pic 1)* and finishing with a crepe. Cover with plastic wrap *(pic 2)* and refrigerate overnight or until the crème pâtissiére is firm. (This is important as otherwise the crepe stack is hard to slice and serve.)

2 Meanwhile, to make the vanilla syrup, combine 125 ml (4 fl oz/½ cup) water with the sugar, vanilla bean and seeds, and lemon zest in a small saucepan. Stir over medium heat until the sugar dissolves. Increase the heat and simmer for 5 minutes or until slightly reduced and syrupy *(pic 3)*. Remove the vanilla bean and lemon zest. Set aside to cool to room temperature. Stir through the berries.

3 Remove the crepe cake from the refrigerator. Top with some of the berries, dust with icing sugar and drizzle with some of the vanilla syrup. Cut into wedges and serve accompanied by the remaining berries and syrup.

TIP You will need to make a double quantity of the crème pâtissiére recipe on page 23 and then measure the required amount.
　You will also need to make a double quantity of the crepe recipe on page 42-45.

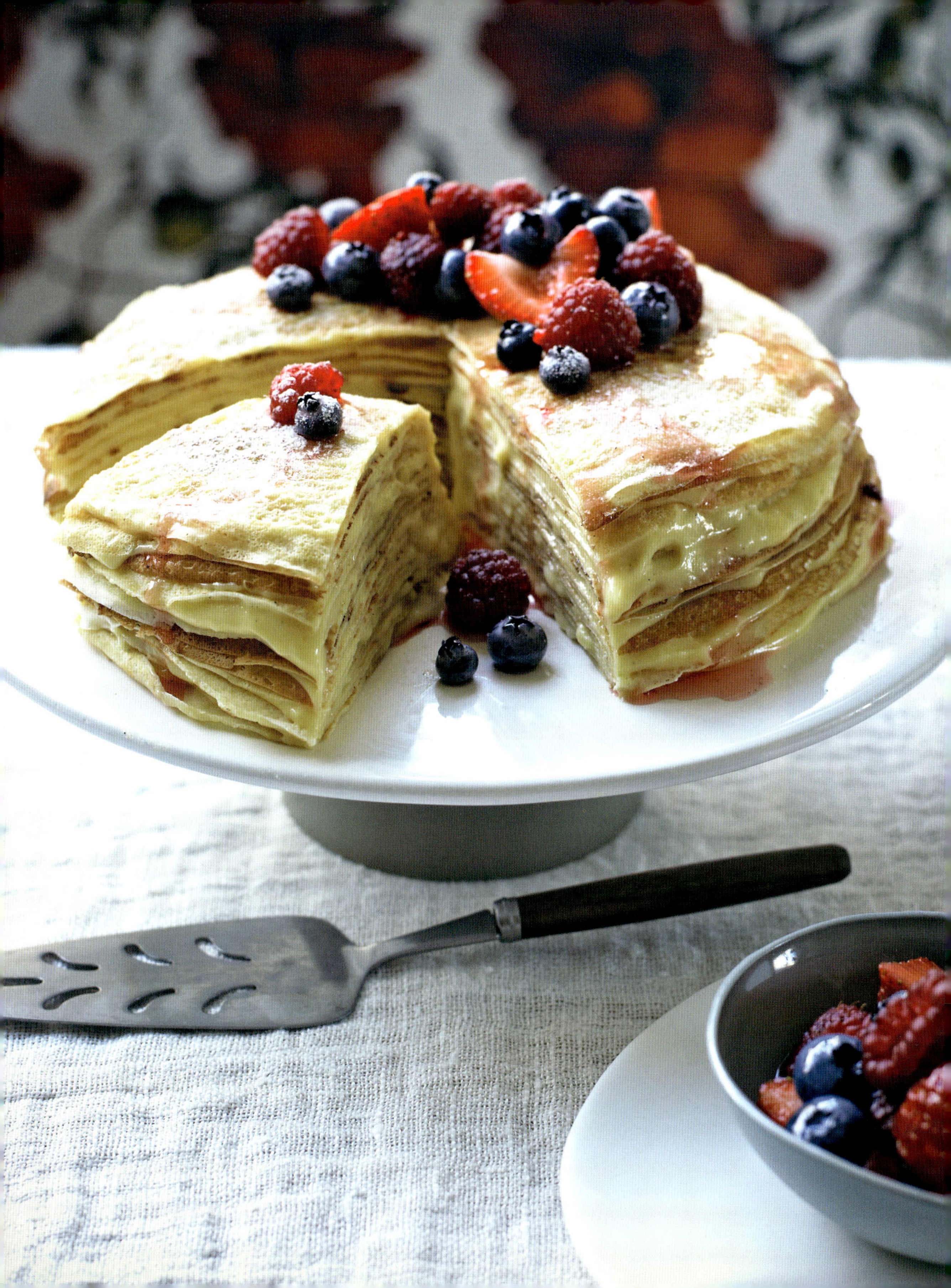

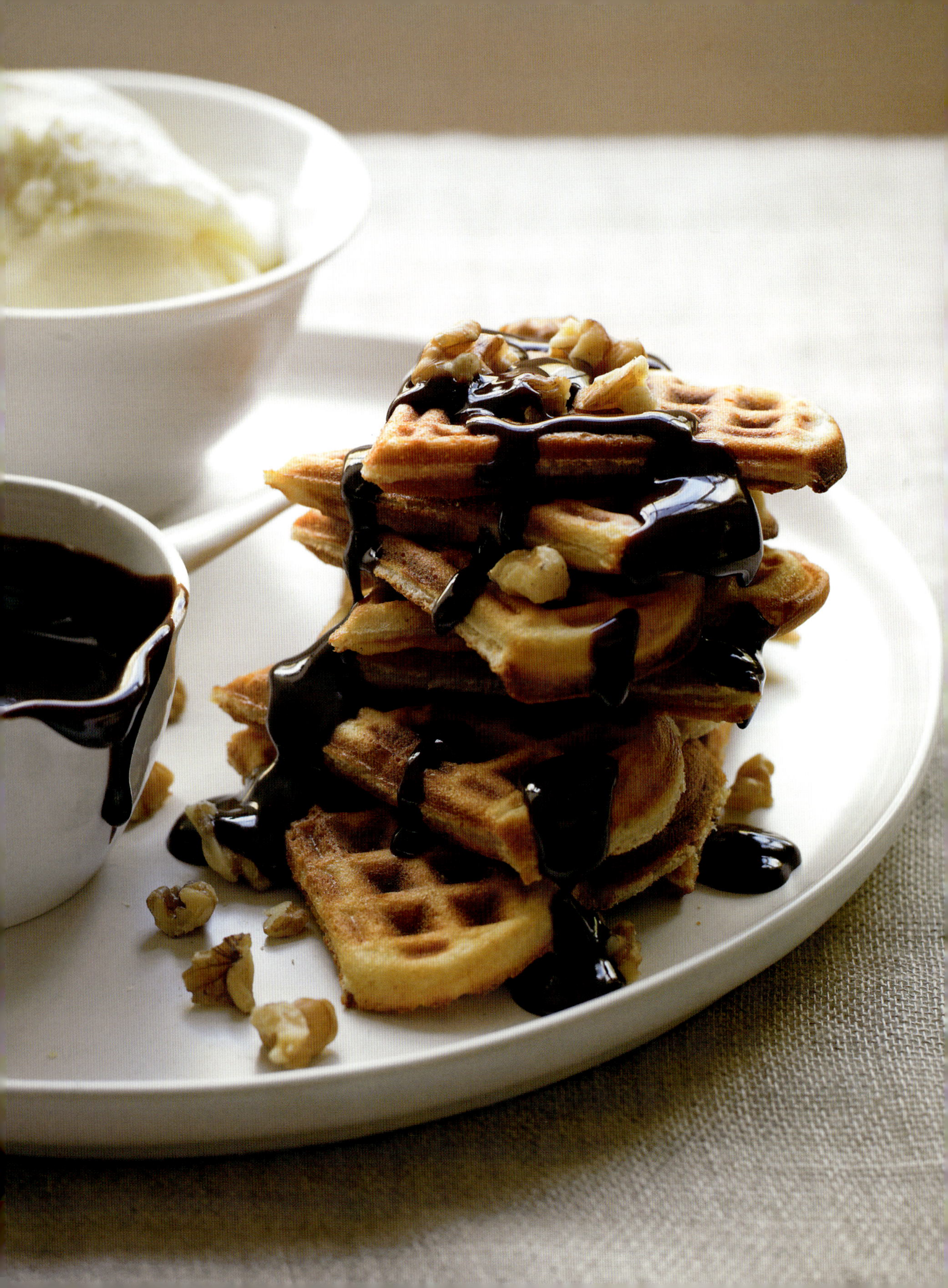

Waffles with chocolate fudge sauce and walnuts

SERVES 6   **PREPARATION TIME** 20 minutes   **COOKING TIME** 40 minutes

260 g (9¼ oz/1¾ cups) plain (all-purpose) flour
1½ teaspoons baking powder
¼ teaspoon salt
75 g (2¾ oz/⅓ cup) caster (superfine) sugar
375 ml (13 fl oz/1½ cups) milk
125 ml (4 fl oz/½ cup) vegetable oil
3 eggs, separated
40 g (1½ oz) butter, melted
1 quantity chocolate fudge sauce (see page 22)
115 g (4 oz/1 cup) walnut halves, coarsely chopped
Vanilla ice cream, to serve

1 Following the manufacturer's instructions, preheat a waffle maker to medium–dark or medium–high setting. Preheat the oven to 70°C (150°F/Gas ¼). Place a wire rack on a baking tray.

2 Sift the flour, baking powder and salt together into a medium bowl. Stir in the sugar until combined. Whisk the milk, oil and egg yolks together in a medium bowl until combined. Use a balloon whisk to whisk the milk mixture into the dry ingredients until just smooth.

3 Use an electric mixer with a whisk attachment to whisk the egg whites in a clean, dry medium bowl until firm peaks form. Use a spatula to gently fold one-third of the egg whites into the batter *(pic 1)*. Add the remaining egg whites and fold until just combined.

4 When the waffle maker is hot enough (see tip), brush both cooking surfaces with a little of the melted butter *(pic 2)*. Pour 125 ml (4 fl oz/½ cup) of the batter into the waffle machine *(pic 3)*, close the lid and cook for 3 minutes or until golden and cooked through. Transfer the waffle to the wire rack on the baking tray and place in the oven to keep warm. Repeat with the remaining melted butter and batter to make 11 more waffles.

5 Drizzle the warm waffles with the hot chocolate fudge sauce, sprinkle with walnuts and serve with vanilla ice cream.

TIP Cooked waffles can be frozen in an airtight container, separated with non-stick baking paper or freezer wrap, for up to 3 months. Thaw and reheat in the toaster.
For sweeter waffles, increase the sugar to 110 g (3¾ oz/½ cup).

Custards and Batters

Banana fritters with lime syrup

Banana and lime are a terrific match and these tropical flavours shine in this remake of an old favourite. The key to the crisp light coating on the bananas is using iced water and rice flour to make the batter.

SERVES 4   **PREPARATION TIME** 20 minutes   **COOKING TIME** 20–22 minutes

160 g (5¾ oz/1 cup) white rice flour
110 g (3¾ oz/¾ cup) self-raising flour
1 teaspoon baking powder
4 firm, ripe medium bananas
Vegetable or peanut oil, for deep-frying
Icing (confectioners') sugar, to dust
Vanilla ice cream (optional), to serve

LIME SYRUP
75 g (2¾ oz/⅓ cup) caster (superfine) sugar
2 tablespoons lime juice
1 kaffir lime (makrut) leaf, very finely shredded (optional)

1 Combine the rice flour, 75 g (2¾ oz/½ cup) of the self-raising flour and the baking powder in a medium bowl and make a well in the centre. Add 500 ml (17 fl oz/2 cups) iced water and use a balloon whisk to stir, gradually incorporating the flour mixture until a smooth batter forms. Set aside for 10 minutes.

2 Meanwhile, to make the lime syrup, combine the sugar, lime juice, lime leaves and 80 ml (2½ fl oz/⅓ cup) water in a small saucepan and stir over medium heat until the sugar dissolves. Bring to a simmer and cook for 3–5 minutes or until thickened slightly. Remove from the heat and set aside to cool slightly.

3 Half-fill a medium saucepan with oil and heat over medium–high heat until the oil reaches 170°C (325°F) on a sugar thermometer, or until a cube of bread dropped into the oil turns golden brown in 20 seconds.

4 Meanwhile, place a wire rack on a baking tray. Cut the bananas into thirds. Place the remaining self-raising flour in a separate bowl. Toss the bananas, one piece at a time, in the flour to coat lightly and then dip in the batter, allowing any excess to drain off *(pic 1)*. Add to the hot oil *(pic 2)*, 4 pieces at a time so you don't overcrowd the pan, and cook for 3–4 minutes, turning often, or until golden brown and crisp. Use a slotted spoon to remove the banana pieces from the hot oil, gently tapping the spoon on the edge of the pan to remove excess oil, and then transfer to the wire rack *(pic 3)*. Repeat with the remaining banana pieces, flour and batter.

5 Serve immediately, drizzled with lime syrup, dusted with icing sugar and accompanied by ice cream, if desired.

Mastering the Basics: Desserts

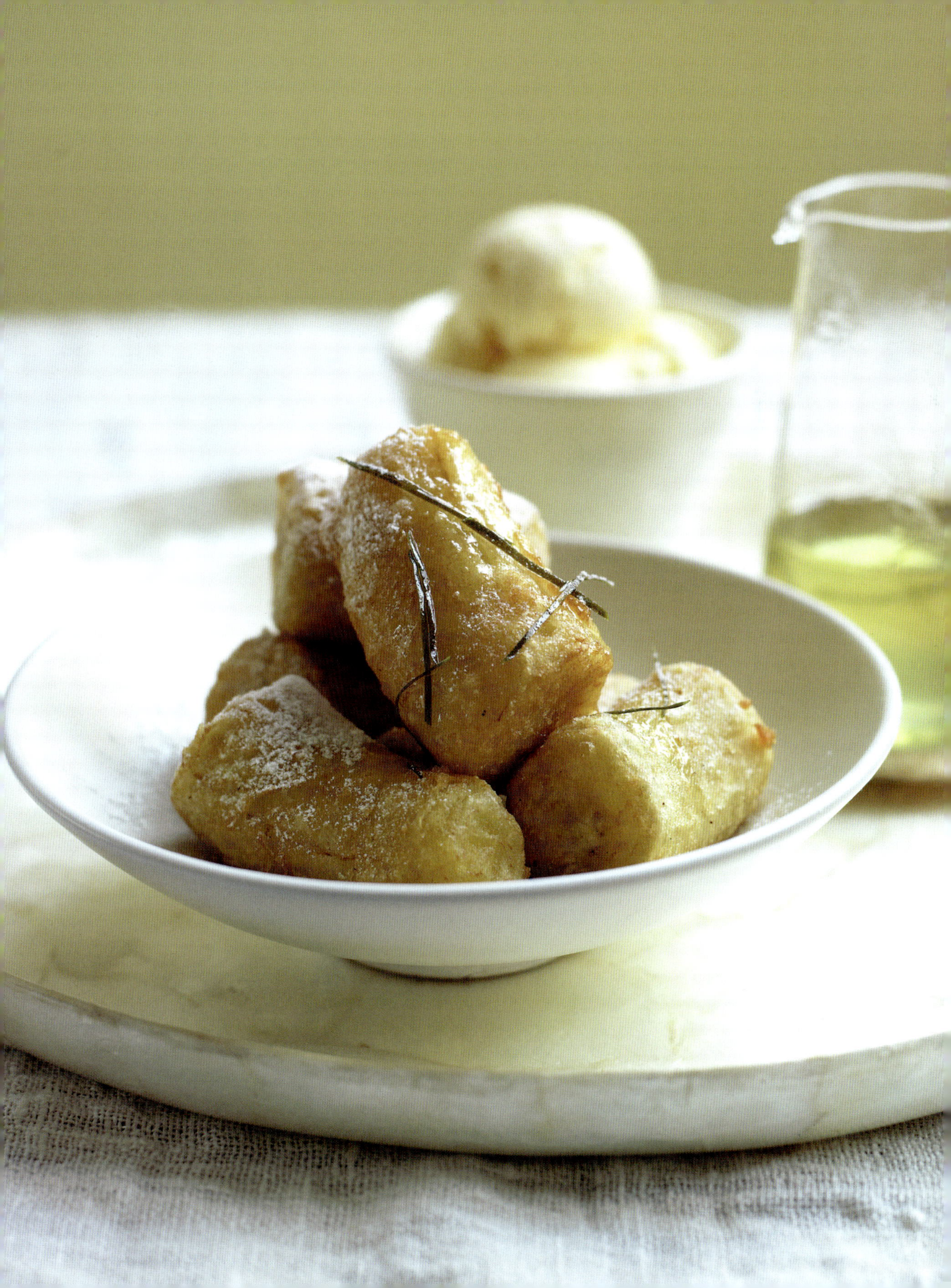

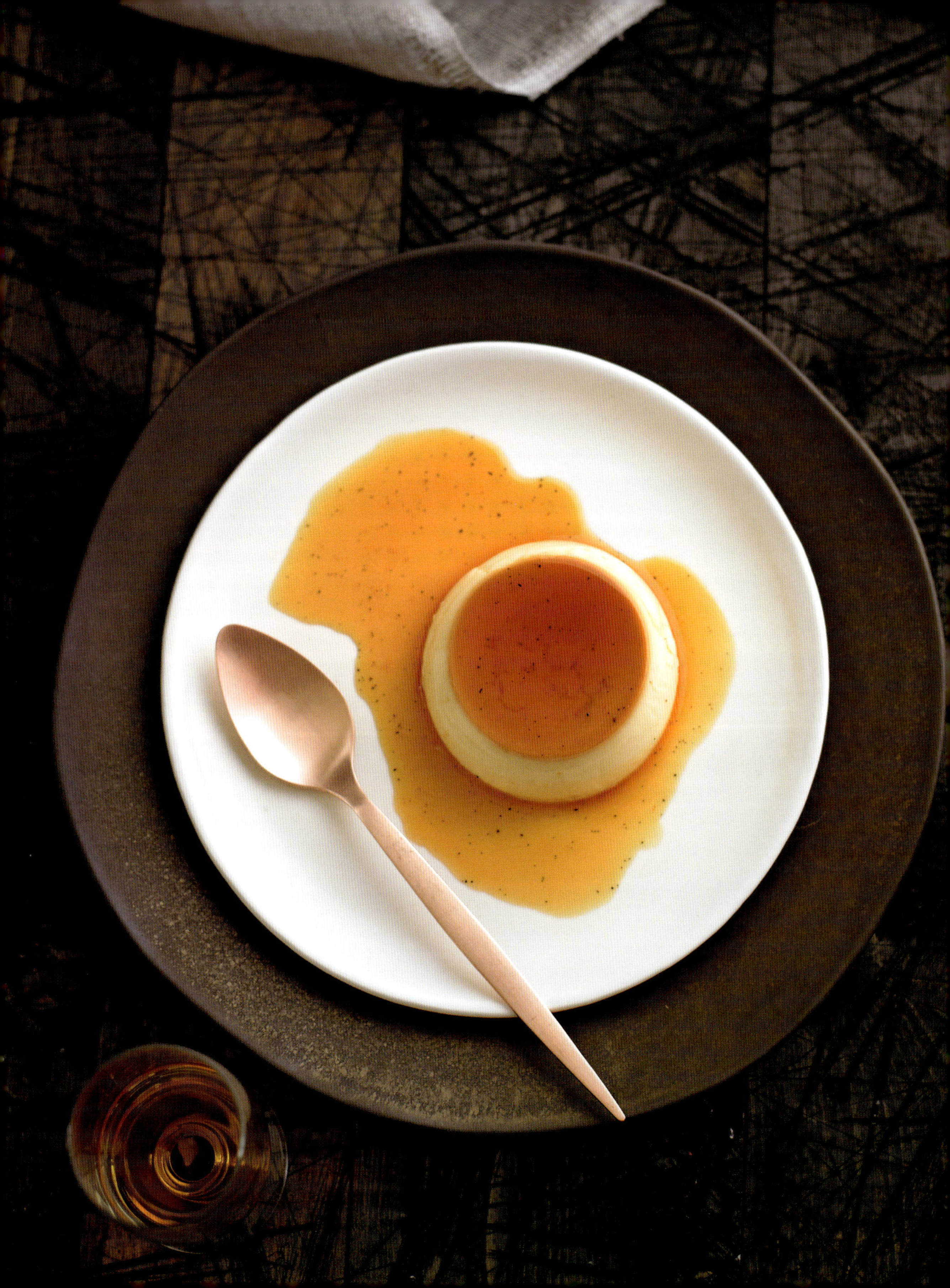

Crème caramel

If you're out to impress, this dish will do the trick. It's another classic French dessert, though there are variations on this silky smooth baked custard from both Spain (flan) and Italy (crema caramella).

SERVES 6 **PREPARATION TIME** 15 minutes (+ 30 minutes standing, cooling, and 2 hours chilling)
COOKING TIME 50 minutes

220 g (7¾ oz/1 cup) caster (superfine) sugar
600 ml (21 fl oz) milk
1 vanilla bean, split lengthways and seeds scraped
4 eggs
2 egg yolks

1 Combine 175 g (6 oz) of the sugar with 80 ml (2½ fl oz/⅓ cup) water in a small saucepan and stir over low heat until the sugar dissolves. Increase the heat to medium–high and bring to the boil. Boil for 6–7 minutes or until the mixture turns a deep caramel colour. Working quickly and taking care as the mixture will spit, remove the pan from the heat and add 2 tablespoons cold water. Return the pan to the heat and bring to a simmer, swirling the pan to combine well, and cook for 2 minutes or until smooth. Place six 185 ml (6 fl oz/¾ cup) dariole moulds or heatproof ramekins in a roasting pan and divide the caramel evenly among them *(pic 1)*. Set aside for 30 minutes to allow the caramel to set. Preheat the oven to 160°C (315°F/Gas 2–3).

2 Heat the milk and vanilla seeds in a small saucepan over medium heat until almost simmering. Remove from the heat. Use a balloon whisk to whisk the eggs and egg yolks together in a large bowl until combined. Add the remaining sugar and the hot milk and stir to combine well. Strain the mixture through a fine sieve into a jug *(pic 2)*.

3 Divide the mixture among the moulds, then fill the roasting pan with enough hot water to come halfway up the sides of the moulds. Bake for 35 minutes or until the custards are set, but still a little wobbly in the centre when the moulds are shaken gently. Remove from the pan and cool to room temperature. Cover each mould with plastic wrap, then refrigerate for 2 hours or until chilled.

4 To serve, use your fingertip to gently press all around the top of a custard to loosen it from the side of the mould *(pic 3)*. Invert onto a serving plate and shake quickly, but gently, until the custard is released from the mould. Repeat with the remaining crème caramels. Serve immediately.

VARIATIONS

Orange crème caramel: Stir the finely grated zest of 1 orange into the strained custard before baking.

Rum crème caramel: Use 540 ml (18½ fl oz) milk and stir 80 ml (2½ fl oz/⅓ cup) rum into the custard before baking.

Espresso crème caramel: Heat 20 g (¾ oz/¼ cup) finely ground espresso beans with the milk, then stand for 30 minutes to infuse. Strain the milk through a fine sieve before adding to the egg mixture.

Custards and Batters

Buttermilk pancakes with strawberry and vanilla compote

These American-style pancakes use buttermilk to give them a slightly tangy flavour and wonderful lightness. If you don't have buttermilk, reduce the quantity by 1 tablespoon and use regular milk with 1 teaspoon lemon juice or white vinegar added. The compote can also be served with vanilla ice cream.

SERVES 4 (makes 12 pancakes)   **PREPARATION TIME** 20 minutes   **COOKING TIME** 55 minutes–1 hour 10 minutes

- 225 g (8 oz/1½ cups) self-raising flour
- 150 g (5½ oz/1 cup) plain (all-purpose) flour
- 55 g (2 oz/¼ cup) caster (superfine) sugar
- 750 ml (26 fl oz/3 cups) buttermilk
- 2 eggs, lightly whisked
- 80 g (2¾ oz) butter, melted and cooled, plus melted butter, extra, to grease
- Icing (confectioners') sugar, to dust

STRAWBERRY AND VANILLA COMPOTE

- 55 g (2 oz/¼ cup) caster (superfine) sugar
- 500 g (1 lb 2 oz) strawberries, hulled and halved
- 1 vanilla bean, split lengthways and seeds scraped

1 To make the strawberry and vanilla compote, combine the sugar with 60 ml (2 fl oz/¼ cup) water in a small saucepan and stir over medium heat until the sugar dissolves. Add the strawberries and vanilla seeds and cook for 5 minutes or until the strawberries start to soften but aren't falling apart *(pic 1)*. Remove from the heat and set aside to cool slightly.

2 Preheat the oven to 120°C (235°F/Gas ½). Sift the self-raising and plain flours together into a medium bowl. Stir in the sugar and make a well in the centre. Use a balloon whisk to whisk together the buttermilk, eggs and butter. Add to the flour mixture and stir with the whisk until a smooth batter forms.

3 Heat a 21 cm (8¼ inch) non-stick frying pan or crepe pan over medium heat. Brush with a little melted butter to lightly grease. Add 80 ml (2½ fl oz/⅓ cup) of the batter *(pic 2)* and cook over medium heat for 2–3 minutes or until bubbles appear on the surface and the pancake is lightly golden underneath *(pic 3)*. Use a spatula to turn the pancake over and cook for a further 2 minutes or until lightly golden and cooked through. Transfer to a heatproof plate, cover loosely with foil and place in the oven to keep warm. Repeat with the remaining batter to make 11 more pancakes, transferring them to the oven to keep warm as you go. (You may need to stir a little extra buttermilk into the batter towards the end of cooking, as it will thicken slightly on standing.)

4 Serve the warm pancakes topped with the strawberry and vanilla compote and dusted with icing sugar.

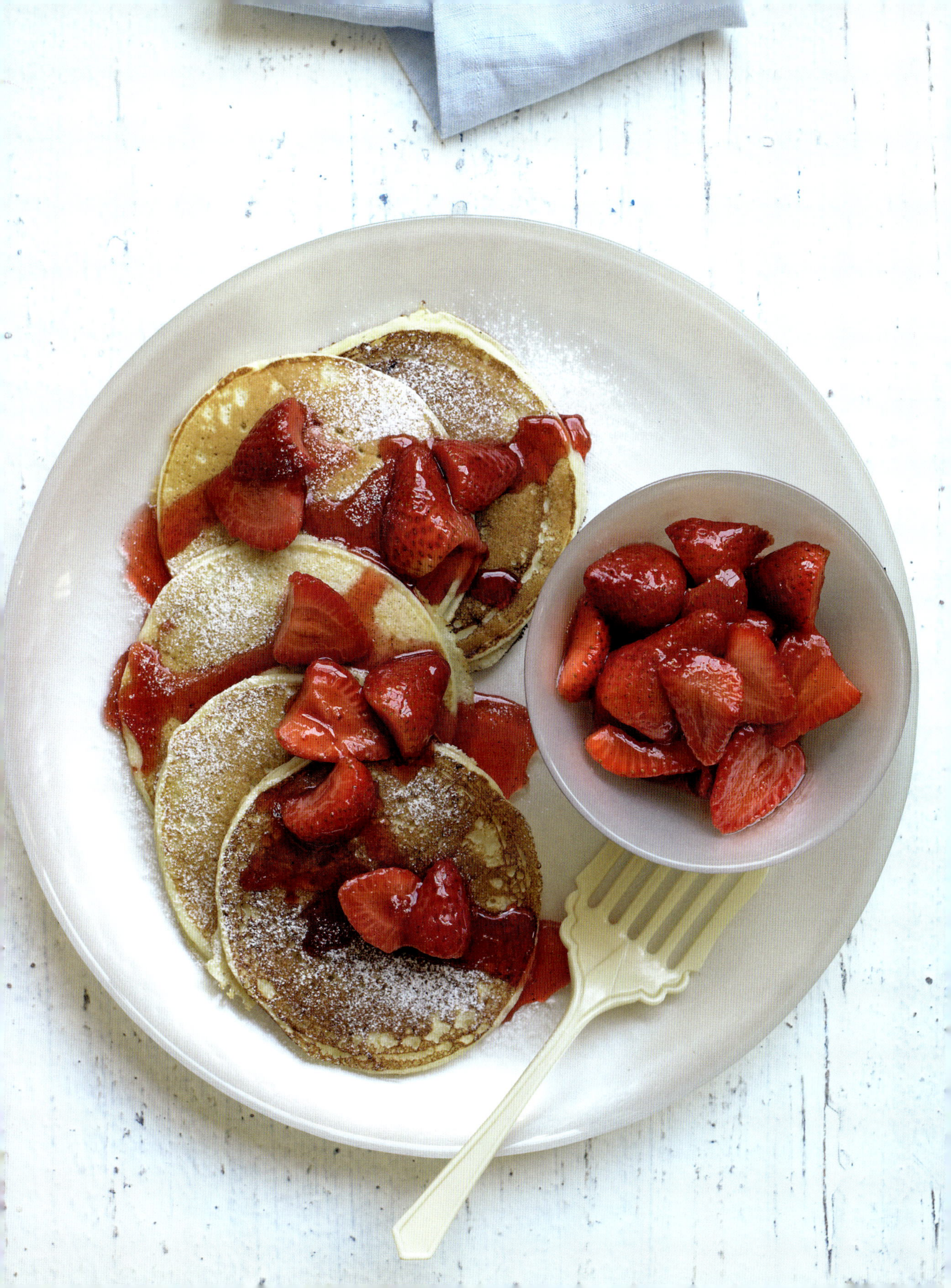

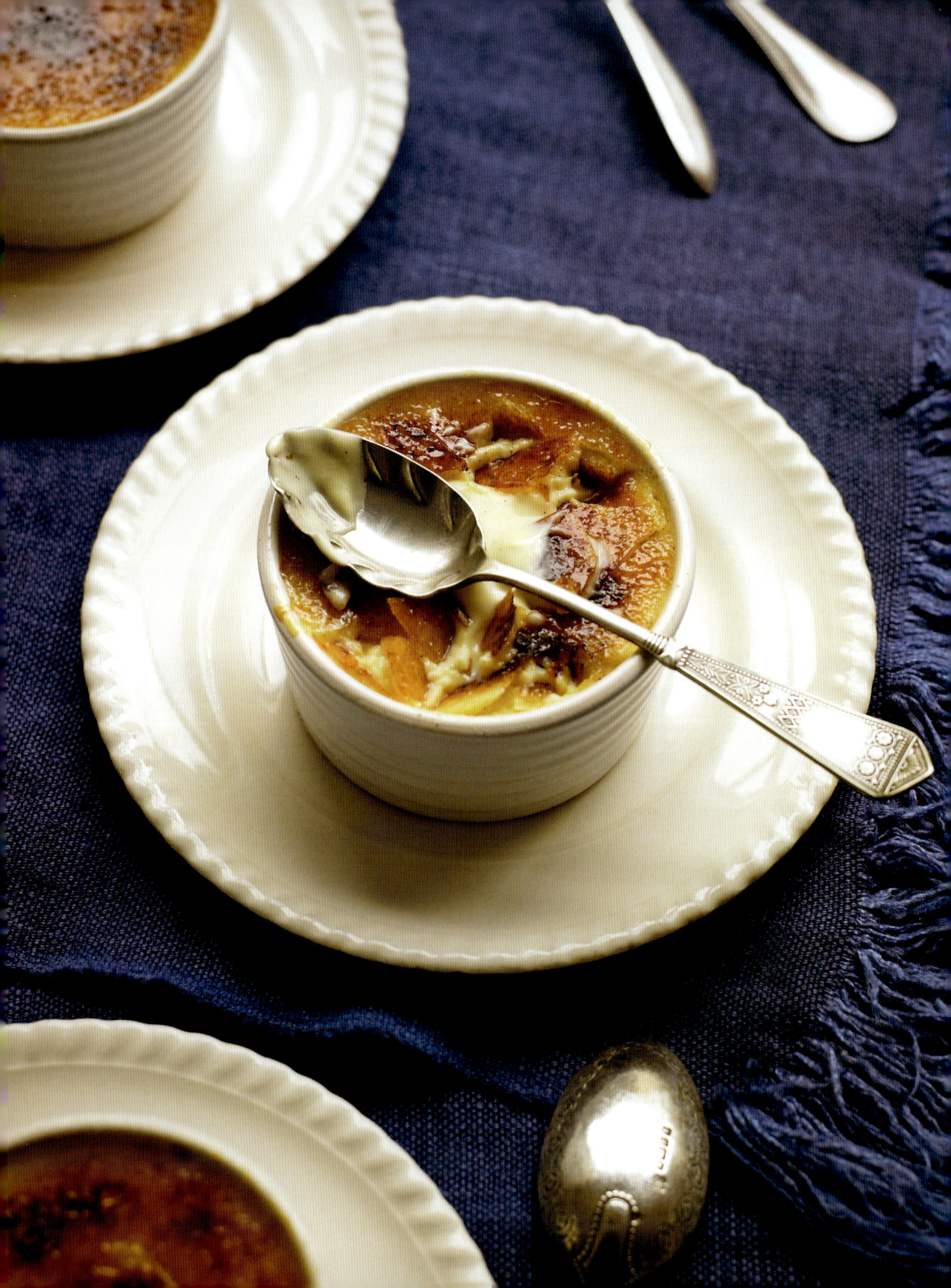

Crème brulée

Perennially popular, this heavenly combination of chilled baked custard with a brittle topping of caramelised sugar is a staple on most bistro menus. Translated literally as 'burnt cream' it's surprisingly simple to make at home (particularly if you have a kitchen blowtorch, though this is not essential).

MAKES 6   **PREPARATION TIME** 15 minutes (+ 20 minutes standing and 3 hours chilling)   **COOKING TIME** 25 minutes

750 ml (26 fl oz/3 cups) pouring (whipping) cream
1 vanilla bean, split lengthways and seeds scraped
6 egg yolks
75 g (2¾ oz/⅓ cup) caster (superfine) sugar, plus 110 g (3¾ oz/½ cup), extra, to sprinkle

1 Preheat the oven to 160°C (315°F/Gas 2–3). Place six 160 ml (5¼ fl oz/⅔ cup) heatproof ramekins in a large roasting pan.

2 Put the cream and vanilla seeds in a medium saucepan and bring almost to the boil. Remove from the heat.

3 Use a balloon whisk to whisk the egg yolks and sugar in a large bowl until combined. Whisk in the hot cream mixture until just combined (you don't want it to be frothy). Strain the custard into a jug and divide evenly among the ramekins. Use a tablespoon to remove any air bubbles from the surface of each custard *(pic 1)*.

4 Add enough boiling water to the roasting pan to reach halfway up the sides of the ramekins. Bake for 20 minutes or until the custards are set, but still a little wobbly in the centre when the ramekins are shaken gently. Transfer the custards to a wire rack and set aside for 15 minutes to cool slightly, then place in the refrigerator, uncovered, for 3 hours or until well chilled.

5 Sprinkle the custards evenly with the extra sugar *(pic 2)* and use a kitchen blowtorch (see tip) to caramelise the sugar *(pic 3)*. Set aside for 5 minutes to allow the caramel to cool and set before serving. If you don't have a blowtorch, put the extra sugar and 2 tablespoons water in a small heavy-based saucepan over low heat and cook, stirring, for 2 minutes, until the sugar dissolves. Bring to the boil, brushing down the side of the pan often with a pastry brush dipped in water to remove any sugar crystals. Cook, without stirring, for 5 minutes or until the syrup is deep golden. Remove from the heat and allow the bubbles to subside. Pour evenly over the chilled custards and set aside for 1 minute or until the caramel sets.

VARIATION

Vanilla and strawberry crème brulée: Spread 2 teaspoons of strawberry jam over the base of each ramekin before adding the custard mixture.

TIP The most efficient way to caramelise the sugar layer on top of a crème brulée is scorching it with a small kitchen blowtorch. These are available from speciality kitchenware stores.

Custards and Batters

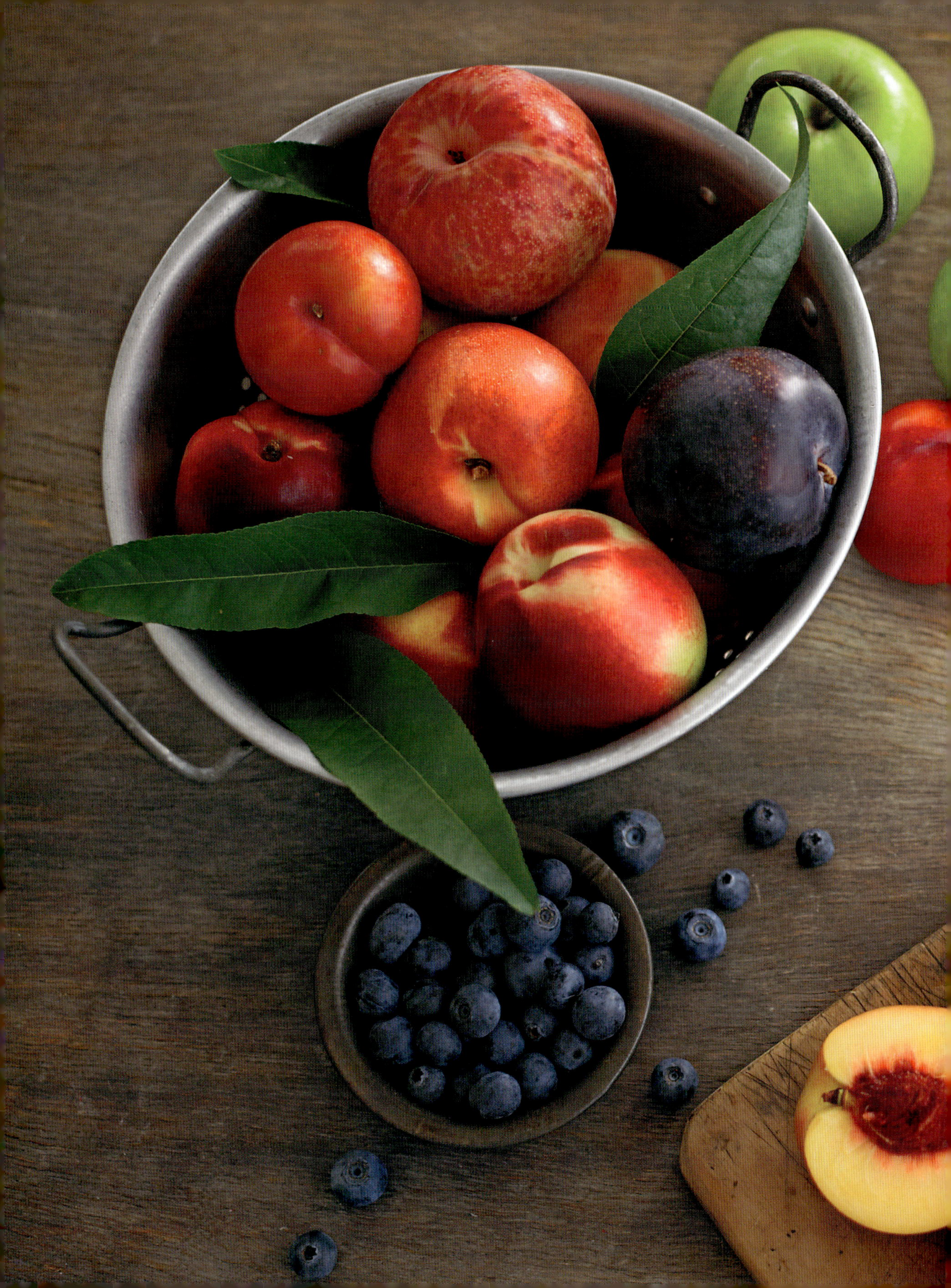

Fruit Desserts

Poached summer fruits in vanilla cinnamon syrup

SERVES 8 **PREPARATION TIME** 20 minutes (+ cooling) **COOKING TIME** 50 minutes

550 g (1 lb 4 oz/2½ cups) caster (superfine) sugar
1 vanilla bean, split lengthways and seeds scraped *(pic 1)*
2 cinnamon sticks
125 ml (4 fl oz/½ cup) brandy
4 firm, ripe freestone peaches, quartered and stones removed
4 large firm, ripe freestone plums, halved and stones removed
6 firm, ripe apricots, halved and stones removed
400 g (14 oz) cherries, pitted
Whipped cream or vanilla ice cream, to serve

1 Combine the sugar with 1.25 litres (44 fl oz/5 cups) water in a large saucepan. Add the vanilla bean and seeds, cinnamon sticks and brandy. Stir over medium–low heat until the sugar dissolves. Bring to a simmer, then simmer for 5 minutes.

2 Add the peaches and plums and simmer very gently over medium–low heat for 5–6 minutes or until the fruits soften slightly *(pic 2)*. Add the apricots and cherries. Bring to a gentle simmer, then cook for 4–5 minutes or until the all the fruits have softened, making sure the apricots and plums don't collapse.

3 Use a slotted spoon to carefully transfer all the fruit to a tray or large dish *(pic 3)*. Bring the cooking liquid to a boil, then boil gently over medium heat for 15–20 minutes or until thickened slightly and reduced by about half. Remove from the heat and cool to room temperature (refrigerate to reduce the cooling time if you like).

4 Pour the syrup over the fruit and serve with whipped cream or ice cream.

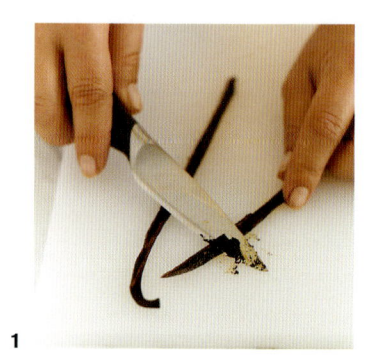

> **TIP** This dessert will keep in an airtight container in the refrigerator for up to 4 days. The recipe can easily be halved to serve 4.

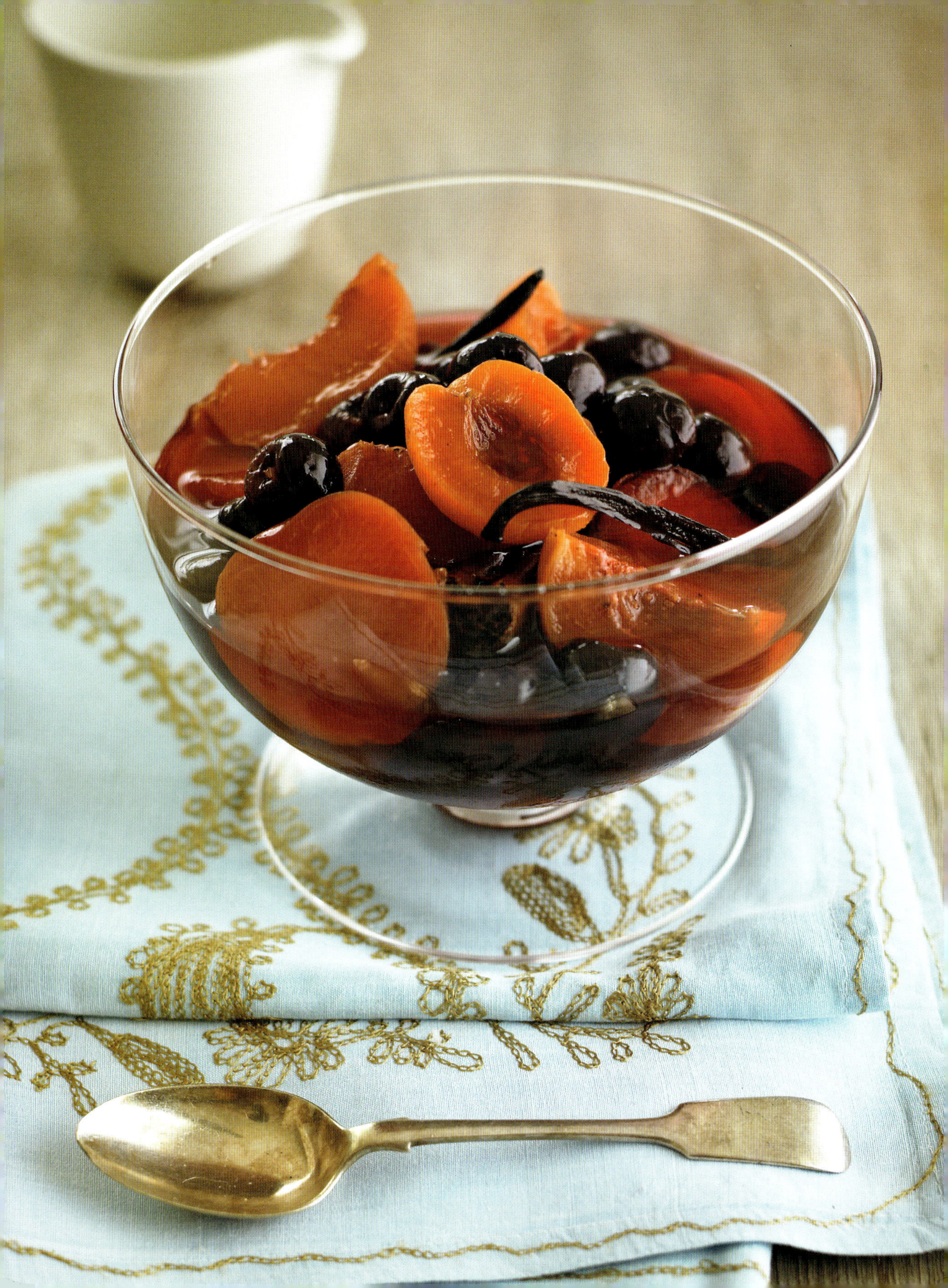

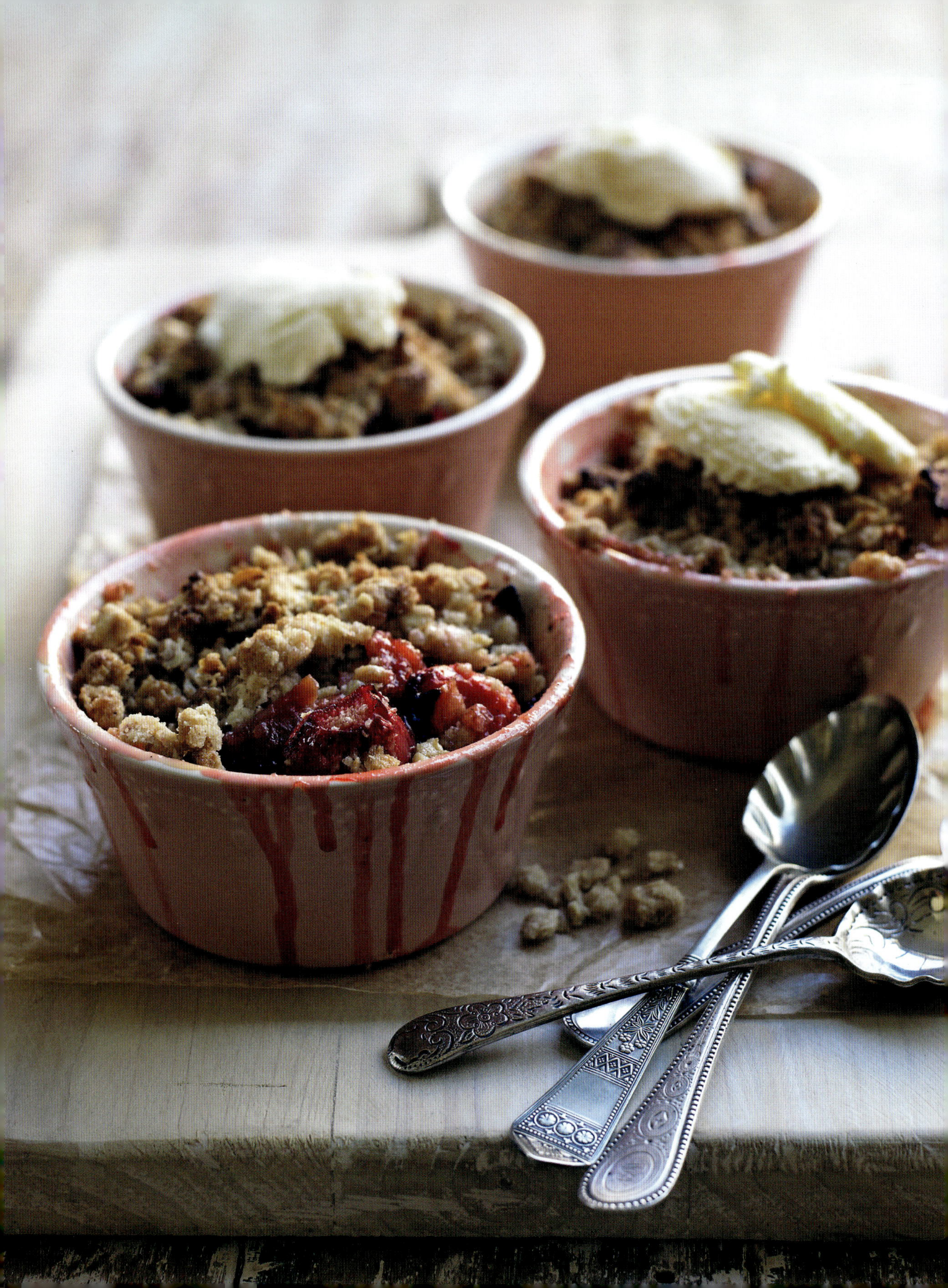

Rhubarb, apple and strawberry crumble

If you haven't put these winter fruits together before, you're in for a treat. They match up beautifully in this warming crumble, with the slightly tart flavour offset perfectly by the sweet, cinnamon-infused topping.

SERVES 6–8 **PREPARATION TIME** 15 minutes **COOKING TIME** 30–35 minutes

600 g (1 lb 5 oz) granny smith apples
2 teaspoons lemon juice
350 g (12 oz) trimmed rhubarb
250 g (9 oz) strawberries, hulled, large berries halved
1 vanilla bean, split lengthways and seeds scraped
140 g (5 oz/²⁄₃ cup) sugar
Vanilla ice cream, to serve

CRUMBLE TOPPING

75 g (2¾ oz/¾ cup) rolled (porridge) oats
75 g (2¾ oz/½ cup) plain (all-purpose) flour
110 g (3¾ oz/½ cup) sugar
½ teaspoon ground cinnamon
90 g (3¼ oz) chilled unsalted butter, diced

1 Preheat the oven to 200°C (400°F/Gas 6).

2 Peel the apples and cut into 1.5–2 cm (⅝–¾ inch) pieces. Toss the apples and lemon juice together in a large bowl. Cut the rhubarb into 2.5 cm (1 inch) lengths *(pic 1)*. Add to the apple with the strawberries, vanilla seeds and sugar and toss to combine *(pic 2)*. Transfer to six 250 ml (9 fl oz/1 cup) heatproof ramekins or dishes.

3 To make the crumble topping, put the oats, flour, sugar and cinnamon in a medium bowl and mix to combine. Use your fingertips to rub in the butter *(pic 3)* until well combined. Sprinkle the crumble topping evenly over the fruit in the ramekins or dishes.

4 Bake for 30–35 minutes, until golden and bubbling. Cover with foil if the topping is browning too quickly. Serve with vanilla ice cream.

TIP You can also cook this crumble in a 1.5 litre (52 fl oz/6 cup) ovenproof dish. Cook at the same temperature for 50–60 minutes.

Fruit Desserts

Berry and passionfruit pavlova

Every cook should be able to whip up a pavlova. They are a great standby recipe, as they require few ingredients, the preparation is quick and uncomplicated, and they're universally popular. You can top the cream with whatever fruit is in season or simply sprinkle with grated dark chocolate.

SERVES 8   **PREPARATION TIME** 20 minutes (+ cooling)   **COOKING TIME** 1 hour 20 minutes

4 egg whites, at room temperature
220 g (7¾ oz/1 cup) caster (superfine) sugar
1 tablespoon cornflour (cornstarch)
1 teaspoon white vinegar

TOPPING
300 ml (10½ fl oz) thickened (whipping) cream
2 passionfruit, halved, pulp removed
250 g (9 oz) strawberries, hulled and sliced
125 g (4½ oz/1 cup) raspberries

1 Preheat the oven to 110°C (225°F/Gas ½). Mark a 20 cm (8 inch) circle on a piece of non-stick baking paper. Turn the paper over and place it on a baking tray. Brush the paper with a little melted butter and dust with a little flour *(pic 1)*.

2 Place the egg whites in a clean, dry, large mixing bowl. Use an electric mixer with a whisk attachment to whisk until soft peaks form. With the motor running, gradually add the sugar, whisking well after each addition. Continue to whisk for 6–7 minutes, until the mixture is very thick and glossy.

3 Fold the sifted cornflour and the vinegar through the meringue mixture *(pic 2)*. Spoon the mixture onto the tray and use a spatula to spread it out, using the marked circle as a guide *(pic 3)*. Smooth the sides or create swirls, as desired.

4 Bake for 1 hour 20 minutes or until the meringue is crisp, but not coloured. Turn the oven off. Cool completely in the oven, with a wooden spoon keeping the door slightly ajar.

5 To serve, use an electric mixer with a whisk attachment or a balloon whisk to whisk the cream in a medium bowl until soft peaks form. Spread the cream over the top of the pavlova and then spoon half the passionfruit pulp over the cream. Top with half the strawberries and raspberries. Drizzle the remaining passionfruit pulp over the top and serve accompanied by the remaining berries.

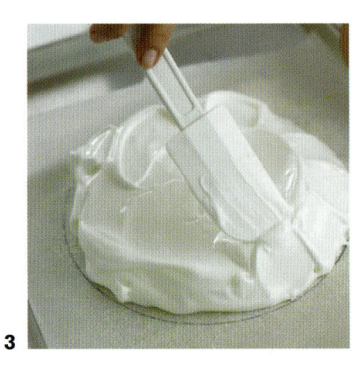

TIP It is best to make pavlova on a dry day with low humidity, as humidity in the air can cause the meringue to 'weep'.

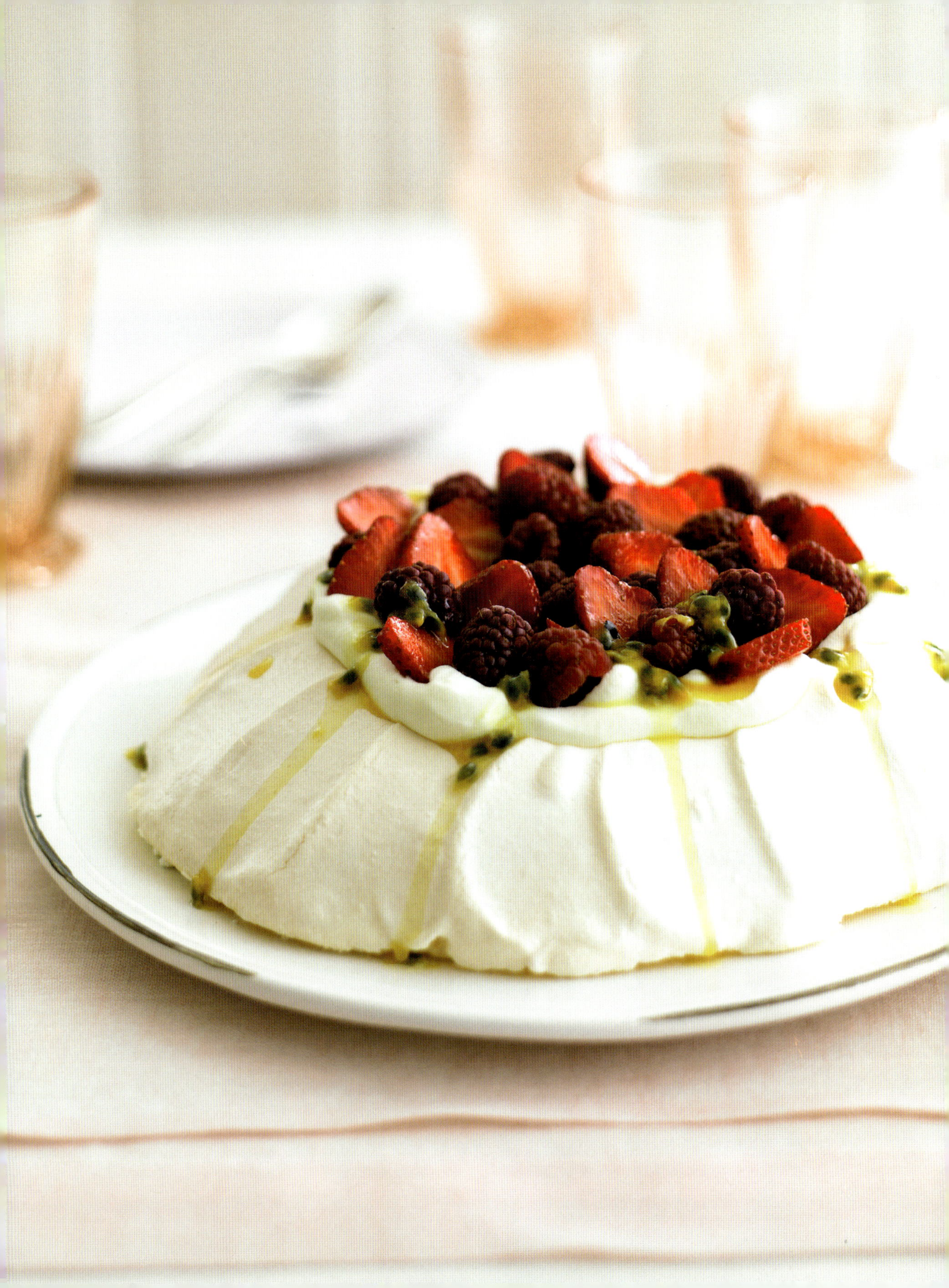

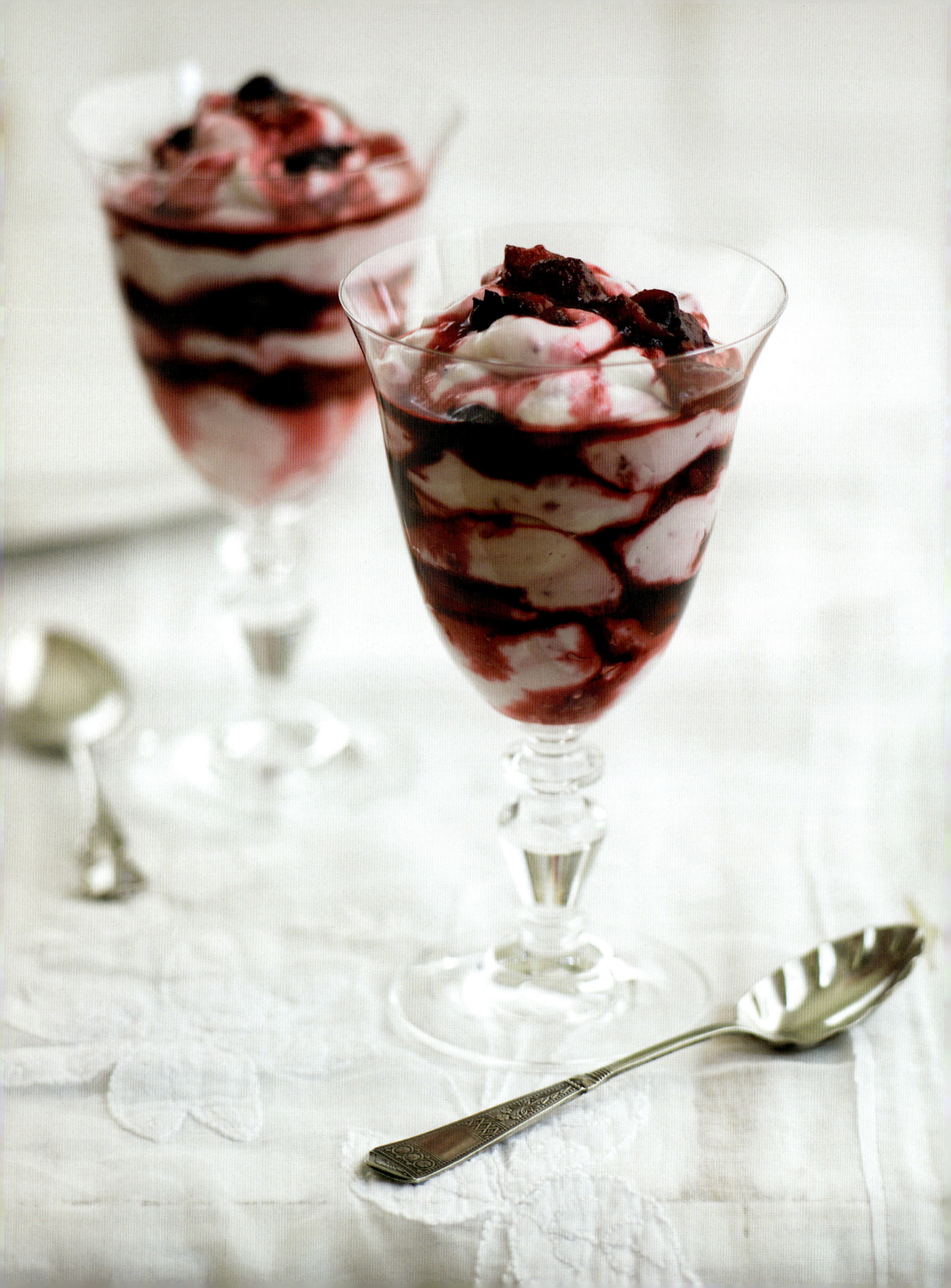

Mixed berry fool

There's nothing to indicate this dessert was so named for being a cheat's version of a dessert, or because it's so simple to pull together that even a fool could make it. But whatever the case, its simplicity, pretty presentation, adaptability and refreshing flavour make it a favourite.

SERVES 4   **PREPARATION TIME** 12 minutes (+ cooling and chilling)   **COOKING TIME** 5 minutes

100 g (3½ oz) strawberries, hulled and coarsely chopped
185 g (6½ oz/1½ cups) raspberries
75 g (2¾ oz) blueberries
220 g (7¾ oz/1 cup) caster (superfine) sugar
500 ml (17 fl oz/2 cups) thickened (whipping) cream

1 Put the strawberries in a medium saucepan with the raspberries, blueberries and sugar. Place over low heat and stir gently until the sugar dissolves *(pic 1)*. Increase the heat to medium–low and bring to a simmer. Simmer for 4–5 minutes or until the liquid has reduced slightly and the berries begin to collapse *(pic 2)*. Set aside to cool to room temperature, then cover and refrigerate until well chilled.

2 Use an electric mixer with a whisk attachment or a balloon whisk to whisk the cream in a medium bowl until very soft peaks form. Drizzle half the berry mixture over the cream and then partially fold through to create a swirled effect *(pic 3)*.

3 Spoon the cream mixture into serving glasses, layering with the remaining berry mixture and finishing with berry mixture. Serve immediately.

TIP Any other berries, such as blackberries, youngberries, boysenberries and loganberries can be used to make this fool.

Fruit Desserts

Mini pavlovas with caramelised figs

These simple-to-make mini pavlovas have just the right amount of wow factor. The meringue is infused with a caramel flavour courtesy of the brown sugar and the caramelised figs make an elegant topping.

SERVES 4   **PREPARATION TIME** 30 minutes (+ 2–3 hours cooling)   **COOKING TIME** 35 minutes

3 egg whites, at room temperature
110 g (3¾ oz/½ cup) caster (superfine) sugar
60 g (2¼ oz/¼ cup, firmly packed) light brown sugar
½ teaspoon natural vanilla extract
1 teaspoon white vinegar
250 ml (9 fl oz/1 cup) thickened (whipping) cream
Icing (confectioners') sugar, to dust
2 tablespoons slivered almonds, toasted

CARAMELISED FIGS
20 g (¾ oz) butter
1 tablespoon light brown sugar
4 fresh figs, trimmed, cut into thirds

1 Preheat the oven to 160°C (315°F/Gas 2–3). Grease 2 baking trays and line with non-stick baking paper.

2 Use an electric mixer with a whisk attachment to whisk the egg whites in a clean, dry medium bowl until soft peaks form. Gradually add the combined sugars, 1 tablespoon at a time, whisking well after each addition *(pic 1)*, until the mixture is thick and glossy. Add the vanilla and vinegar and whisk for 30 seconds or until combined.

3 Use a metal spoon to drop one-quarter of the meringue mixture onto a prepared tray. Use the back of the spoon to spread the mixture out slightly and then make a slight indent in the top *(pic 2)*. Repeat with the remaining meringue mixture to make 4 mini pavlovas in total.

4 Bake for 30 minutes or until they are crisp and sound hollow when tapped on the base. Turn the oven off. Cool completely in the oven, with a wooden spoon keeping the door slightly ajar.

5 Use an electric mixer with a whisk attachment to whisk the cream in a medium bowl until soft peaks form. Cover and refrigerate until needed.

6 To make the caramelised figs, melt the butter in a medium frying pan over medium–high heat until foaming. Add the sugar and cook, stirring, for 1 minute or until it dissolves. Add the figs, cut side down, and cook for 3–4 minutes each side or until caramelised *(pic 3)*. (The cooking time will depend on the ripeness of the figs.)

7 To serve, place the mini pavlovas on serving plates, dust lightly with icing sugar, top with the cream and figs and sprinkle with the almonds.

TIP The pavlovas can be made up to 4 days ahead. Keep in an airtight container in a cool place.

Mastering the Basics: Desserts

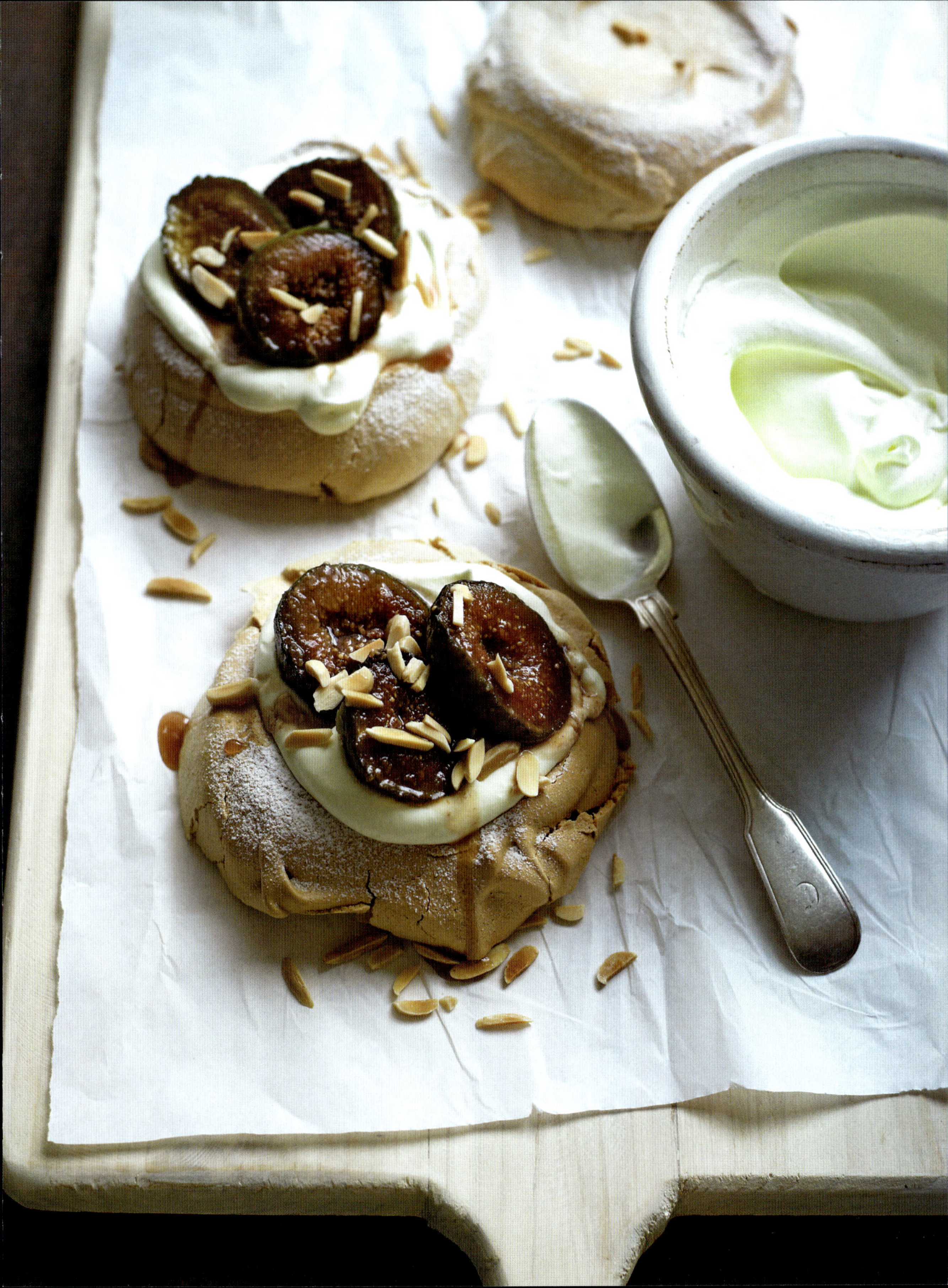

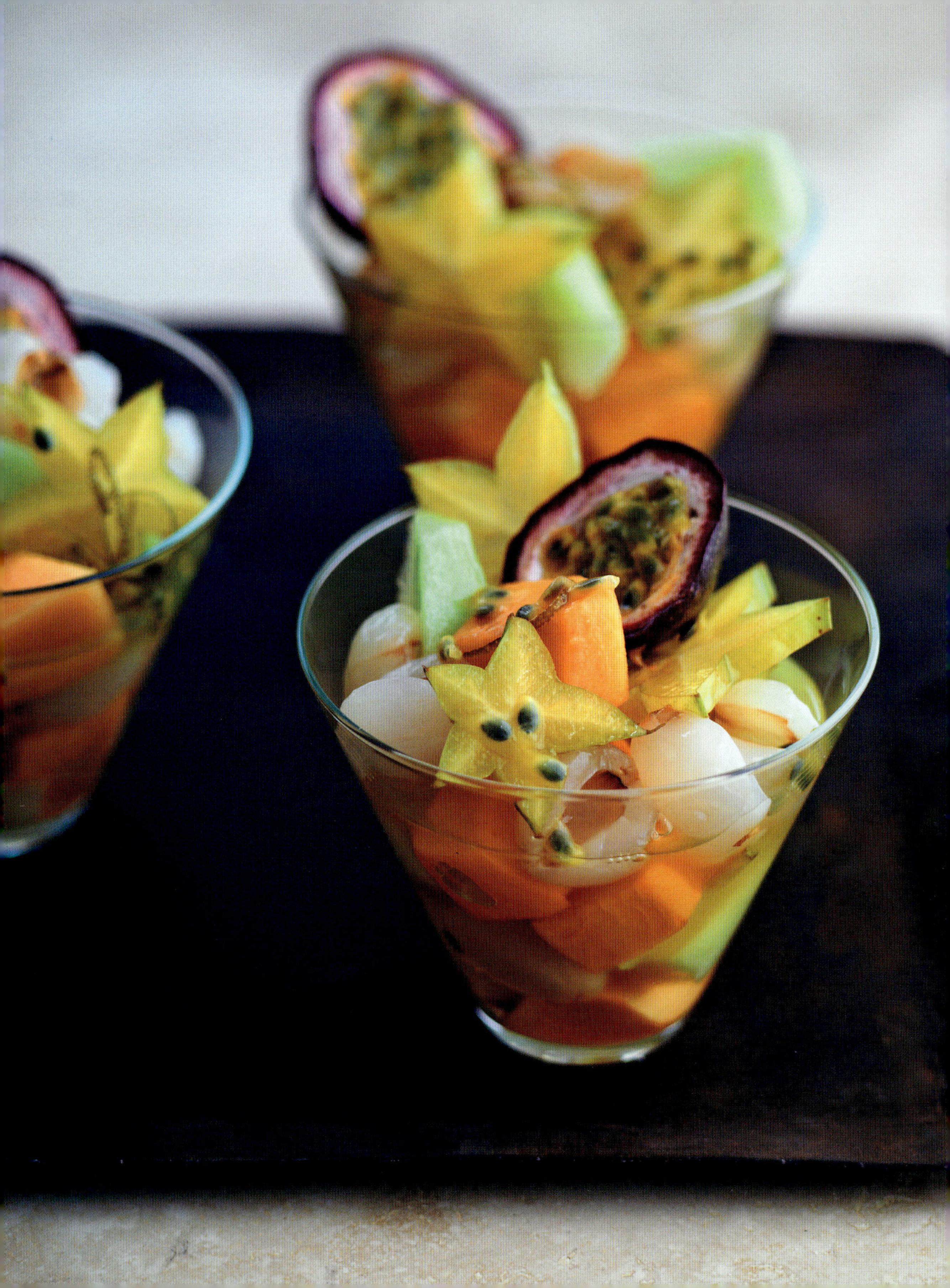

Tropical fruit salad

A stunning combination of fruits from the tropics, this fruit salad is anything but ordinary. With a refreshing lemongrass and lime syrup, it would make a great ending to an Asian-inspired meal.

SERVES 6 **PREPARATION TIME** 25 minutes (+ cooling) **COOKING TIME** 10 minutes

½ honeydew melon
½ rockmelon
½ papaya
30 lychees
2 starfruit
6 passionfruit

LEMONGRASS AND LIME SYRUP
4 lemongrass stems
295 g (10½ oz/1⅓ cups) caster (superfine) sugar
2 limes

1 To make the lemongrass and lime syrup, trim the very tops of the lemongrass, remove and discard the outer layers, then cut each stem in half and bruise using the flat side of a large, heavy knife *(pic 1)*. Put the lemongrass, sugar and 330 ml (11¼ fl oz/1⅓ cups) water in a small saucepan. Use a zesting tool to remove the zest from the limes (see page 35) and add to the pan *(pic 2)*. Juice the limes, strain the juice and add to the pan.

2 Stir the syrup over low heat until the sugar dissolves. Increase the heat to medium and bring to a simmer. Simmer for 8 minutes or until thickened slightly to a light syrup consistency *(pic 3)*. Set aside to cool completely (place the syrup in the refrigerator to reduce the cooling time, if you like).

3 Thickly slice the melons and papaya. Remove and discard the seeds and skin, then slice the flesh into bite-sized pieces. Peel the lychees, cut in half and remove the seeds. Slice the starfruit and halve the passionfruit.

4 Divide the melons, papaya, lychees and starfruit among 6 serving glasses or bowls. Spoon the pulp from half a passionfruit over the fruit and place the remaining passionfruit halves on top. Drizzle with the lemongrass and lime syrup, and serve.

Fruit Desserts

Pan-fried stone fruit

Make the most of the fabulous stone fruits that are available over summer by tossing them in sugar (you can also use caster/superfine sugar if you like) and pan-frying them. Firm, ripe fruit will give the best result. Pineapple and banana are also delicious cooked this way.

SERVES 4   **PREPARATION TIME** 5 minutes   **COOKING TIME** 4 minutes

2 mangoes
2 yellow freestone nectarines
2 white freestone peaches
2 freestone plums
330 g (11½ oz/1½ cups, firmly packed) light brown sugar
Mascarpone cheese or vanilla ice cream, to serve

1 Cut the cheeks from the mangoes and spoon the flesh from the skin in one piece *(pic 1)*. (Reserve the remaining mango flesh for another use.) Cut the nectarines, peaches and plums in half and remove the stones.

2 Line a baking tray with non-stick baking paper. Have a wide spatula and tongs ready for cooking and a bowl of cold water nearby in case you burn yourself with the hot sugar.

3 Spread the sugar on a plate. Press the cut side of each piece of fruit into the sugar to cover generously *(pic 2)*.

4 Preheat a large non-stick frying pan over medium heat. Working quickly, place half the sugar-coated fruit in the frying pan, cut side down. Cook for 1 minute *(pic 3)*, lightly shaking the pan occasionally to ensure the sugar caramelises evenly. (The sugar gets very hot, so be careful.) Use the spatula and tongs to transfer the fruit to the lined tray. Slowly add a little water to the pan — it will spit slightly, but will cook off any burnt sugar immediately. Pour away the water and dry the pan with paper towels. Reheat the pan and repeat the process to cook the remaining fruit.

5 Serve warm or at room temperature with mascarpone or ice cream.

TIP You can also cook this fruit on a barbecue flat plate — just be ready with some water to rinse and scrape the flat plate as soon as you have finished, as it can be challenging to clean later.

Mastering the Basics: Desserts

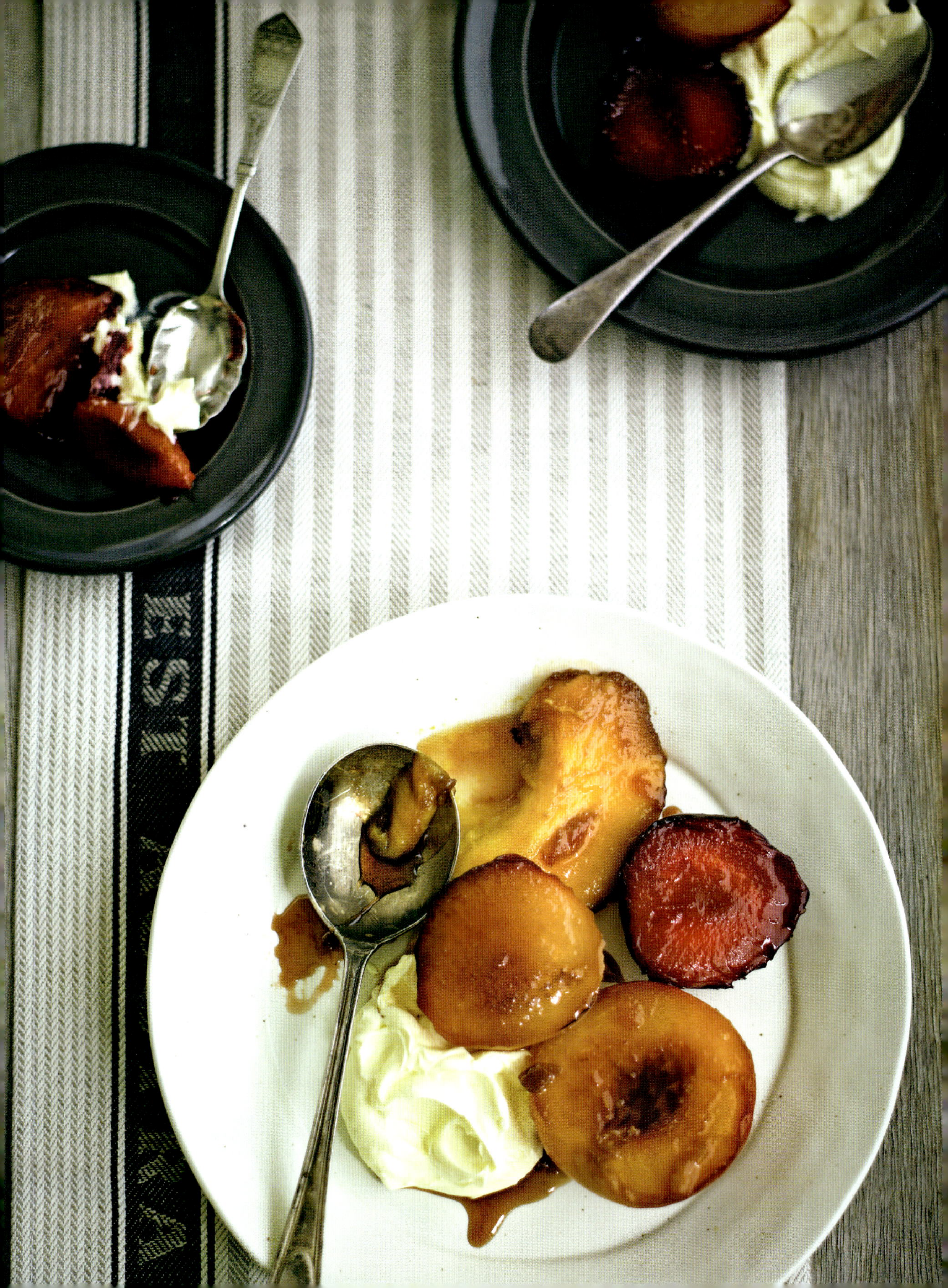

Preparing fruit

Pitting cherries

Removing the seeds from cherries is made easy with a cherry pitter (these are also handy for pitting olives). There are many varieties, some of which have a 'splatter guard' to keep the juices from spraying everywhere as you remove the seeds.

1 Remove the stem from the cherries. Place a cherry, stem side up, in a cherry pitter (available from large supermarkets, variety stores and kitchenware stores).
Press the handles of the cherry pitter together to push the seed out through the base of the cherry.

Coring apples, pears and quinces

All three of these autumn/winter fruits will often require coring before they are used in desserts. Remember to brush the cut surfaces of these fruits with a little lemon juice as soon as they are cut so they don't discolour.

> **TIP** If the fruit is not being used whole, use a small sharp knife to cut it into quarters and slice away the core from each piece. Use as directed.

Apples To core a whole apple, hold the fruit firmly on a chopping board and insert an apple corer through the top, straight down to the base. Remove the corer and the core of the apple will come away with it. Any remaining core or seeds can be removed using a small sharp knife.

Pears To core a whole pear and leave the stem intact, hold the pear gently, but firmly, so as not to bruise it, and use a small teaspoon or melon baller to scoop out the core from the underside of the fruit.

Quinces To core a quince, cut the fruit in half lengthways. Hold the fruit firmly in your hand and use the point of a small sharp knife to cut around the core and loosen it. Use the knife or a small teaspoon to scoop out the core. This method can also be used for apple and pear halves.

Removing seeds from a pomegranate

The seeds of a pomegranate are surrounded by a tough, bitter membrane that needs to be detached from the seeds before they can be used.

1 Use a small sharp knife to score the fruit into quarters. Use your hands to break the fruit into halves and then quarters, using the score lines as a guide.

2 Bend the skin back on itself and allow the seeds to drop into a bowl. Any seeds that remain attached to the membrane can be gently removed, taking care not to puncture them, with a teaspoon or your fingers.

3 If you need to extract the juice from the seeds, crush them with the back of a spoon in a sieve set over a bowl.

Preparing pineapple

Pineapples are generally served as wedges or rings. The tough core is often discarded, but this is a matter of taste.

1 Use a large sharp knife to remove the base and top. Stand the fruit upright and cut downwards to remove the skin. If desired, use a small sharp knife to remove the eyes in lines around the edge of the pineapple.

2 For wedges, use a large sharp knife to cut the pineapple in half and then into wedges of the desired thickness. Cut away the core if you like. The pineapple can then be cut into small chunks, if desired.

3 To cut into rings, slice the pineapple and then use a small round cutter to cut out the core and remove.

Fruit Desserts

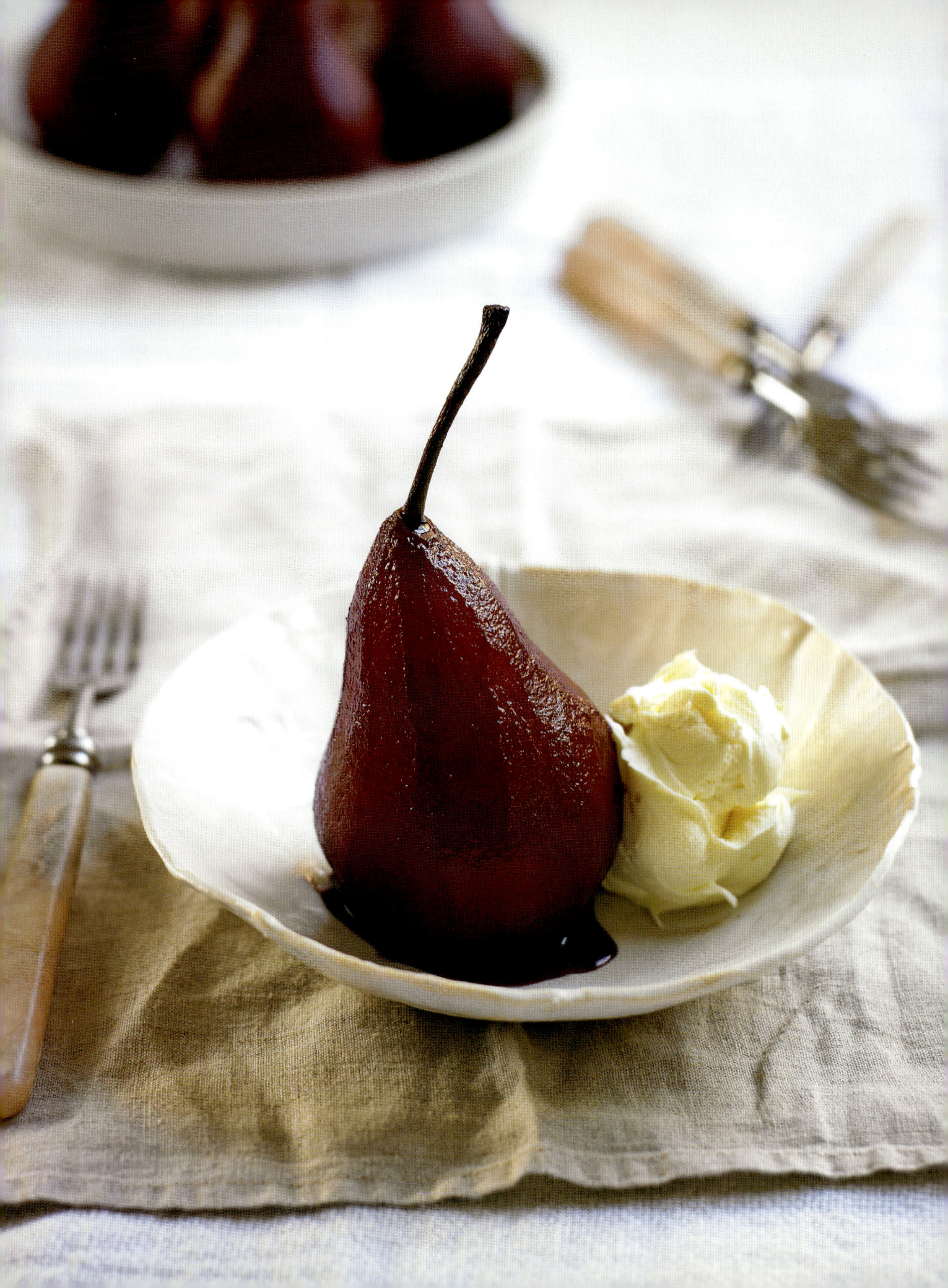

Pears poached in red wine

With their striking deep-red colour and mellow spice-infused syrup, these poached pears make a sublime dessert. A good-quality, lighter-style red wine will give the best result.

SERVES 6   **PREPARATION TIME** 15 minutes (+ cooling)   **COOKING TIME** 1 hour 10 minutes–1 hour 25 minutes

750 ml (26 fl oz/3 cups) red wine
370 g (13 oz/1²⁄₃ cups) caster (superfine) sugar
2 cinnamon sticks
2 cm (¾ inch) piece ginger, peeled and thinly sliced
2 star anise
1 teaspoon whole cloves
6 firm, ripe beurre bosc pears
Mascarpone cheese or whipped cream, to serve

1 Combine the red wine, sugar and 750 ml (26 fl oz/3 cups) water in a large saucepan. Add the cinnamon sticks *(pic 1)*. Place the ginger, star anise and cloves on a piece of muslin (cheesecloth) large enough to enclose them, then tie up with kitchen string to make a pouch. Add to the pan and bring to a simmer. Cover and reduce the heat to medium–low.

2 Meanwhile, peel the pears *(pic 2)* and then, working from the base and using a small teaspoon or melon baller, remove the cores, leaving the stems intact. Add the pears to the pan and top up with a little more water if necessary to just cover them. Gently place a small plate or saucer over the pears to keep them submerged *(pic 3)*. Simmer the pears gently over low heat for 45–60 minutes or until they are tender. (The cooking time will depend upon the ripeness of the pears.)

3 Use a slotted spoon to carefully transfer the pears to a large bowl or platter. Bring the cooking liquid to a simmer and simmer for 20 minutes or until reduced and slightly syrupy. Remove the spice pouch and the cinnamon sticks and discard. Set aside to cool. Serve the pears and syrup at room temperature with mascarpone or whipped cream.

Fruit Desserts

Zabaglione with caramelised figs

This classic Italian dessert of whisked eggs, sugar and Marsala is often served warm but is equally delicious at room temperature. Caramelised figs make a beautiful accompaniment, as do fresh strawberries or roasted peaches or plums.

SERVES 4   **PREPARATION TIME** 10 minutes   **COOKING TIME** 10 minutes

8 egg yolks, at room temperature
110 g (3¾ oz/½ cup) caster (superfine) sugar
125 ml (4 fl oz/½ cup) Marsala
4 firm ripe figs, halved
55 g (2 oz/¼ cup) caster (superfine) sugar, extra

1 Add about 5 cm (2 inches) of water to a medium saucepan and bring to a simmer. Put the egg yolks and sugar in a heatproof bowl that will fit snugly over the saucepan later (make sure the base of the bowl doesn't touch the water). Use electric hand-held beaters with a whisk attachment to whisk for 3 minutes until thick and pale *(pic 1)*. Add the Marsala and whisk to combine.

2 Place the bowl over the saucepan of simmering water and whisk constantly for 5–6 minutes, until very thick and increased in volume *(pic 2)*, scraping down the side of the bowl with a spatula when necessary. Spoon the zabaglione into 4 individual glasses, about 125 ml (4 fl oz/½ cup) in capacity.

3 Heat a non-stick frying pan over medium–high heat. Sprinkle the figs with the extra sugar and place, cut side down, in the pan. Cook for 1–2 minutes or until caramelised underneath *(pic 3)*.

4 Serve the zabaglione accompanied by the caramelised figs.

Mastering the Basics: Desserts

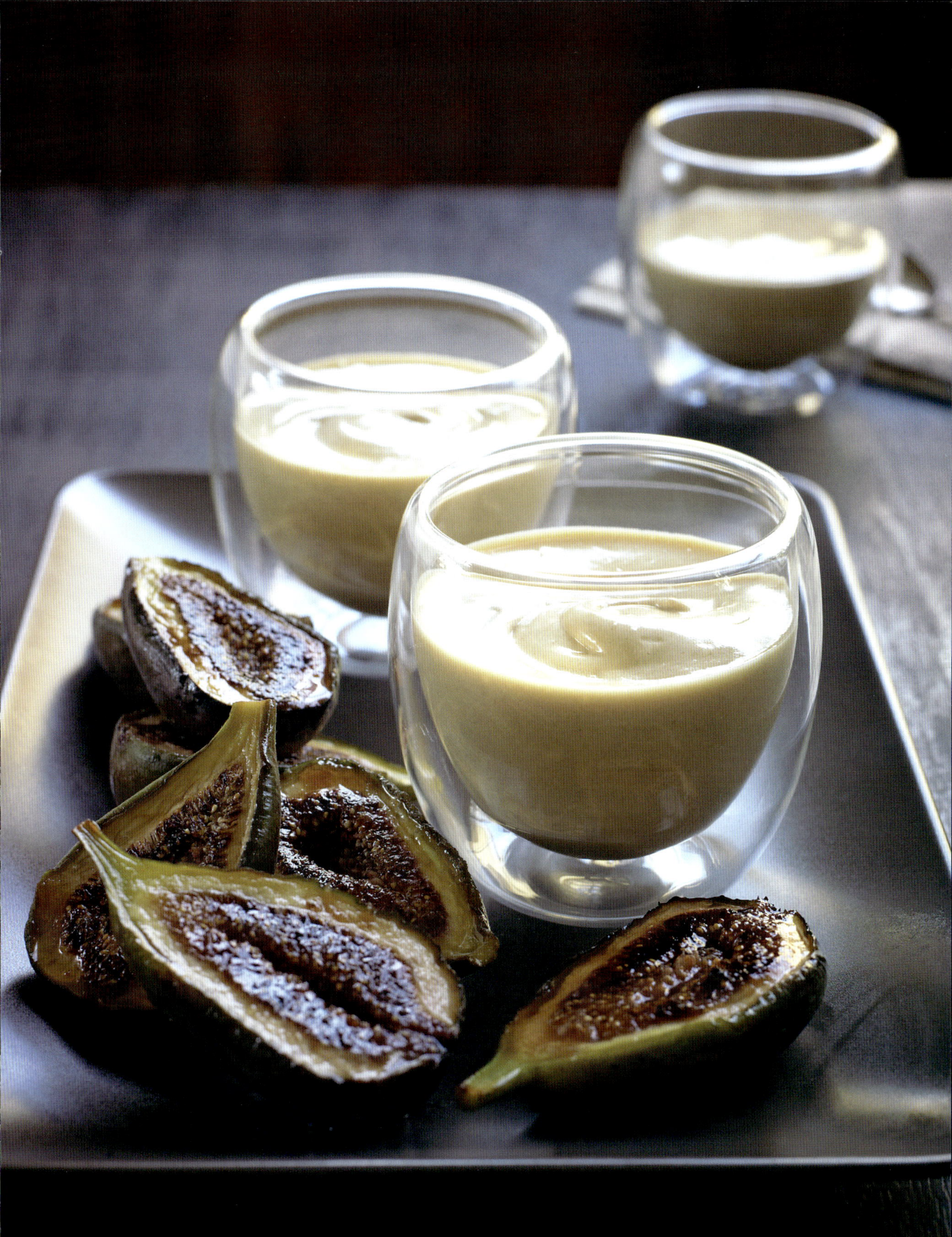

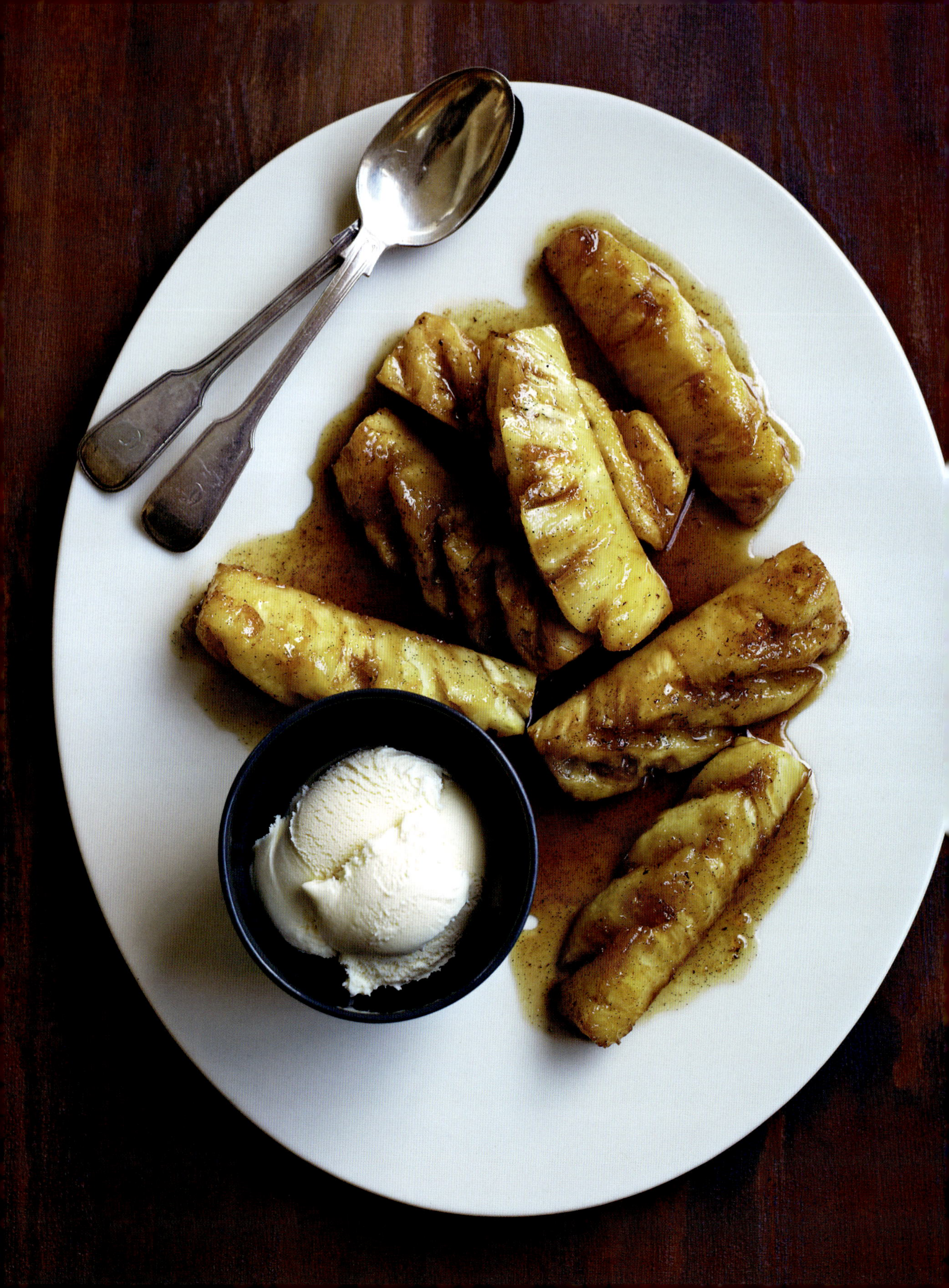

Flambéd pineapple

Flambéing sweet and juicy wedges of pineapple creates a simple fruit dessert with a touch of drama. When you flambé food, you ignite the alcohol to burn it off and give the food a slightly singed flavour.

SERVES 4   **PREPARATION TIME** 20 minutes   **COOKING TIME** 10 minutes

---

1 small pineapple, top removed (about 900 g/2 lb) or ½ large pineapple
110 g (3¾ oz/½ cup, firmly packed) light brown sugar
60 g (2¼ oz) unsalted butter, chopped
1 vanilla bean, split lengthways and seeds scraped
60 ml (2 fl oz/¼ cup) white rum
Vanilla ice cream, to serve

1 Use a sharp knife to trim the ends of the pineapple, then remove the skin. Use a small sharp knife to remove the eyes by cutting diagonal lines from the top to the base of the pineapple *(pic 1)*. Cut into 3–4 cm (1¼–1½ inch) thick wedges and cut away the core *(pic 2)*. (You will need 8 wedges, about 8 cm/3¼ inches long each.) Pat the pineapple dry with paper towels.

2 Rub half the brown sugar over half the pineapple, to cover all sides. Heat a large non-stick frying pan over medium heat and add half the butter and half the vanilla seeds. When the butter has melted, add the sugar-coated pineapple wedges and cook for 1 minute each side or until caramelised *(pic 3)*. Add half the rum to the pan, then remove from the heat and ignite with a long match. Return to the heat and cook for a further minute.

3 Transfer the pineapple to a serving dish and drizzle with the sauce from the pan. Cover with foil to keep warm and set aside. Clean the pan and repeat the cooking process with the remaining pineapple, sugar, vanilla seeds and rum. Serve warm, with vanilla ice cream.

TIP This recipe works best when cooked in two batches.

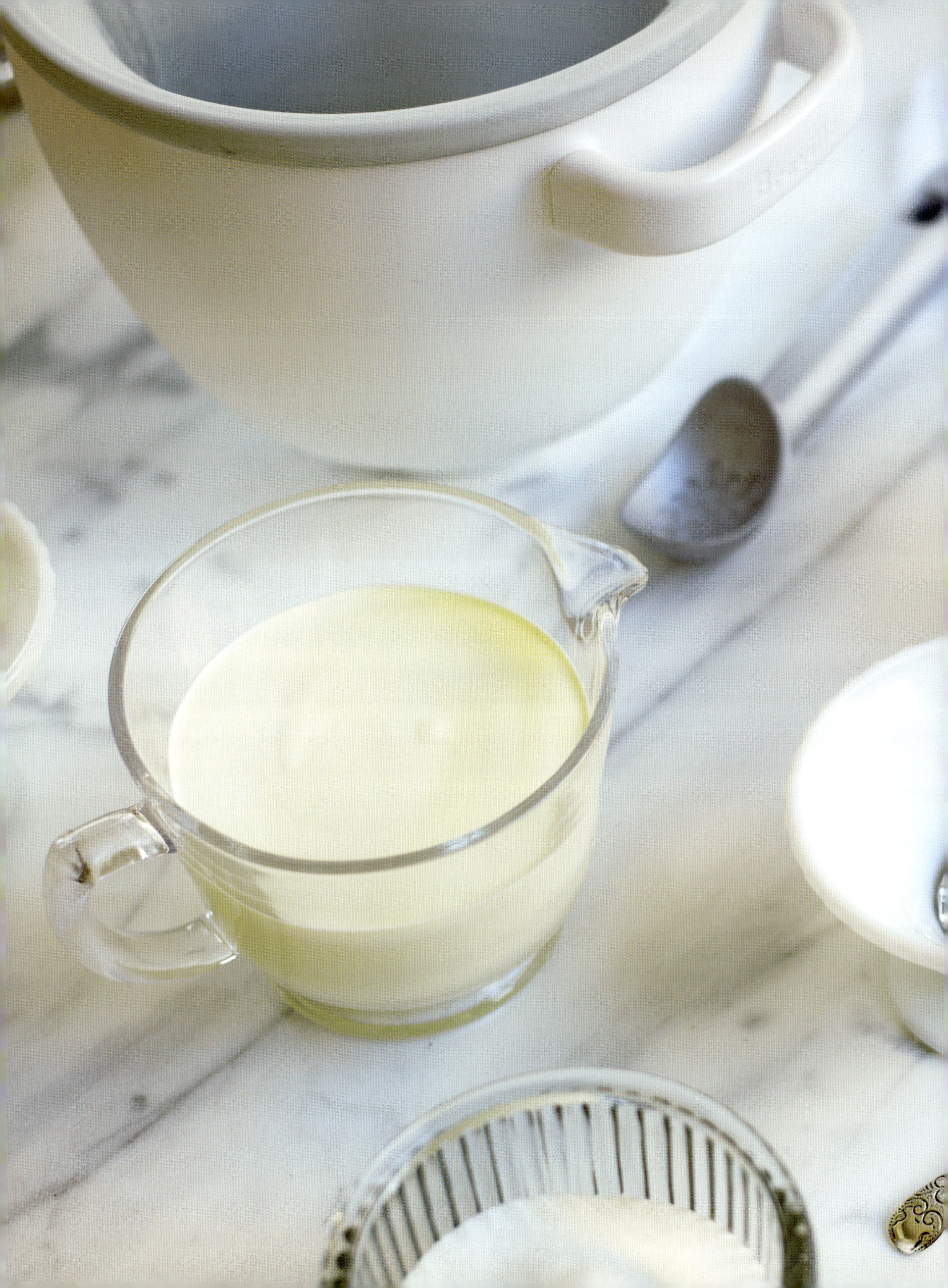

Cold Desserts

Cherry and pistachio parfait

SERVES 10   **PREPARATION TIME** 35 minutes (+ cooling and 1 hour chilling)   **COOKING TIME** 10–15 minutes
FREEZING TIME 6 hours

110 g (3¾ oz/½ cup) caster (superfine) sugar
2 eggs, at room temperature
4 egg yolks, at room temperature
300 ml (10½ fl oz) thickened (whipping) cream
1 vanilla bean, split lengthways and seeds scraped
45 g (1¾ oz/⅓ cup) pistachios, finely chopped
Fresh cherries, to serve

CHERRY SYRUP
250 g (9 oz) cherries, pitted
110 g (3¾ oz/½ cup) caster (superfine) sugar
1 tablespoon lemon juice

1 To make the cherry syrup, place the cherries, sugar and lemon juice in a small saucepan. Stir over medium–low heat until the sugar dissolves. Increase the heat to medium and bring to a simmer, then simmer for 3 minutes or until syrupy. Transfer to a bowl and leave to cool to room temperature.

2 Pour the cherry mixture into a sieve set over a heatproof bowl to drain, reserving the syrup. Finely chop the cherries. Refrigerate the syrup and cherries separately.

3 Grease a 1.75 litre (61 fl oz/7 cup) loaf (bar) tin and line the base and sides with two strips of non-stick baking paper, with each strip extending over two opposite sides. Combine the sugar with 125 ml (4 fl oz/½ cup) water in a small saucepan over low heat and stir until the sugar dissolves. Increase the heat and bring to the boil. Place a sugar thermometer in the syrup and boil until it reaches 117°C (243°F) (soft ball stage) *(pic 1)*.

5 Meanwhile, place the eggs and egg yolks in a medium heatproof bowl and use an electric mixer with a whisk attachment to whisk until very thick and pale. With the motor running on medium–high, pour the hot sugar syrup in a steady stream onto the egg mixture, whisking constantly until incorporated *(pic 2)*. Increase the speed to high and whisk for a further 5 minutes or until the mixture has cooled to room temperature. Transfer to a large bowl.

6 Use an electric mixer to whisk the cream and vanilla seeds until very soft peaks form. Gently fold the cream into the egg mixture with the pistachios until just combined *(pic 3)*.

7 Spread the chopped cherries over the base of the prepared tin. Pour over the pistachio mixture and smooth the surface. Cover with the overhanging paper, then plastic wrap and freeze for 6 hours or until frozen.

8 About 1 hour before serving, place serving plates and a tray in the freezer to chill. To unmould the parfait, loosen it from the tin using the paper lining and invert onto the chilled tray. Use a sharp knife, dipped in boiling water and then dried, to cut the parfait into slices. Serve on the chilled plates with the cherry syrup and fresh cherries.

TIP You can also make this parfait in 10 lightly greased 160 ml (5¼ fl oz/⅔ cup) metal dariole moulds or ceramic ramekins. Small plastic yoghurt containers or freezer-proof teacups can also be used.

Mastering the Basics: Desserts

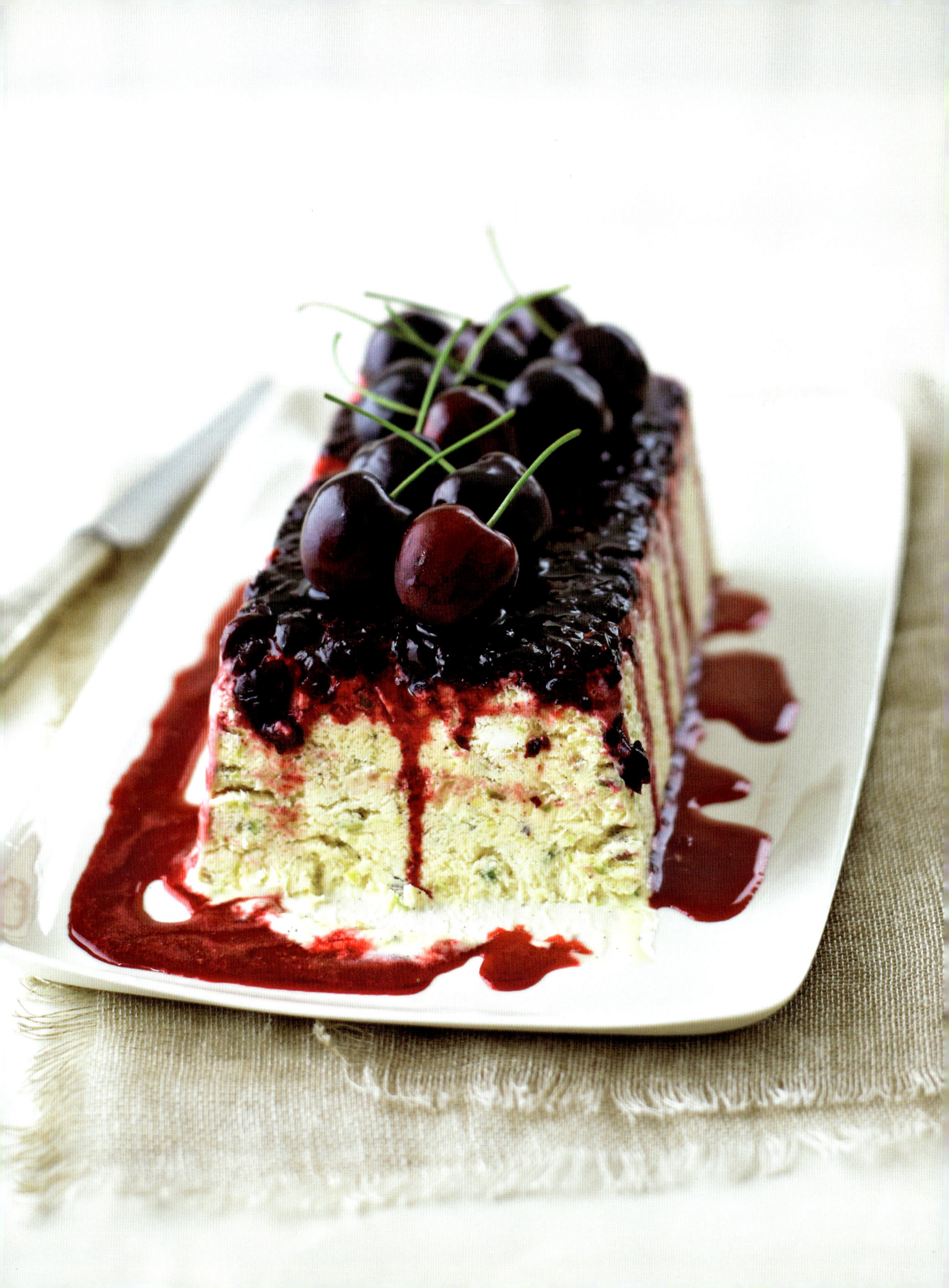

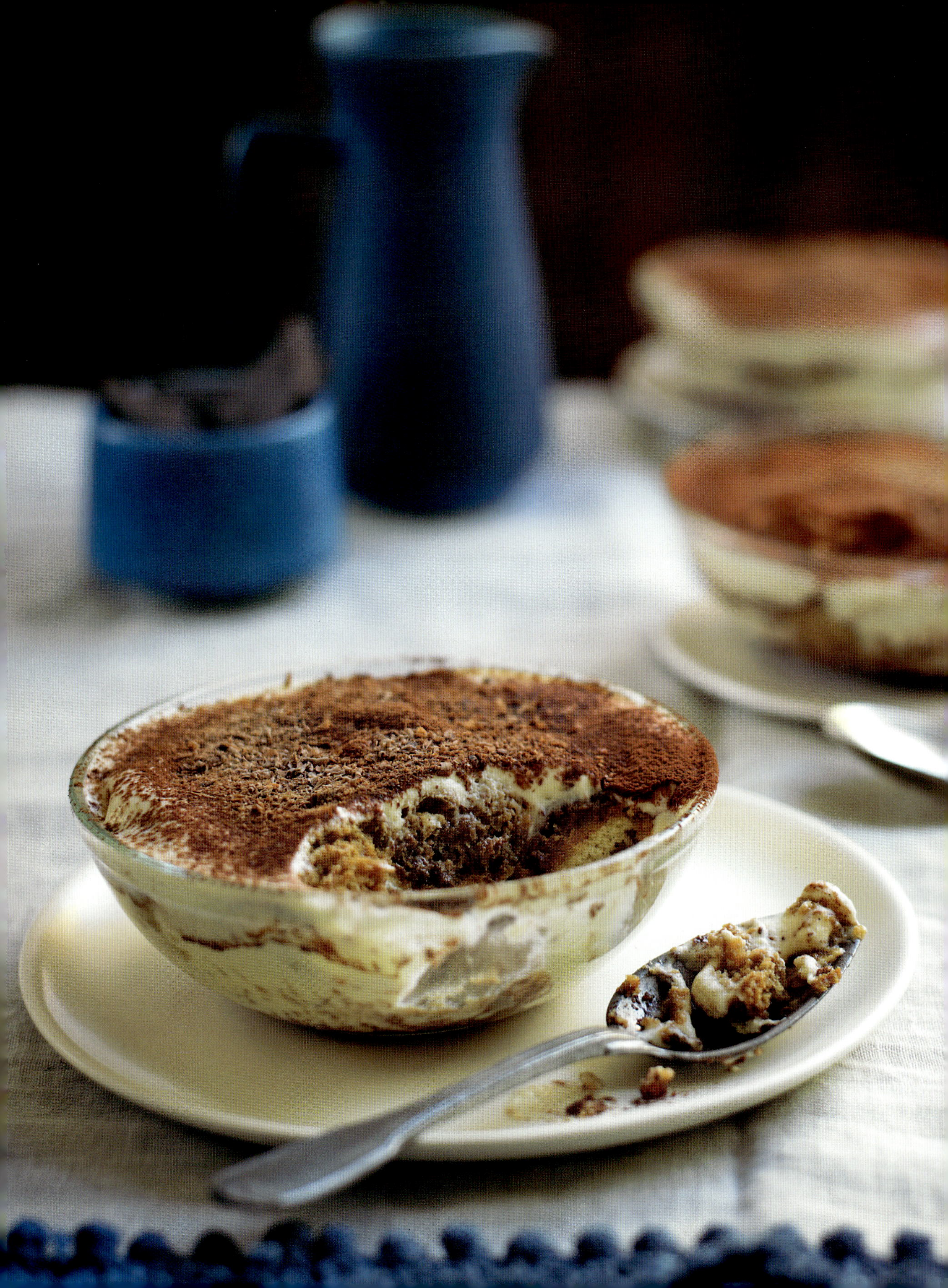

Tiramisu

This immensely popular Italian dessert translates as 'pick-me-up' and with its mouthwatering combination of chocolate, coffee, liqueurs, mascarpone and sweet biscuits, the name is well deserved. Use an Italian-style mascarpone if you can, as these have a wonderfully light texture.

SERVES 6 **PREPARATION TIME** 25 minutes (+ 1–2 hours chilling) **COOKING TIME** nil

60 g (2¼ oz) piece dark chocolate (70% cocoa solids)
185 ml (6 fl oz/¾ cup) freshly made strong espresso coffee, cooled to room temperature
2½ tablespoons coffee liqueur (such as Kahlua)
2 tablespoons Marsala
1 teaspoon natural vanilla extract
3 eggs, at room temperature, separated
75 g (2¾ oz/⅓ cup) caster (superfine) sugar
300 g (10½ oz) mascarpone cheese
150 g (5½ oz) savoiardi biscuits (lady fingers) (see tip)
Unsweetened cocoa powder, for dusting

1 Place the chocolate in the freezer (this will make it easier to grate). Combine the coffee, coffee liqueur, Marsala and vanilla in a wide bowl and set aside.

2 Use an electric mixer with a whisk attachment to whisk the egg yolks and sugar in a medium bowl until just thick and pale. Use a large metal spoon or spatula to gently fold in the mascarpone until just combined and smooth. Wash and thoroughly dry the whisk attachment and then whisk the egg whites in a clean, dry medium bowl until soft peaks form. Add to the mascarpone mixture and fold together until just combined *(pic 1)*.

3 Working with one at a time, briefly dip both sides of the biscuits in the coffee mixture and then place on a baking tray *(pic 2)*. Finely grate the chocolate and place in a bowl.

4 To assemble, use a fine sieve to dust the bases of six 250 ml (9 fl oz/1 cup) capacity dishes with cocoa and then sprinkle with one-quarter of the grated chocolate. Top with one-third of the mascarpone mixture and then use half the biscuits to make a single layer of biscuits in each dish — gently pressing them into the mascarpone and breaking them up to fit, if necessary *(pic 3)*. Dust with cocoa and sprinkle with one-third of the remaining chocolate. Top with half the remaining mascarpone mixture, and the remaining biscuits. Sprinkle with cocoa and half the remaining chocolate, and finish with the remaining mascarpone mixture. Refrigerate for 1–2 hours for the flavours to blend and the mascarpone mixture to firm slightly.

5 Dust with cocoa and sprinkle with the remaining chocolate to serve.

TIP Savoiardi biscuits are also known as sponge finger biscuits and are available from the biscuit section of the supermarket or from continental delicatessens.

Cold Desserts

Lemon gelato

MAKES about 1.2 litres (42 fl oz)   **SERVES** 8–10   **PREPARATION TIME** 15 minutes (+ 10 minutes standing, and cooling, refrigerating and churning)   **COOKING TIME** 15 minutes   **FREEZING TIME** 2 hours

1 litre (35 fl oz/4 cups) milk
Finely grated zest of 1 lemon
10 egg yolks, at room temperature
220 g (7¾ oz/1 cup) caster (superfine) sugar
125 ml (4 fl oz/½ cup) strained fresh lemon juice

1 Combine the milk and zest in a small saucepan and bring almost to the boil. Set aside for 10 minutes to infuse.

2 Use an electric mixer with a whisk attachment to whisk the egg yolks and sugar in a medium bowl until thick and pale *(pic 1)*. Whisk in the milk mixture until smooth.

3 Strain the mixture into a medium saucepan *(pic 2)* and then use a wooden spoon to stir over medium–low heat until the mixture coats the back of the spoon (do not let the mixture boil or it will curdle). Remove from the heat, cover the surface with plastic wrap and cool to room temperature. Refrigerate until cold. Stir in the lemon juice.

4 Pour the lemon custard into an ice-cream machine and churn following the manufacturer's instructions *(pic 3)*. Transfer the churned gelato to an airtight container and freeze for 2 hours or until firm.

TIP To make without an ice-cream machine, place the mixture in a shallow non-reactive metallic container in the freezer until it freezes around the edges. Remove and transfer to a chilled metallic bowl. Use an electric mixer to beat until smooth. Return to the container and freeze until set.

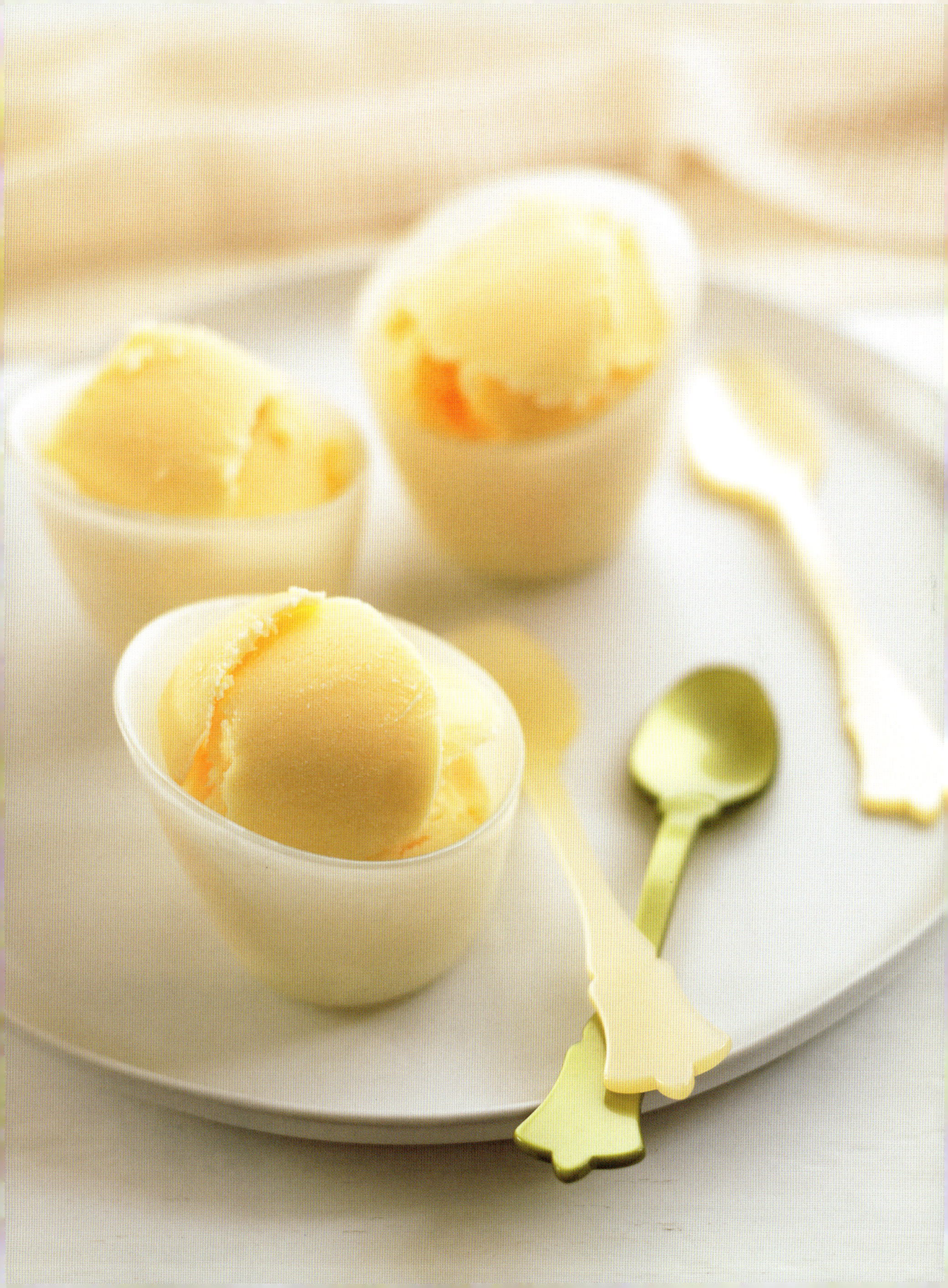

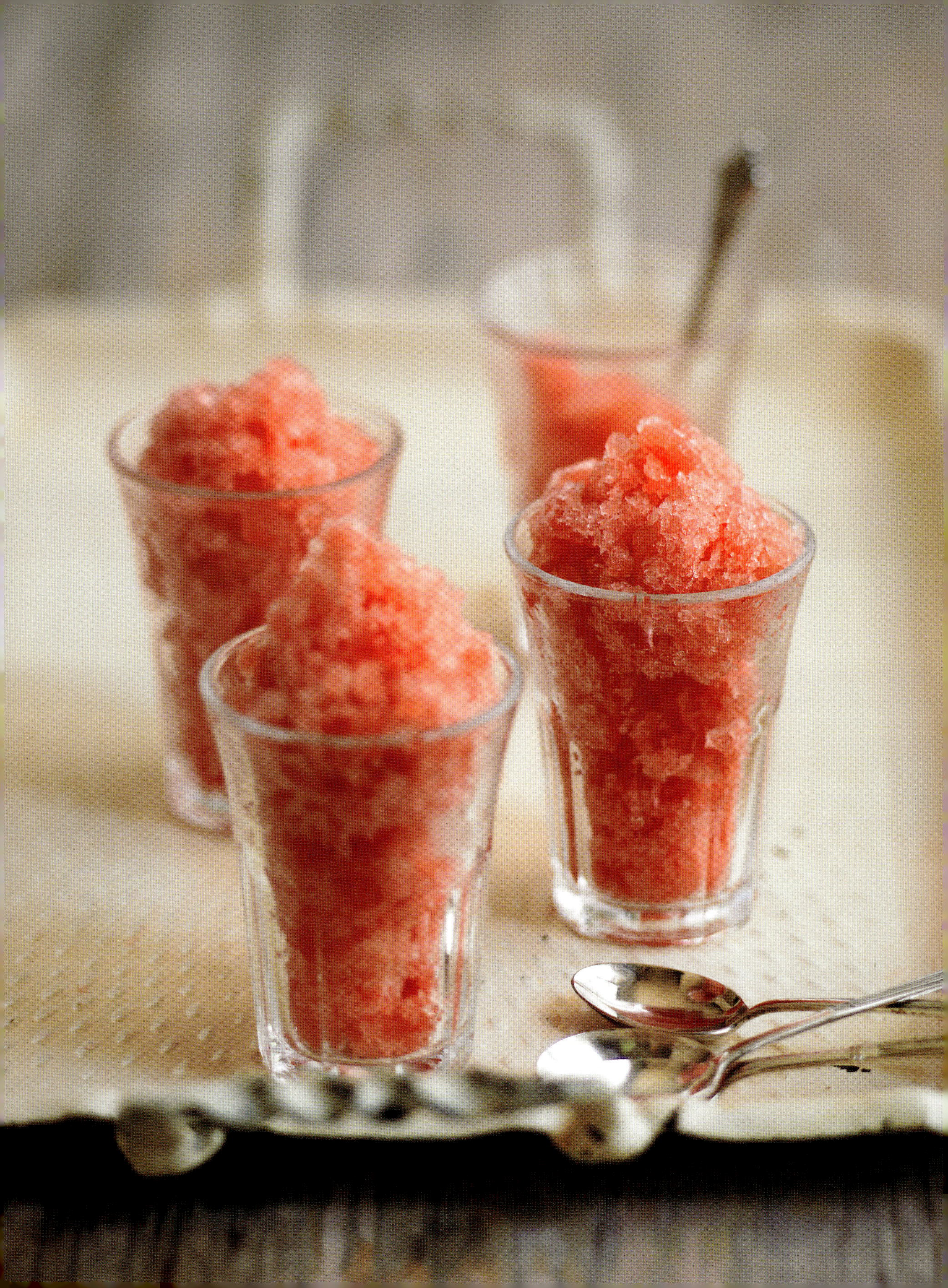

Watermelon and rosewater granita

A granita is a traditional ice dessert that is usually flavoured with fruit juice, coffee or wine. This version, reminiscent of the Middle East, is delicate and refreshing, with a subtle fragrance of rosewater to complement the sweetness of the watermelon.

SERVES 4   **PREPARATION TIME** 15 minutes   **COOKING TIME** nil   **FREEZING TIME** 4–6 hours

1.2–1.4 kg (2 lb 10 oz–3 lb 2 oz) wedge seedless watermelon
75 g (2¾ oz/⅓ cup) caster (superfine) sugar
2 tablespoons lemon juice
1 teaspoon rosewater, or to taste

1 Slice the watermelon and cut the flesh away from the rind *(pic 1)*, discarding the skin and rind. Weigh the flesh — you will need 700 g (1 lb 9 oz). Roughly chop the flesh.

2 Process the watermelon flesh, sugar and lemon juice in a food processor until smooth and well combined.

3 Transfer the watermelon mixture to a fine sieve set over a bowl and use a large spoon to push it through the sieve *(pic 2)*. Discard any pulp. Add the rosewater and stir to combine.

4 Pour the watermelon mixture into a square 20 cm (8 inch) cake tin. Freeze for 2–3 hours or until partially frozen. Use a fork to scrape the mixture to break it up into small ice crystals. Return to the freezer for a further 2–3 hours, scraping every hour *(pic 3)* to form small, even ice crystals, or until completely frozen. Return to the freezer until ready to serve.

5 Scrape the mixture with a fork before spooning into glasses to serve.

Cold Desserts

Dark chocolate mousse

Chocolate mousse is a winner with children and adults alike, and this rich, intense and indulgent version is sure to become a family favourite that's also perfect for entertaining.

SERVES 8–10   **PREPARATION TIME** 15 minutes (+ 3 hours chilling)   **COOKING TIME** 5 minutes

300 g (10½ oz) dark chocolate (70% cocoa solids)
500 ml (17 fl oz/2 cups) thickened (whipping) cream
6 egg yolks, at room temperature
110 g (3¾ oz/½ cup) caster (superfine) sugar
Amaretti biscuits and raspberries, to serve

1 Place the chocolate in a heatproof bowl over a saucepan of simmering water (make sure the base of the bowl doesn't touch the water) and stir occasionally until melted. Remove the bowl from the pan and set aside to cool.

2 Meanwhile, use an electric mixer with a whisk attachment to whisk the cream in a medium mixing bowl until soft peaks form. Set aside and clean the whisk attachment.

3 Put the egg yolks and sugar in another medium mixing bowl and use the cleaned whisk attachment to whisk for about 5 minutes or until very pale and thick *(pic 1)*.

4 Add the cooled chocolate to the egg yolk mixture and use a balloon whisk to whisk until just combined *(pic 2)*. Add the cream and whisk until just combined. Spoon the mousse into a serving bowl *(pic 3)*, cover and refrigerate for 3 hours or until set.

5 Serve spoonfuls of mousse with the amaretti biscuits and raspberries.

VARIATIONS

Choc-orange mousse: Whisk in 80 ml (2½ fl oz/⅓ cup) of Grand Marnier, or another orange liqueur, after the cream.

Espresso chocolate mousse: Whisk in 80 ml (2½ fl oz/⅓ cup) very strong, freshly made espresso coffee and 1 tablespoon of brandy after the cream.

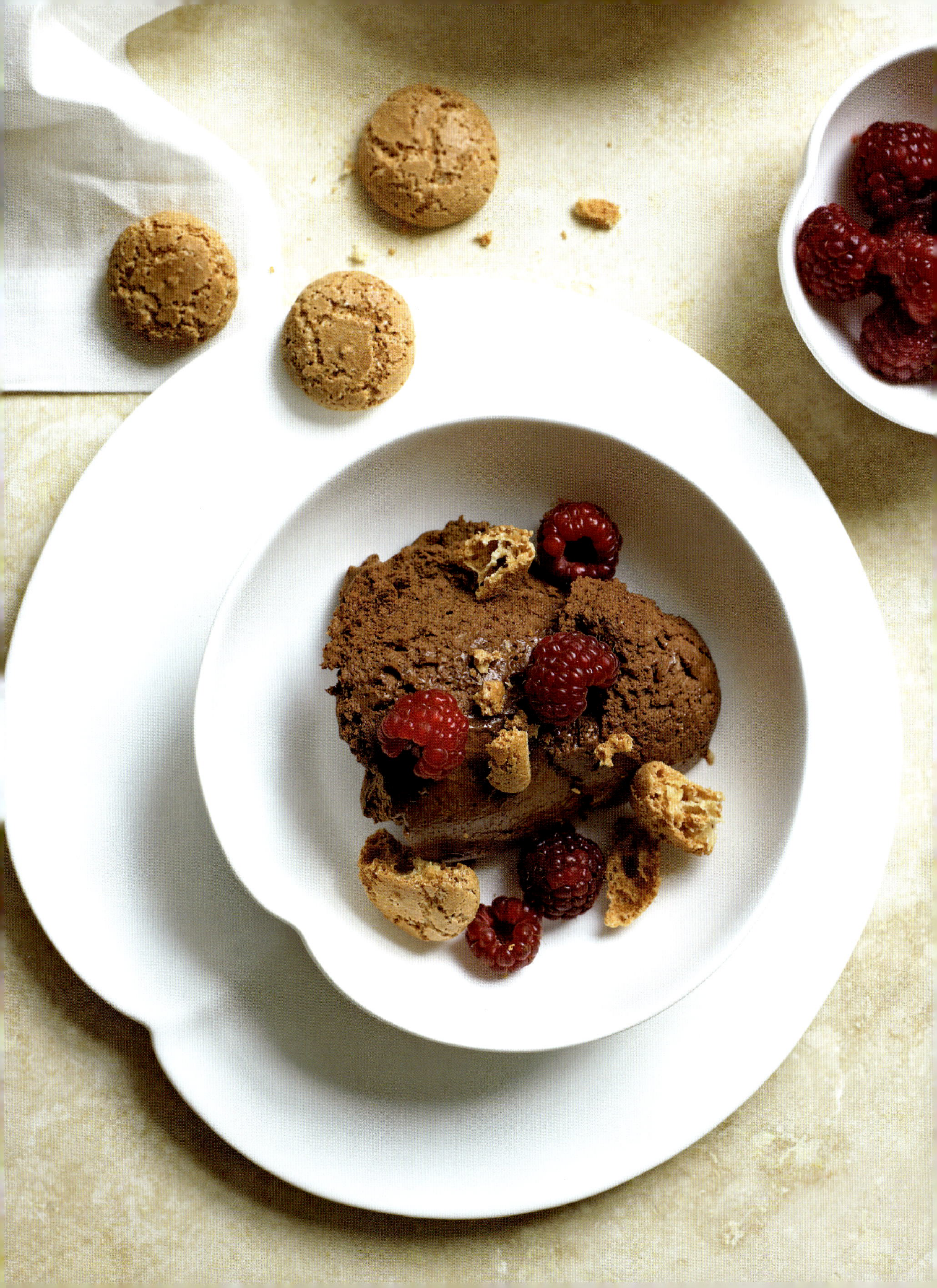

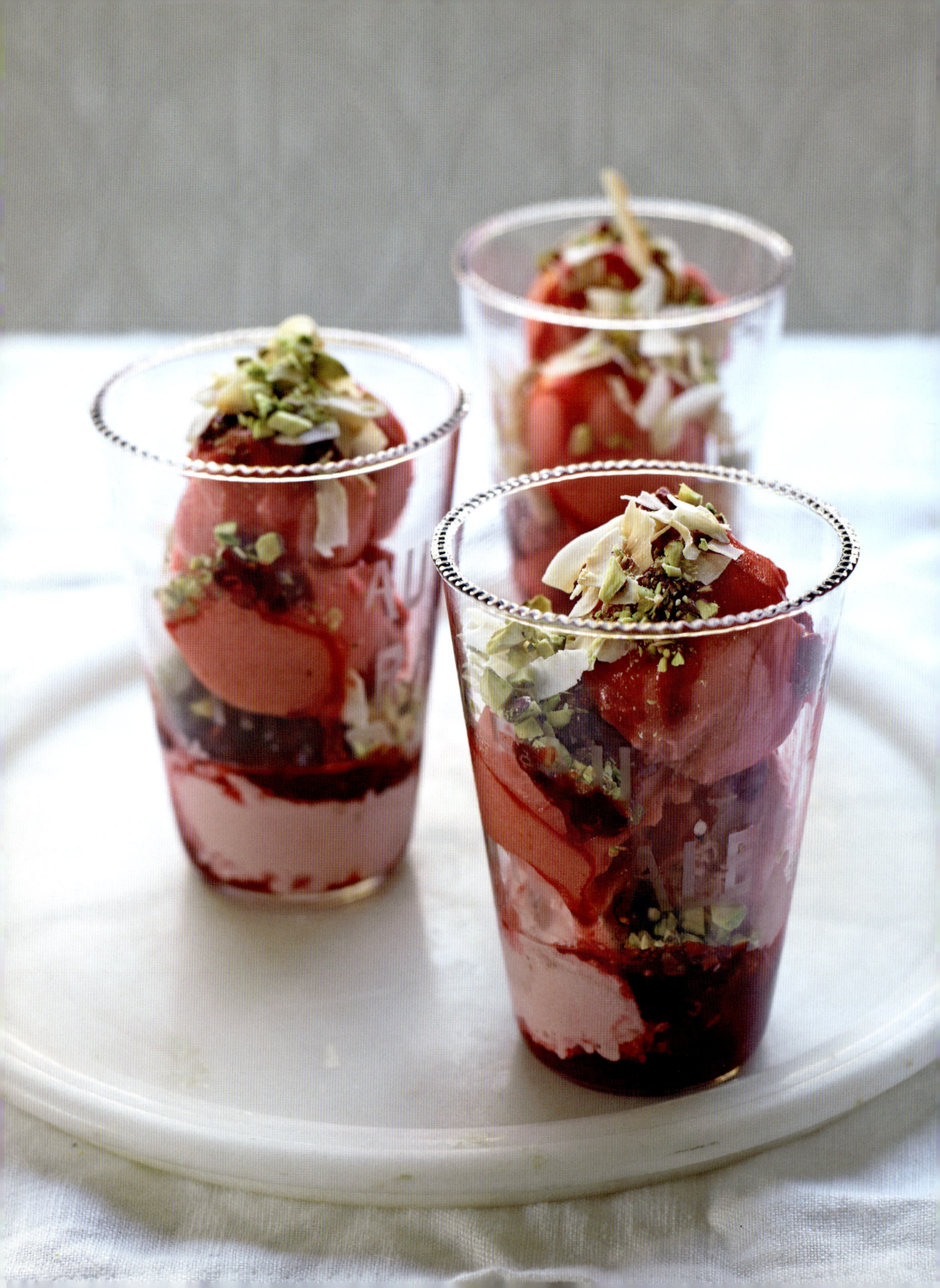

Berry sundae

This is one of those great desserts that you can pull together at the drop of a hat, but it looks impressive and tastes delicious. The combination of creamy ice cream and refreshing sorbet works beautifully, and the toasted coconut and pistachios provide extra flavour and crunch.

SERVES 6   **PREPARATION TIME** 10 minutes   **COOKING TIME** 3–5 minutes

30 g (1 oz/½ cup) flaked coconut
500 ml (17 fl oz/2 cups) good-quality berry ice cream
500 ml (17 fl oz/2 cups) good-quality berry sorbet
125 g (4½ oz) fresh or thawed frozen raspberries
2½ tablespoons pistachios, toasted and coarsely chopped

RASPBERRY SAUCE
200 g (7 oz) fresh or thawed frozen raspberries
40 g (1½ oz/⅓ cup) icing (confectioners') sugar

1 Preheat the oven to 180°C (350°F/Gas 4). Spread the coconut over a baking tray and toast for 3–5 minutes or until the edges are light golden *(pic 1)*. Set aside to cool.

2 To make the raspberry sauce, put the raspberries in a medium bowl and use a fork to roughly crush them *(pic 2)*. Sift the icing sugar over the crushed raspberries and mix to combine.

3 Place 2 scoops of ice cream in each of 6 serving glasses or bowls and spoon over half the raspberry sauce, dividing it evenly among them. Add 2 scoops of sorbet to each glass or bowl and spoon over the remaining raspberry sauce *(pic 3)*. Top with raspberries, coconut and pistachios. Serve immediately.

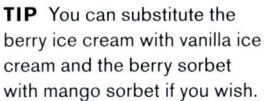

TIP You can substitute the berry ice cream with vanilla ice cream and the berry sorbet with mango sorbet if you wish.

Cold Desserts

Frozen Desserts

There's far more to frozen desserts than ice cream alone. The Italians and French have some delicious alternatives, and sorbet, gelato, frozen yoghurt and granita should all be added to the mix. Frozen desserts are the perfect do-ahead dessert and a great choice when the weather is warm.

What's in a name?

Frozen yoghurt is simply based on yoghurt, sugar and flavourings, such as fruit purées. Its texture isn't as smooth as ice cream due to the lack of cream in the mixture, and it has a refreshing tangy flavour.

Granita, like sorbet, is usually based on a sugar syrup with the addition of a flavouring such as a fruit purée or juice, wine or coffee. The partially frozen mixture is scraped with a fork as it freezes to create large, uniformly sized ice crystals that provide its characteristic granular texture.

Ice cream is generally based on a stirred custard mixture of eggs, milk and/or cream, and sugar with the addition of various flavourings such as vanilla, chocolate or fruit purées. Italian ice cream is called gelato.

Parfait is a French concoction involving a custard-based ice cream mixture with whipped cream folded through. It is often frozen without being churned.

Semifreddo is an Italian frozen dessert similar to ice cream, but with a very high cream and/or sugar content which gives it a very smooth texture. Its rich character also means that it freezes to a softer consistency than traditional ice cream giving the illusion that it isn't as cold, hence the Italian translation of 'half cold'. The term semifreddo can also be used to describe a chilled or semi-frozen dessert made from ice cream, cake, custards, whipped cream and/or fruit.

Sorbet is generally based on a sugar syrup, or a sweetened fruit juice or purée, to which other flavourings are added. Sorbets have a high water content and no fat, making them a refreshing frozen dessert option.

Using an ice-cream machine

1 Always chill an ice-cream, sorbet or gelato mixture well before churning to reduce the churning time and to make sure the churning process is complete before the machine becomes too warm.

2 Don't fill the machine's bowl more than two-thirds full, as the mixture will increase in volume while it is being stirred and frozen.

3 The amount of time a mixture will take to churn depends upon the type and combination of ingredients in it, as well as the efficiency of the machine. Thirty minutes should generally be enough to churn a mixture to a thick, smooth consistency.

4 When the mixture has finished churning, immediately transfer it to a freezer-proof container (either metal, ceramic or plastic), cover well and place in the freezer until firm.

Making frozen desserts by hand

A smooth texture is what you're after for home-made ice creams, gelati and sorbets. This is determined by the size of ice crystals that form during freezing — the smaller the ice crystals, the smoother the texture. An ice-cream machine stirs the mixture constantly while freezing it and this prevents large ice crystals from forming.

It is possible to make smooth-textured ice creams, gelati and sorbets without an ice-cream machine. Pour the prepared mixture into a freezer-proof container, seal well and freeze for 2–4 hours, until partially frozen (it will be firm around the edges but still relatively soft in the centre). Transfer the mixture to a food processor bowl and process until it is smooth but not melted (alternatively, put it in a chilled mixing bowl and use an electric mixer to beat) — this will break up the ice crystals and help create a smooth texture. Transfer the mixture immediately back to the freezer-proof container, reseal and freeze until it is completely frozen. Check the consistency of the mixture — depending on the type of frozen dessert it is and the combination of ingredients used, you may need to repeat the processing/beating process once or twice to reach the desired consistency.

Storing frozen desserts

Make sure all frozen desserts are tightly sealed when storing as they can easily pick up other flavours. The richer the mixture (the more cream, sugar and alcohol it contains), the longer it will keep for. Home-made ice creams, semifreddos, gelati and parfaits will keep well for up to 2 weeks. Sorbets, granitas and frozen yoghurts are best served within a week of making (granitas will often need scraping before serving as they solidify easily).

Peach ripple semifreddo

This summery semifreddo makes the most of the peach season with a tangy ripple of puréed fruit. You do not need an ice-cream machine to make this recipe.

MAKES 1.25 litres (44 fl oz/5 cups) **SERVES** 8–10 **PREPARATION TIME** 25 minutes (+ cooling and chilling)
COOKING TIME 15 minutes **FREEZING TIME** overnight

500 g (1 lb 2 oz/2¼ cups) caster (superfine) sugar, plus 110 g (3¾ oz/½ cup), extra
460 g (1 lb ¼ oz) firm, ripe yellow peaches (see tip), halved and stoned
2 eggs, at room temperature
4 egg yolks, at room temperature
375 ml (13 fl oz/1½ cups) pouring (whipping) cream
1 vanilla bean, split lengthways and seeds scraped

1 Put the sugar and 500 ml (17 fl oz/2 cups) water in a medium saucepan and stir over medium heat until the sugar dissolves. Increase the heat and bring to the boil. Add the peaches and simmer gently for 5 minutes. The skins should start to come off. Remove from the heat and set aside to cool for 10 minutes, then use a slotted spoon to transfer the peaches to a bowl. Reserve the syrup for serving. Peel away and discard the skins. Set the flesh aside to cool to room temperature, then transfer to a food processor bowl and process until smooth. Return to the bowl, cover and place in the refrigerator.

2 Combine the eggs, egg yolks and extra sugar in a heatproof bowl over a saucepan of simmering water (make sure the base of the bowl doesn't touch the water). Use electric hand-held beaters with a whisk attachment to whisk for 6 minutes or until thick and pale *(pic 1)*. Remove from the heat and whisk for 5 minutes or until the mixture has cooled to room temperature.

3 Put the cream and vanilla seeds in a medium bowl and use an electric mixer with a whisk attachment to whisk to very soft peaks. Use a large metal spoon or spatula to gently fold the whipped cream into the egg mixture until just combined *(pic 2)*.

4 Pour half of the semifreddo mixture into a square 20 cm (8 inch) freezer-proof container. Dot with half the peach purée and use a palette knife to swirl through to create a ripple effect *(pic 3)*. Pour over the remaining semifreddo mixture and dot with the remaining peach purée, swirling to create a ripple effect as before. Freeze overnight or until completely frozen. Serve the semifreddo in scoops with the reserved syrup spooned over, if desired.

TIP It's important that the peaches are ripe, both for flavour and so that the skins will start to peel away without having to overcook them.

100 Mastering the Basics: Desserts

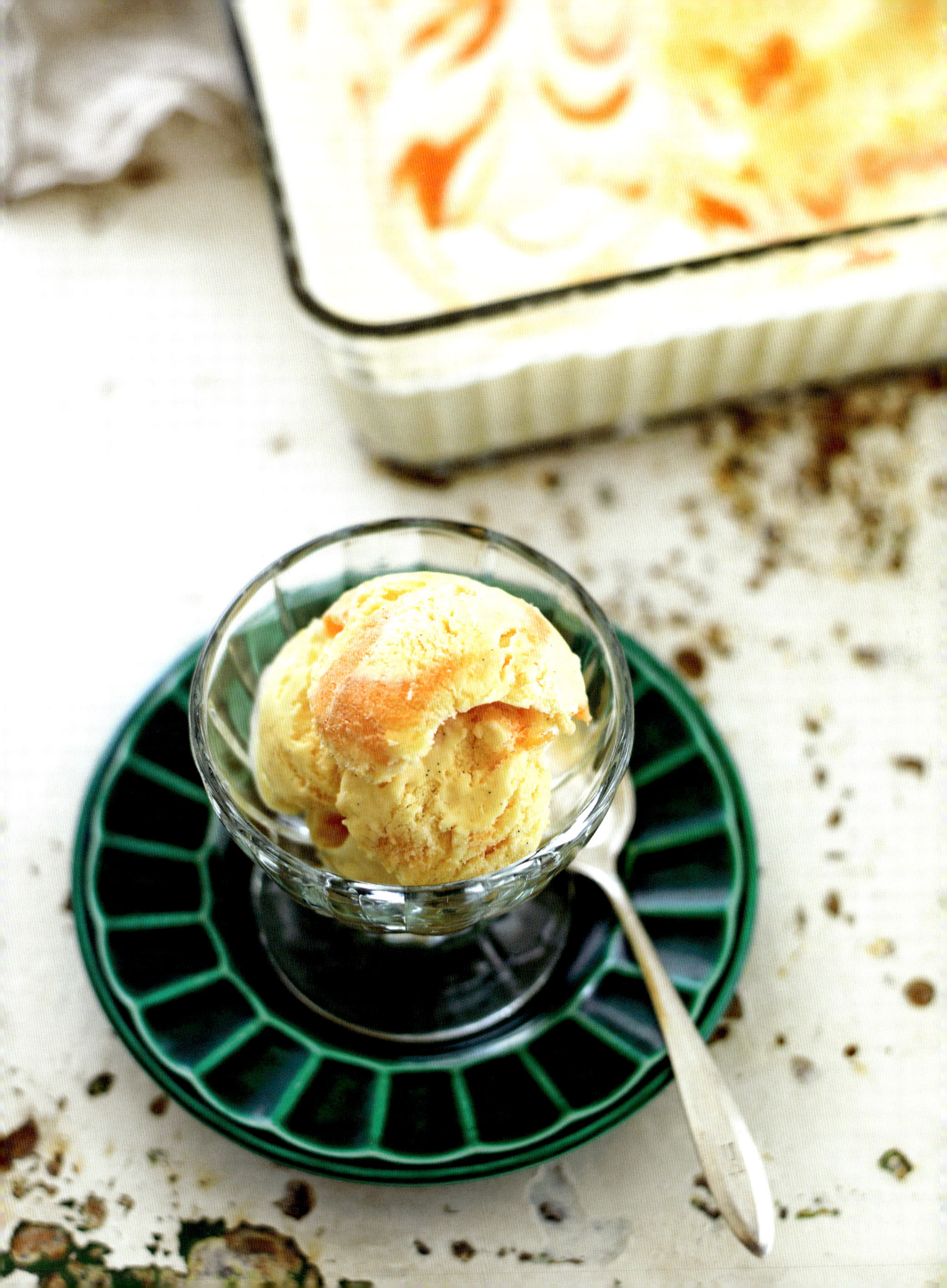

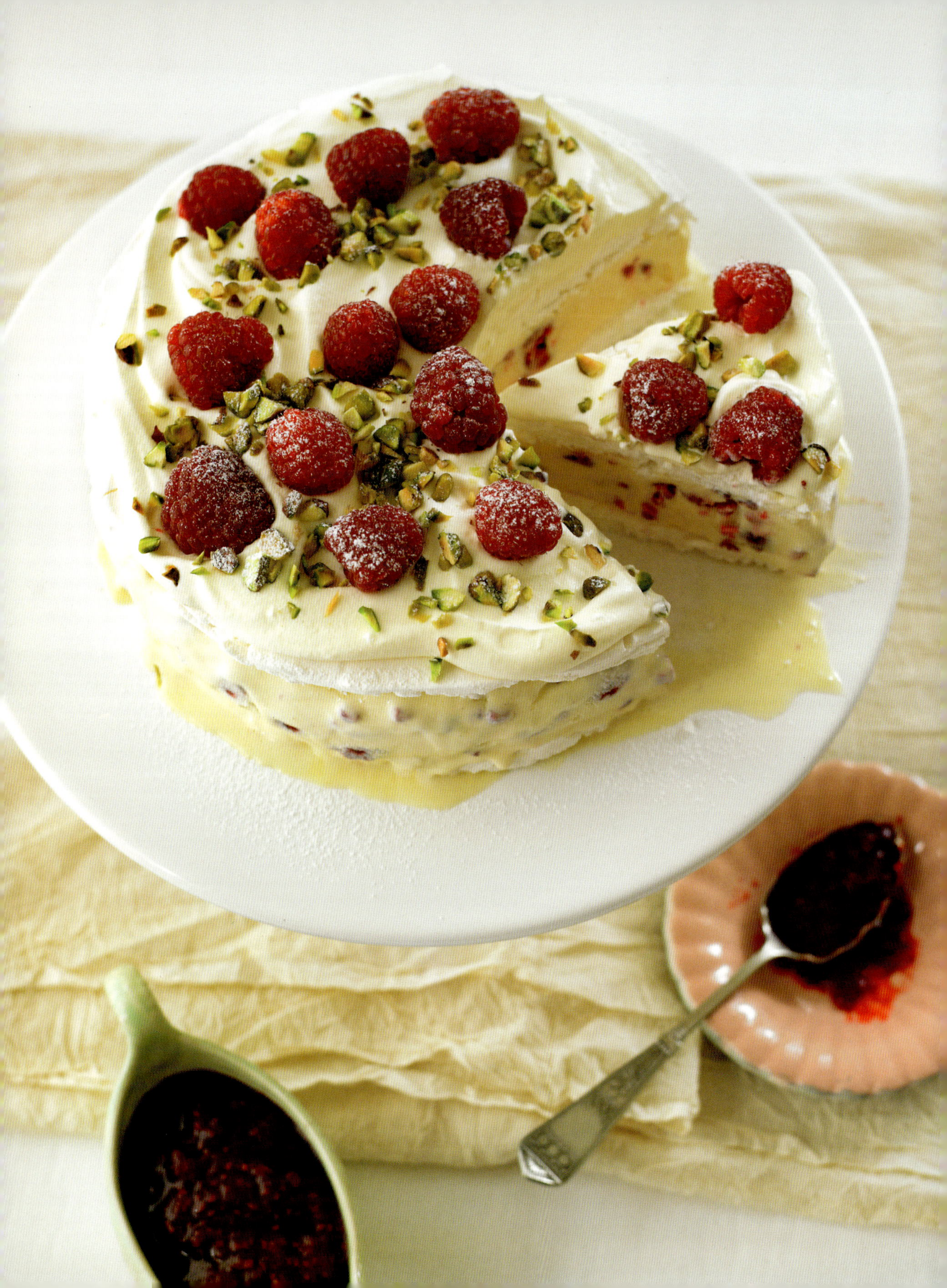

Raspberry and vanilla vacherin

SERVES 10 **PREPARATION TIME** 40 minutes (+ cooling and standing) **COOKING TIME** 2 hours 15 minutes **FREEZING TIME** 3 hours

3 egg whites, at room temperature
220 g (7¾ oz/1 cup) caster (superfine) sugar
600 ml (21 fl oz) vanilla ice cream
125 g (4½ oz) frozen raspberries
125 ml (4 fl oz/½ cup) thickened (whipping) cream
2 tablespoon pistachios, toasted and finely chopped
125 g (4½ oz/1 cup) fresh raspberries, to serve
Icing (confectioners') sugar, to dust

RASPBERRY COULIS
250 g (9 oz) frozen raspberries
2 tablespoons caster (superfine) sugar
1 tablespoon lemon juice

1 Preheat the oven to 150°C (300°F/Gas 2). Mark two 18 cm (7 inch) circles on a piece of non-stick baking paper. Turn the paper over and place on a large baking tray.

2 Use an electric mixer with a whisk attachment to whisk the egg whites and 2 tablespoons of the caster sugar until soft peaks form. With the motor running, add 110 g (3¾ oz/½ cup) of the remaining caster sugar, 1 tablespoon at a time, whisking well after each addition, until very thick and glossy. Use a spatula or large metal spoon to fold in the remaining caster sugar until well combined.

3 Divide the meringue between the two marked circles and use a palette knife to spread evenly *(pic 1)*. Bake for 8 minutes until starting to set. Reduce the oven temperature to 90°C (190°F/Gas ½) and bake for a further 2 hours, until crisp and dry all the way through. Transfer to a wire rack to cool.

4 Meanwhile, to make the raspberry coulis, put all the ingredients in a medium saucepan over medium heat and cook, covered, for 3 minutes. Stir until the sugar dissolves and the raspberries break down. Increase the heat and bring to the boil. Reduce the heat to low and simmer for 5 minutes.

5 Line a round 20 cm (8 inch) spring-form cake tin with non-stick baking paper. Place a meringue disc in the tin, trimming to fit if necessary *(pic 2)*.

6 Scoop the ice cream into a large bowl and set aside at room temperature for 5–10 minutes, until softened slightly but not melted. Add the frozen raspberries and quickly stir through until evenly distributed. Spoon the mixture into the tin, gently pressing down with the back of the spoon to remove any air pockets *(pic 3)*. Top with the remaining meringue disc, trimming to fit if necessary. Cover with plastic wrap and freeze for 3 hours or until firm.

7 To serve, use an electric mixer with a whisk attachment to whisk the cream until soft peaks form. Remove the vacherin from the freezer, remove from the tin and transfer to a chilled serving plate. Spread with the whipped cream, sprinkle with the pistachios and top with the fresh raspberries. Dust with icing sugar and serve with the coulis.

TIP You may need to stand the vacherin at room temperature for 5–10 minutes to allow it to soften slightly before serving. Use a large sharp knife, dipped in hot water and dried, to cut it.

Cold Desserts   **103**

Mango sorbet

MAKES 1 litre (35 fl oz/4 cups)   **SERVES** 6–8   **PREPARATION TIME** 25 minutes (+ cooling and chilling)
COOKING TIME 5 minutes   **FREEZING TIME** 6 hours

150 g (5½ oz/⅔ cup) caster (superfine) sugar
4 large ripe mangoes (about 475 g/1 lb 1 oz each) (see tip)
125 ml (4 fl oz/½ cup) strained freshly squeezed lime juice

1 Place the sugar and 200 ml (7 fl oz) water in a small saucepan over low heat and stir until the sugar dissolves. Increase the heat to high and bring to the boil. Boil for 1 minute. Pour into a heatproof bowl and set aside until cooled to room temperature (you can put it in the refrigerator to reduce the cooling time).

2 Use a large metal spoon to remove the flesh from the mangoes *(pic 1)*, discarding the skin and stones. Weigh the mango flesh — you will need 950 g (2 lb 2 oz). Place the mango flesh in the bowl of a food processor and process until it is puréed.

3 Transfer the mango purée to a sieve set over a bowl and use a large spoon to push it through to extract as much liquid as possible *(pic 2)*. Discard the mango pulp. Add the cooled sugar syrup and lime juice to the mango juice and stir well. Cover and refrigerate until well chilled.

4 Churn the mango mixture in an ice-cream machine following the manufacturer's instructions *(pic 3)*. Transfer to a freezer-proof container and freeze for 6 hours or overnight, until completely frozen. Serve in scoops.

TIP Make sure you use ripe mangoes that have a strong aroma in this sorbet for the best result.

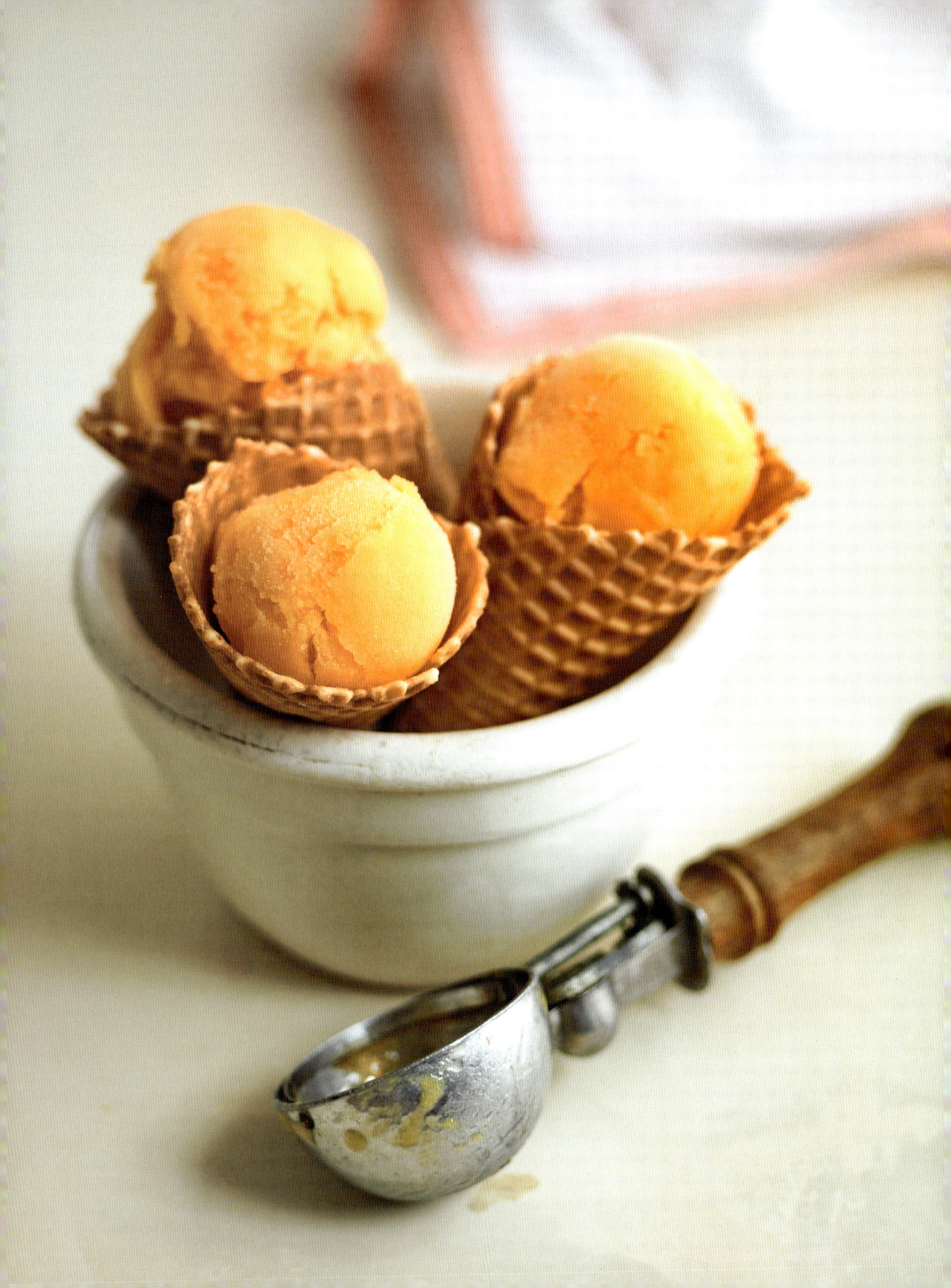

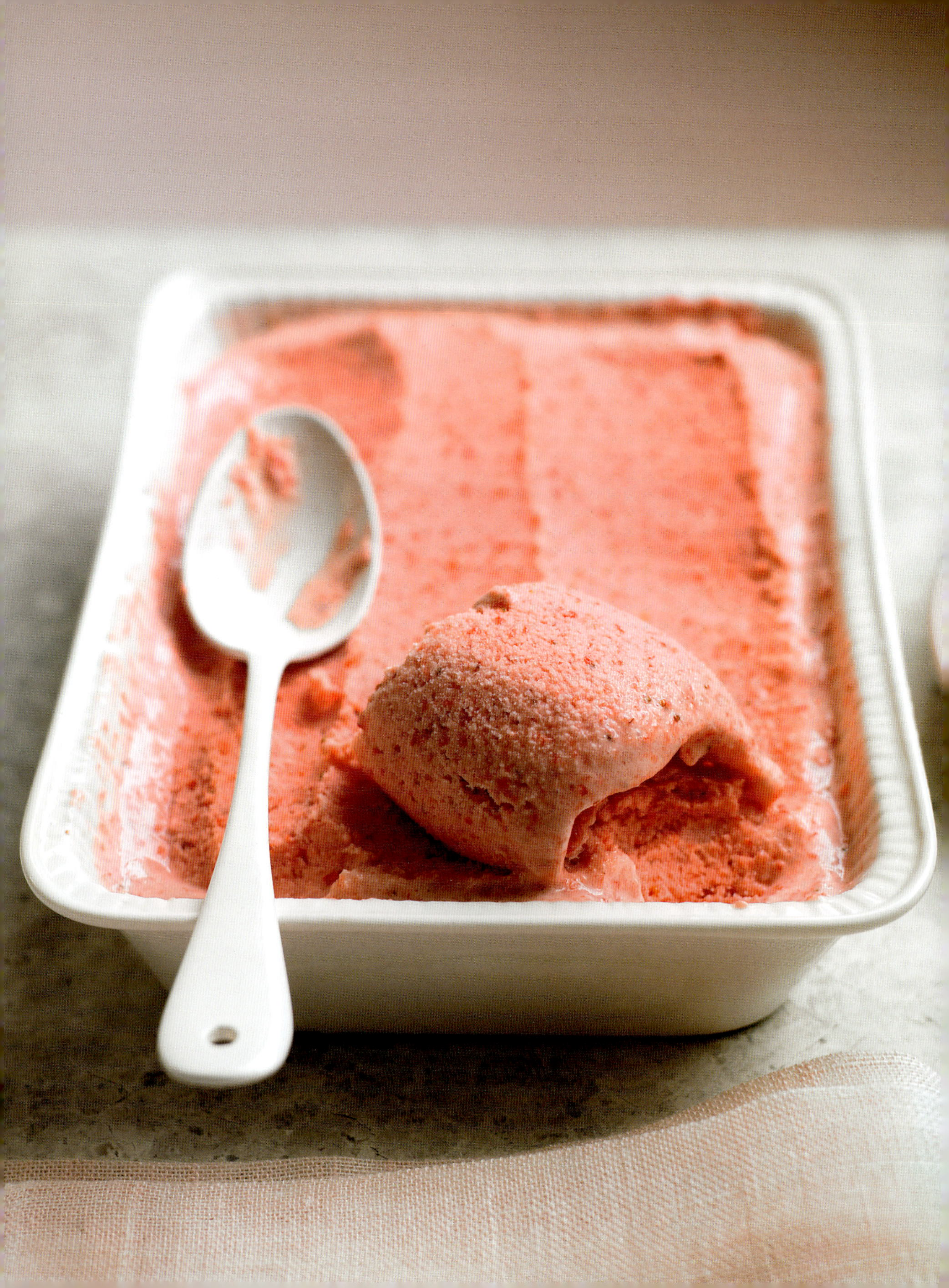

Strawberry frozen yoghurt

To make this sublime dessert more sophisticated, add 2 teaspoons of vodka or a flavoured liqueur towards the end of churning time. Don't go overboard, as it won't freeze properly if you add too much.

MAKES about 650 ml (22½ fl oz) **SERVES** 6–8 **PREPARATION TIME** 15 minutes (+ 2 hours standing, and churning) **COOKING TIME** nil **FREEZING TIME** 2 hours

500 g (1 lb 2 oz) ripe strawberries, hulled and diced
110 g (3¾ oz/½ cup) caster (superfine) sugar
390 g (13¾ oz/1½ cups) full-fat Greek-style yoghurt

1 Combine the strawberries and sugar in a medium bowl *(pic 1)* and set aside, tossing occasionally, for 2 hours or until the sugar dissolves.

2 Transfer the strawberry mixture to a food processor bowl, add the yoghurt *(pic 2)* and process until smooth.

3 Churn the strawberry mixture in an ice-cream machine following the manufacturer's instructions *(pic 3)*. Transfer to an airtight container and freeze for 2 hours or until firm.

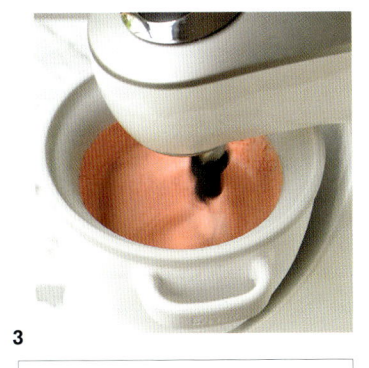

TIP If you don't have an ice-cream machine, freeze the mixture in a metal container until partially frozen. Transfer to a chilled bowl and use an electric mixer to beat until smooth. Return to the container and freeze until set.

Tipsy trifle

This is one of the best trifles you will ever make — rich and completely indulgent. Although it's completely adults only, as the name implies, you can make a kid-friendly version by replacing the sherry with freshly squeezed orange juice.

SERVES 8–10   **PREPARATION TIME** 30 minutes (+ 2 hours chilling)   **COOKING TIME** nil

- 400 g (14 oz) ready-made or home-made plain sponge cake
- 165 g (5¾ oz/½ cup) cherry or berry jam (such as raspberry, strawberry, blackberry)
- 1 quantity crème pâtissiére (see page 23), cooled
- 250 ml (9 fl oz/1 cup) pouring (whipping) cream, lightly whipped
- 375 ml (13 fl oz/1½ cups) sweet sherry
- 250 ml (9 fl oz/1 cup) pouring (whipping) cream, extra, lightly whipped
- 35 g (1¼ oz/⅓ cup) flaked almonds, toasted

1 Use a long serrated knife to split the sponge cake horizontally (cut the cake in half first to make it easier to handle, if necessary). Spread the jam over the bottom layer of cake, top with the remaining layer and then cut the cake into 3.5 cm (1⅓ inch) pieces *(pic 1)*.

2 Use a large metal spoon or spatula to stir the crème pâtissiére in a medium bowl until smooth. Add the cream and fold in until evenly combined.

3 Place one-third of the cake pieces in a 2 litre (70 fl oz/8 cup) glass or ceramic serving bowl, then drizzle with one-third of the sherry *(pic 2)*. Spoon over one-third of the crème pâtissiére mixture *(pic 3)*, spreading it as evenly as possible. Continue to make 2 more layers with the remaining cake, sherry and crème pâtissiére mixture. Cover with plastic wrap and refrigerate for at least 2 hours or until ready to serve.

4 To serve, spread the extra cream over the top of the trifle and sprinkle with the toasted almonds.

TIP This trifle can be made up to 2 days before serving.

Mastering the Basics: Desserts

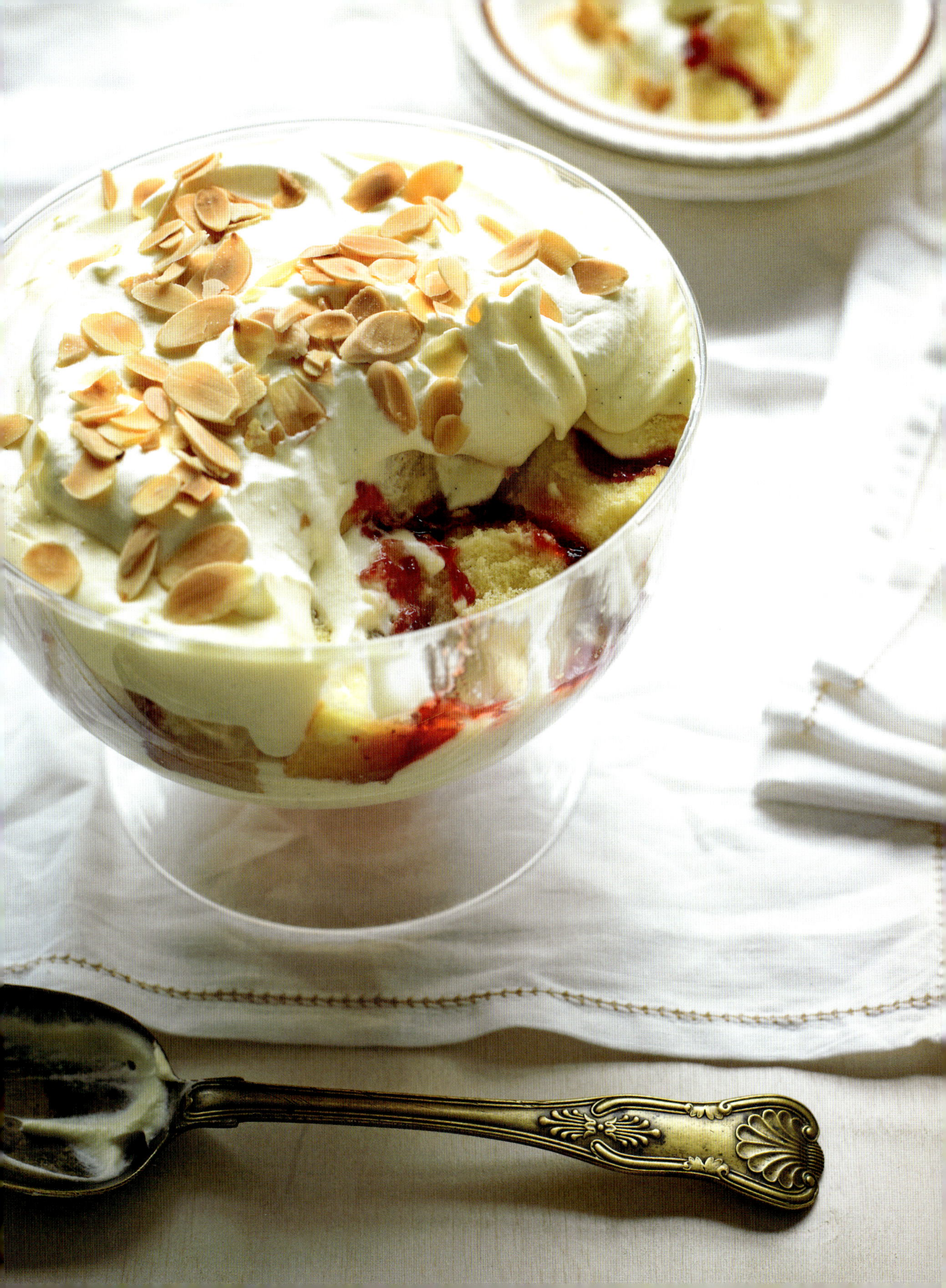

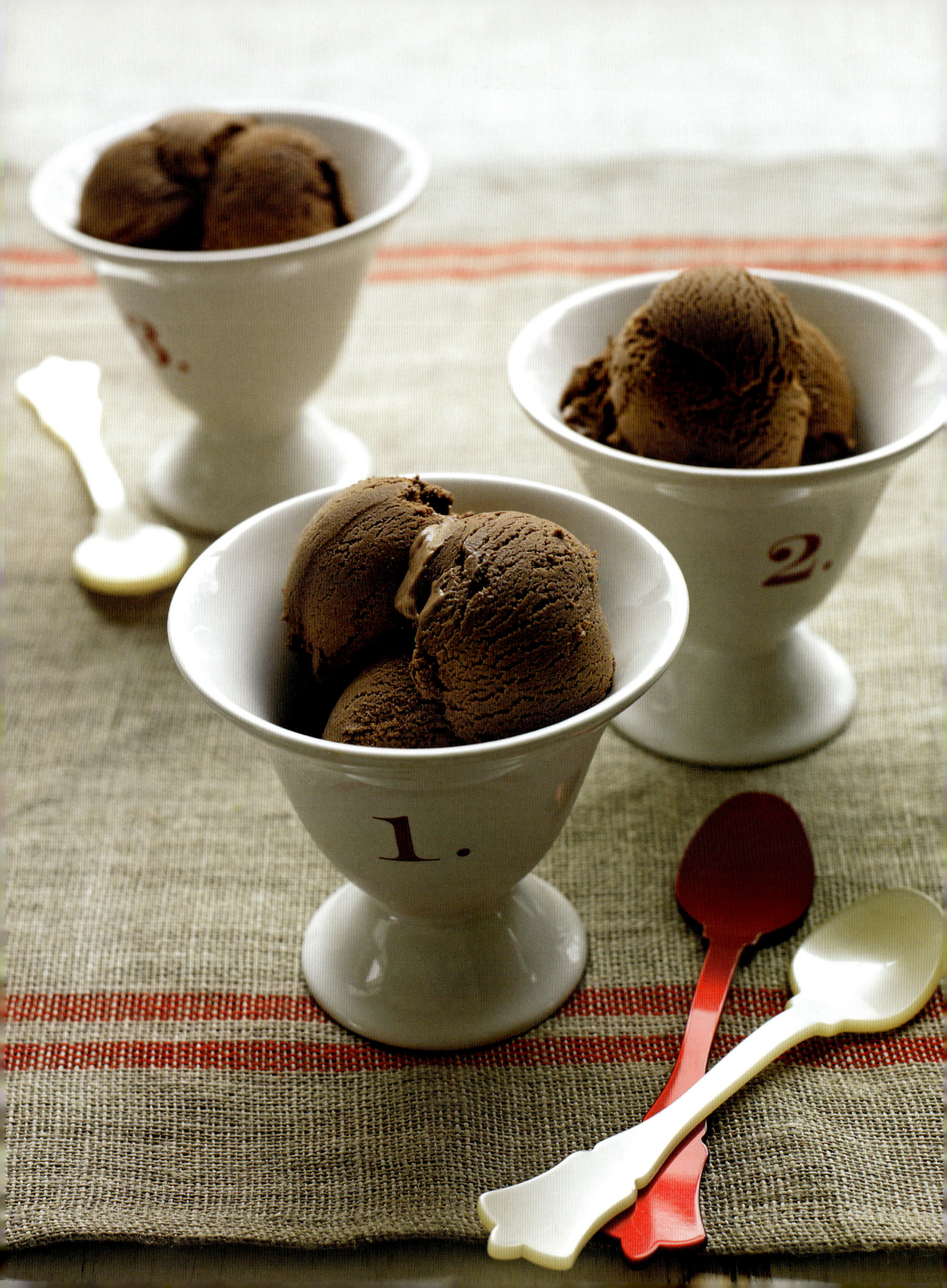
1.
2.

Chocolate ice cream

MAKES 1 litre (35 fl oz/4 cups) **SERVES** 4–6 **PREPARATION TIME** 10 minutes (+ chilling and churning)
COOKING TIME 10 minutes **FREEZING TIME** 3–4 hours

400 ml (14 fl oz) milk
300 ml (10½ fl oz) thickened (whipping) cream
250 g (9 oz) dark chocolate, finely chopped
5 egg yolks, at room temperature
110 g (3¾ oz/⅔ cup) caster (superfine) sugar

1 Put the milk, cream and chocolate in a medium heavy-based saucepan over low heat and cook, stirring constantly, for 3–5 minutes or until the chocolate melts and the mixture is smooth *(pic 1)*. Remove from the heat and set aside.

2 Meanwhile, use an electric mixer with a whisk attachment to whisk the egg yolks and sugar in a medium mixing bowl for 5 minutes or until very thick and pale.

3 Add the egg mixture to the chocolate mixture. Use a wooden spoon to stir constantly over medium–low heat for about 5 minutes or until the custard thickens slightly, coats the back of the spoon and holds its shape when you draw your finger across the spoon *(pic 2)*. Transfer the custard to a bowl and place in the freezer, stirring occasionally, until well chilled but not set.

4 Churn the chilled chocolate mixture in an ice-cream machine following the manufacturer's instructions *(pic 3)*. Transfer to a freezer-proof container and freeze for 3–4 hours, until firm. Serve in scoops.

TIP If you don't have an ice-cream machine, put the mixture in a freezer-proof container, cover and freeze for 3 hours or until partially frozen. Transfer to a food processor bowl and process until smooth. Return to the container, cover and freeze for 3 hours or until set.

Cold Desserts

Pear charlotte

SERVES 8　**PREPARATION TIME** 45 minutes (+ cooling and overnight chilling)　**COOKING TIME** 10 minutes

250 g (9 oz/about 25) savoiardi biscuits (lady fingers)
Dark chocolate sauce (see page 22), to serve

FILLING
160 ml (5¼ fl oz/⅔ cup) milk
½ vanilla bean, split lengthways and seeds scraped
3 egg yolks
55 g (2 oz/¼ cup) caster (superfine) sugar
3 teaspoons powdered gelatine
2 ripe pears (500 g/1 lb 2 oz), peeled, cored and diced
250 ml (9 fl oz/1 cup) thickened (whipping) cream, whipped

BRANDY SYRUP
110 g (3¾ oz/⅔ cup) caster (superfine) sugar
60 ml (2 fl oz/¼ cup) brandy

1 To make the brandy syrup, put the sugar and 250 ml (9 fl oz/1 cup) water in a small saucepan over high heat and bring to the boil, stirring constantly until the sugar dissolves. Set aside to cool, then stir in the brandy.

2 To make the filling, put the milk and vanilla seeds in a small saucepan over high heat and bring almost to the boil. Use an electric mixer with a whisk attachment to whisk the egg yolks and sugar in a large bowl for about 3 minutes or until pale and tripled in volume (a thick ribbon will almost form when the beaters are lifted). Whisk in the milk mixture until combined, then pour into a medium saucepan. Cook, stirring constantly with a wooden spoon, over medium heat for about 5 minutes or until the mixture thickens and coats the back of the spoon (do not boil or the custard will curdle).

3 Meanwhile, sprinkle the gelatine over 2 tablespoons of hot water in a small bowl and stir until the gelatine dissolves. Stir the gelatine mixture into the custard. Stir in a third of the pears and blend until smooth using a stick blender. Refrigerate for 20 minutes or until cool (don't leave the mixture for too long or it will set). Use a large metal spoon or spatula to fold one-third of the pear custard into the whipped cream. Fold in the remaining pear custard until smooth and just combined.

4 To assemble, lightly grease a 2 litre (70 fl oz/8 cup) charlotte mould. Working with one biscuit at a time, dip in the brandy syrup and place around the side of the mould (sugar-side out) *(pic 1)*. Line the base with soaked biscuits, cutting them to fit snugly. Spoon one-third of the pear mixture into the mould and smooth the surface. Add one-third of the remaining diced pears, making sure they are evenly distributed *(pic 2)*. Repeat with the remaining pear mixture and diced pears in 2 batches. Dip the remaining biscuits in the syrup and press lightly into the pear mixture to cover the filling *(pic 3)*. Refrigerate, covered, overnight until set.

5 Turn the charlotte out onto a cake stand or serving plate. Serve in wedges, accompanied by the chocolate sauce.

TIP Pears that are ripe and full of flavour will give the best result. To avoid the pears discolouring, wait until you are ready to use them before peeling and dicing. You could add lemon juice but it will affect the taste.

Mastering the Basics: Desserts

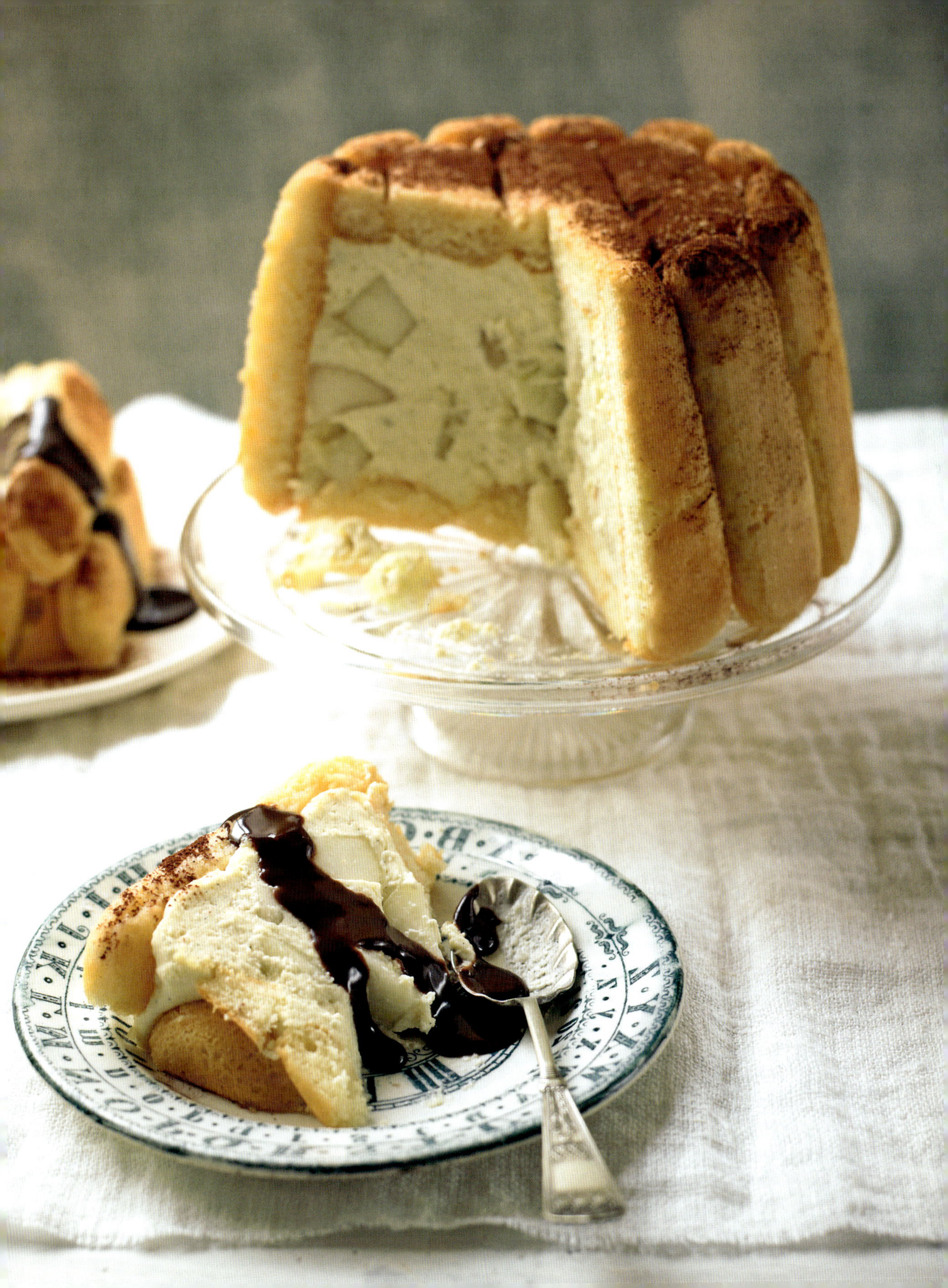

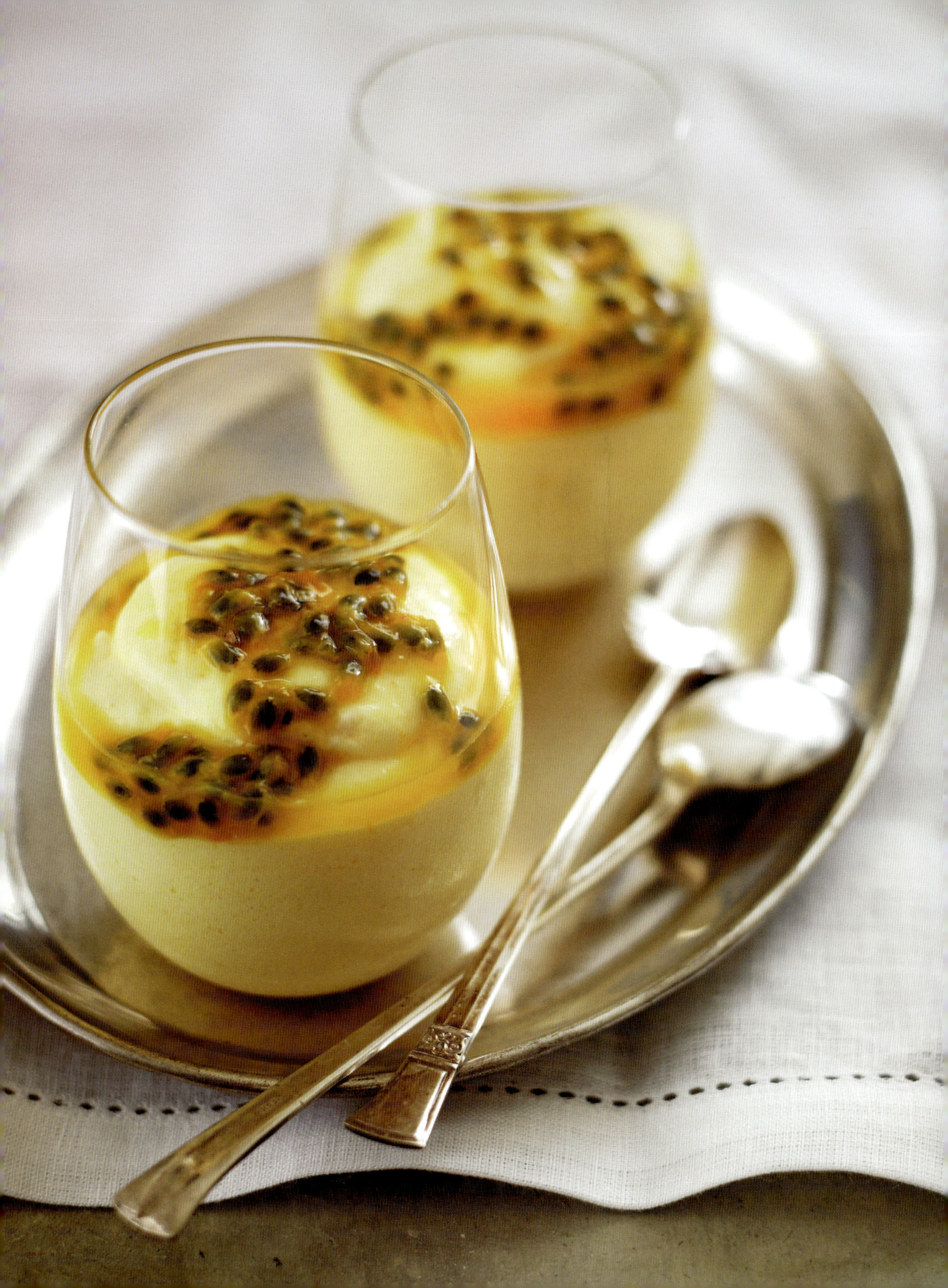

Passionfruit mousse

With its sunny colour and tropical flavour, this memorable mousse is a great way to make the most of passionfruit when they are in season.

SERVES 6   **PREPARATION TIME** 30 minutes (+ cooling and 2–3 hours chilling)   **COOKING TIME** 5 minutes

16 passionfruit, pulp removed, plus 6 extra passionfruit, pulp removed
2 teaspoons powdered gelatine
3 eggs, at room temperature, separated
110 g (3¾ oz/½ cup) caster (superfine) sugar, plus 1½ tablespoons, extra
250 ml (9 fl oz/1 cup) pouring (whipping) cream

1 Push the pulp from the 16 passionfruit through a sieve set over a bowl to extract the juice — you will need 185 ml (6 fl oz/¾ cup). Discard the seeds. Pour half the passionfruit juice into a small heatproof bowl or cup, sprinkle over the gelatine and stand for 5 minutes or until the gelatine has softened. Place the bowl in a saucepan with enough water to come halfway up the side of the bowl. Heat gently over medium–low heat *(pic 1)* until the gelatine dissolves. Remove the bowl from the pan, stir in the remaining passionfruit juice and cool to room temperature.

2 Use an electric mixer with a whisk attachment to whisk the egg yolks and sugar in a medium bowl until thick and pale. Stir in the cooled gelatine mixture *(pic 2)*, then refrigerate for 30 minutes or until just beginning to set.

3 Use electric beaters with a whisk attachment to whisk the cream in a medium bowl until soft peaks form. Clean the whisk attachment. Put the egg whites in a clean, dry medium bowl and whisk until soft peaks form. Use a large metal spoon or spatula to fold the whipped cream through the passionfruit mixture until evenly combined. Add one-third of the egg whites and fold to combine well. Gently fold in the remaining egg whites *(pic 3)*.

4 Divide the mixture evenly among six 250 ml (9 fl oz/1 cup) serving glasses. Cover each with plastic wrap and refrigerate for 2–3 hours or until set.

5 Combine the pulp from the 6 extra passionfruit with the extra sugar in a small bowl and stir until the sugar dissolves. Spoon over the mousse in the glasses and serve.

TIP This mousse can be made up to 1 day ahead of serving.
It is also delicious served topped with sliced strawberries or raspberries instead of the passionfruit pulp.

Gelatine

Gelatine is a tasteless setting agent used in many chilled desserts. It is a crucial ingredient in dishes such as charlottes, jellies and mousses. It gives body to custard-like mixtures so they can hold their shape and also traps air in whisked eggs and cream to retain their light texture.

Powdered versus leaf gelatine

Commercial gelatine used in dessert making is available in two forms: powdered and leaf, or sheet, form. Powdered gelatine is sold in small canisters or sachets, while leaf gelatine is sold as brittle sheets. Leaf gelatine can vary in weight and setting strength so make sure you check the details before using it. Brands and grades of gelatine vary greatly and there is no set rule for substitution for powdered gelatine.

The amount of gelatine required in a recipe is determined by the quantity of mixture to be set and how firm it needs to become. Soft-set, airy mixtures (such as a fruit mousse) will need less gelatine than creamy, more firmly set ones (such as a charlotte). Always follow the recommended quantity in the recipe and remember that any additional gelatine may leave you with a dessert that has a 'rubbery' texture.

Softening and melting gelatine

Before gelatine is added to a mixture, both powdered and leaf gelatine must be softened to swell the gelatine granules so they will dissolve evenly when heated. Powdered gelatine also needs to be dissolved in a little liquid.

To soften and dissolve powdered gelatine, sprinkle it over a small amount of liquid in a heatproof dish and set aside for 5 minutes for it to be absorbed (it will become spongy). Then, place the dish in a saucepan with enough water to come about halfway up the side of the dish. Heat over low heat, without stirring, until the gelatine dissolves and the liquid is clear. Don't stir the mixture while heating it or the gelatine may form 'strings' that will prevent it from dissolving completely. Remove from the pan and use as directed.

To soften leaf gelatine, place it in a bowl of water to cover and set aside to soak for 5 minutes or until it is very soft. Use your hands to squeeze the gelatine to remove any excess water. Add the softened gelatine to the mixture (the mixture needs to be warm) and stir to incorporate.

Unmoulding gelatine desserts

Gelatine desserts need to be loosened from their mould before turning onto a serving plate.

To release small individual desserts (such as panna cotta) from their moulds, gently press down and towards the centre of the dessert with your fingertips to break the seal around the edge. Invert the mould onto a serving plate and gently shake it until the dessert is released.

Larger gelatine desserts are often best released by briefly dipping in hot water to melt the mixture slightly, therefore breaking the seal. Dip the mould in hot water for only a few seconds (metal moulds will need less time than plastic or ceramic ones). Use your fingertips to gently pull the mixture away from the side of the mould to break the seal. Place a serving plate over the top of the mould and invert. Holding the plate and mould firmly together, give a quick shake to release the dessert onto the plate. Give it a few more quick shakes if it sticks. If the dessert doesn't release, rinse a tea towel (dish towel) under hot water and then place over the mould for about 10 seconds before shaking quickly again.

TIP Some fruits, such as raw pineapple and kiwi fruit, contain an enzyme that inhibits gelatine from setting, so avoid these when making desserts that contain gelatine.

Cold Desserts 117

Lemon macaroon and strawberry mousse cake

SERVES 8 **PREPARATION TIME** 40 minutes (+ 30 minutes cooling and 3 hours chilling) **COOKING TIME** 30 minutes

4 egg whites, at room temperature
165 g (5¾ oz/¾ cup) caster (superfine) sugar
1 teaspoon natural vanilla extract
135 g (4¾ oz/1⅓ cups) almond meal
35 g (1¼ oz/¼ cup) plain (all-purpose) flour
1 teaspoon finely grated lemon zest
2 tablespoons strawberry jam
125 ml (4 fl oz/½ cup) thickened (whipping) cream, whisked to firm peaks
95 g (3¼ oz/1 cup) flaked almonds, toasted and lightly crushed, to serve
Strawberries and icing (confectioners') sugar, to garnish

STRAWBERRY MOUSSE
600 ml (21 fl oz) thickened (whipping) cream
180 g (6¼ oz) white chocolate, finely chopped
250 g (9 oz) strawberries, hulled
2 tablespoons strawberry jam
1 tablespoon powdered gelatine

1 Preheat the oven to 180°C (350°F/Gas 4). Grease two 22 cm (8½ inch) spring-form cake tins and line each tin with non-stick baking paper.

2 Put the egg whites in a clean, dry bowl and use an electric mixer with a whisk attachment to whisk until soft peaks form. Gradually add the sugar, whisking well after each addition, until thick and glossy. Whisk in the vanilla.

3 Combine the almond meal, flour and zest. Add to the meringue mixture and use a large metal spoon to fold until just combined. Divide between the tins and smooth the surface. Bake for 18 minutes, until lightly browned. Cool in the tins.

4 To make the strawberry mousse, bring 125 ml (4 fl oz/½ cup) of the cream almost to the boil in a small saucepan. Remove from heat, add the chocolate and set aside for 30 seconds. Stir until melted. Set aside for 30 minutes to cool.

5 Meanwhile, process the strawberries and jam until smooth. Push through a sieve set over a bowl. Discard the seeds. Sprinkle the gelatine over 60 ml (2 fl oz/¼ cup) warm water in a small heatproof jug. Set aside for 5 minutes to soften. Stand the jug in a small saucepan of simmering water and heat gently until the gelatine dissolves *(pic 1)*.

7 Use an electric mixer with a whisk attachment to whisk the remaining cream until firm peaks form. Fold in the strawberry purée, chocolate mixture and gelatine until just combined *(pic 2)*.

8 Remove a macaroon from the tin. Spread the other macaroon, still in the tin, with the jam. Spread the strawberry mousse *(pic 3)* over the jam, then top with the remaining macaroon. Cover and refrigerate for 3 hours or overnight.

9 Remove the cake from the tin. Spread cream over the side, then press almonds onto the cream. Top with strawberries, dust with icing sugar and serve.

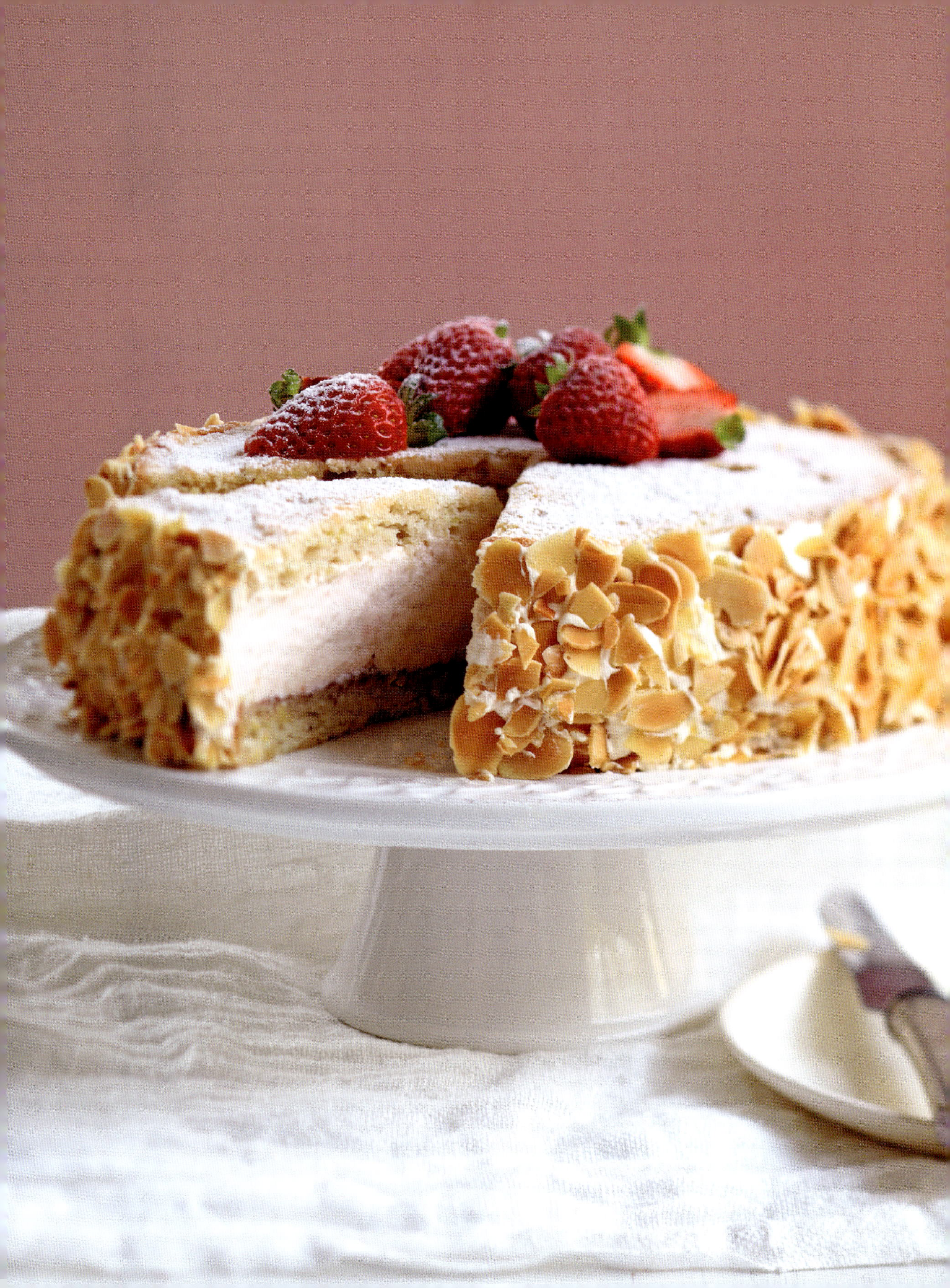

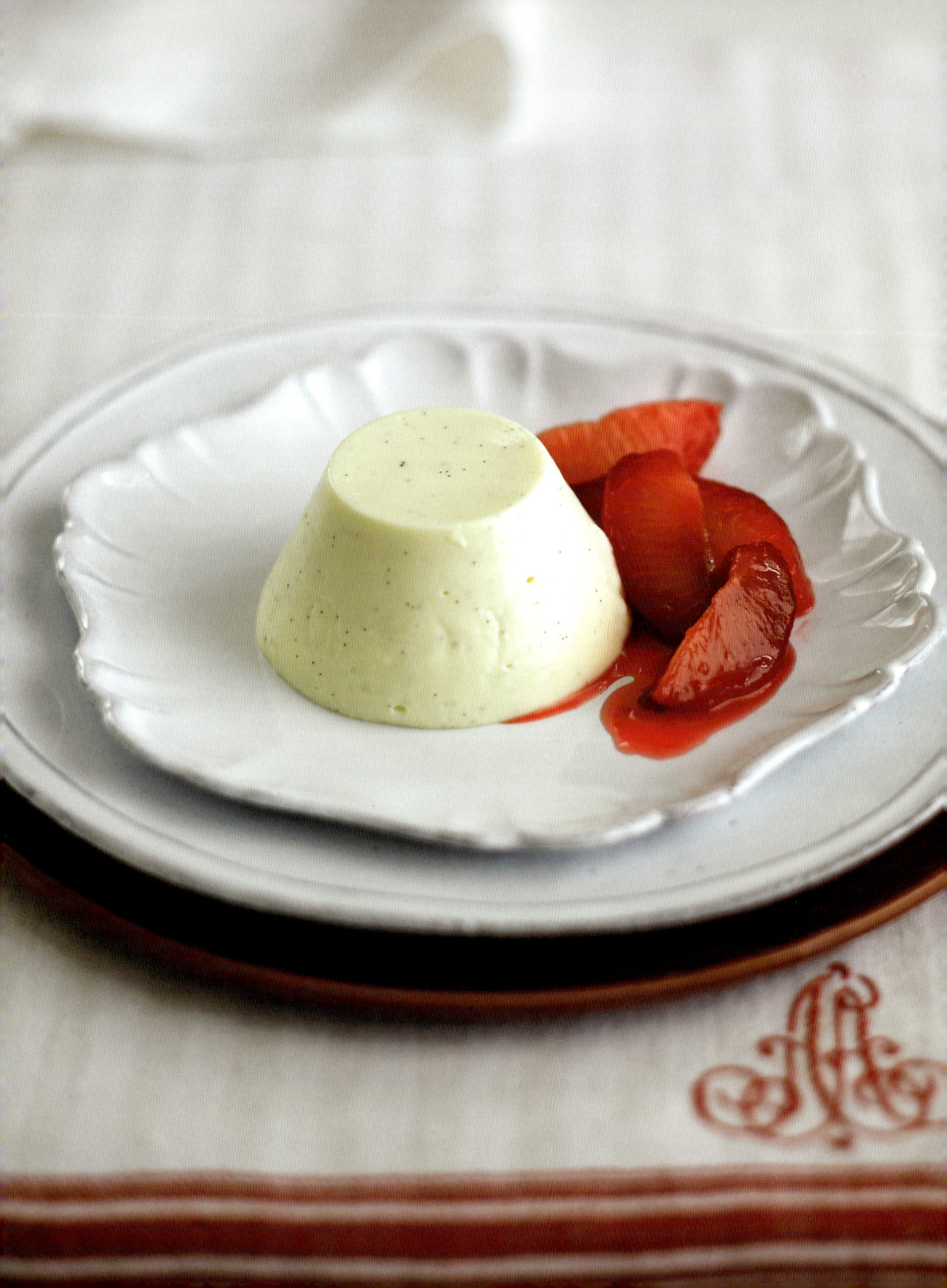

Vanilla panna cotta with poached plums

Panna cotta is an Italian term that translates as cooked cream. However, there's a bit more to this light, silky textured dessert than cream alone. Milk, sugar and flavourings are added, then the hot mixture is set with the addition of gelatine. Poached fruit is a terrific partner for panna cotta.

MAKES 8 **PREPARATION TIME** 15 minutes (+ 1½ hours cooling and 6 hours chilling) **COOKING TIME** 15 minutes

3 teaspoons powdered gelatine
500 ml (17 fl oz/2 cups) pouring (whipping) cream
250 ml (9 fl oz/1 cup) milk
110 g (3¾ oz/½ cup) caster (superfine) sugar
1 vanilla bean, split lengthways and seeds scraped

POACHED PLUMS
295 g (10½ oz/1⅓ cups) caster (superfine) sugar
4 firm, ripe red-fleshed plums, halved and stoned

1 Place 60 ml (2 fl oz/¼ cup) water in a small heatproof bowl and sprinkle over the gelatine. Set aside for 5 minutes to soften. Place the bowl in a saucepan with enough water to come halfway up the side of the bowl. Heat gently over medium–low heat until the gelatine dissolves.

2 Put the cream, milk, sugar and vanilla seeds in a small saucepan and stir with a whisk over medium heat until the sugar dissolves and the vanilla seeds are evenly distributed. Bring to a simmer, then stir in the gelatine mixture *(pic 1)* and simmer, stirring occasionally, for 1 minute. Remove from the heat and strain into a heatproof bowl. Set aside for 30 minutes, stirring occasionally, or until cooled to room temperature. Cover and refrigerate for 1 hour, stirring occasionally, until well chilled and starting to thicken.

3 Transfer the cream mixture to a jug and pour into eight 125 ml (4 fl oz/½ cup) plastic dariole moulds or small glasses *(pic 2)*. Cover each with plastic wrap and then refrigerate for 5 hours or until set.

4 Meanwhile, to make the poached plums, place the sugar and 330 ml (11¼ fl oz/1⅓ cups) water in a medium saucepan and stir over low heat until the sugar dissolves. Increase the heat and bring to the boil. Add the plums and simmer for 2 minutes or until they are just starting to soften. Use a slotted spoon to gently transfer the plums to a clean baking tray, cut side down, and set aside to cool. When they are cool enough to handle, remove and discard the skin. When they are completely cool, cut each half into 4 wedges. Simmer the syrup over medium heat for 5 minutes or until thickened slightly and syrupy. Set aside to cool completely.

5 Use the tip of a sharp knife to create an air pocket down the side of each mould and break the vacuum *(pic 3)*, then unmould the panna cotta onto serving plates. Serve with the poached plums and the syrup.

Cold Desserts **121**

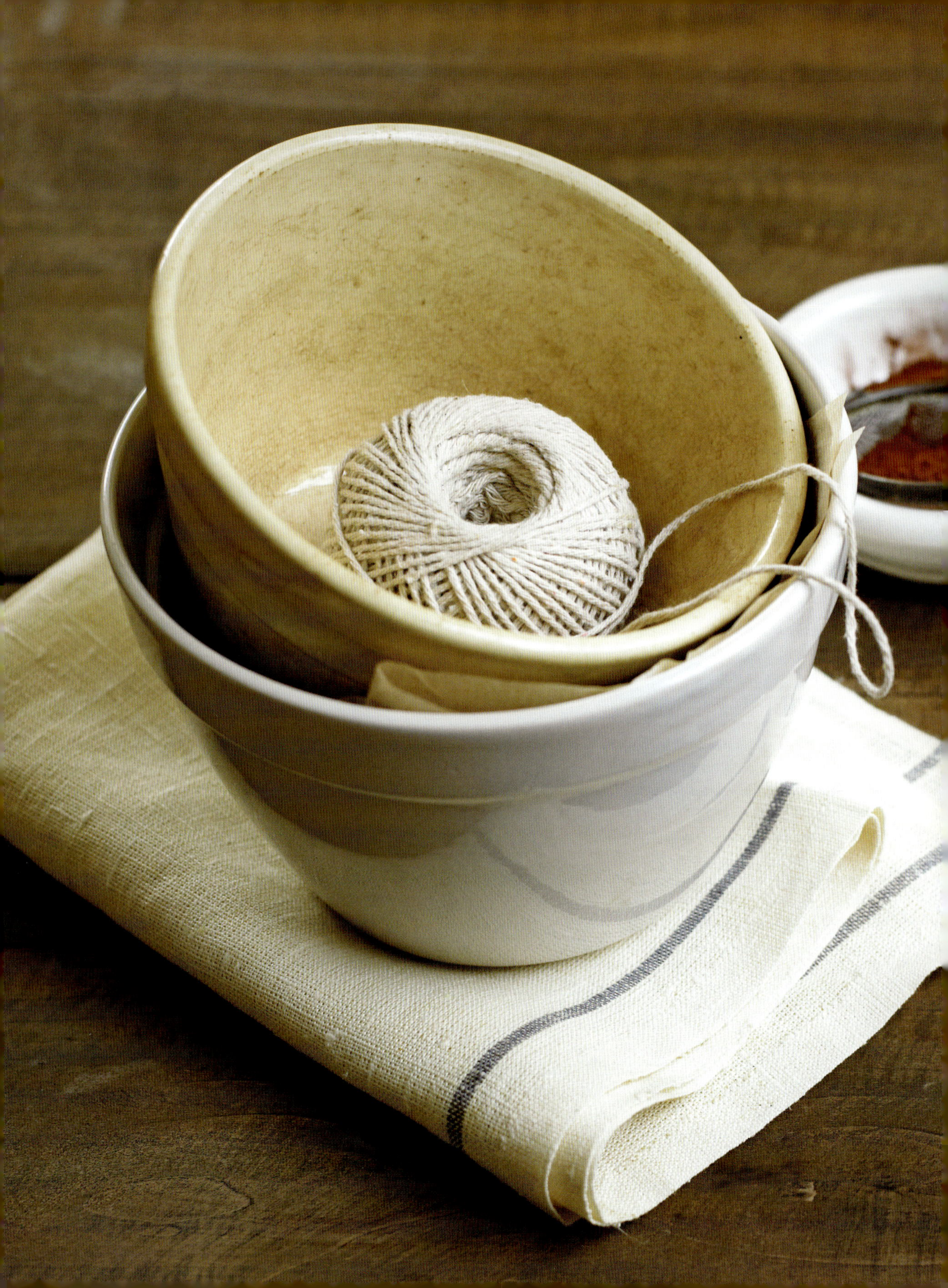

Hot Puddings

Chocolate self-saucing puddings

This is one of those dishes that, when you're making it, doesn't seem like it could possibly work. It looks messy before cooking, but once in the oven it magically transforms into a wonderful cake-like topping over a rich chocolate sauce.

SERVES 4   **PREPARATION TIME** 20 minutes   **COOKING TIME** 25–30 minutes

150 g (5½ oz/1 cup) self-raising flour
220 g (7¾ oz/1 cup) caster (superfine) sugar
55 g (2 oz/½ cup) unsweetened cocoa powder
160 ml (5¼ fl oz/⅔ cup) milk
1 egg, lightly whisked
60 g (2¼ oz) butter, melted and cooled
60 g (2¼ oz) dark chocolate, finely chopped
250 ml (9 fl oz/1 cup) boiling water
Cream or vanilla ice cream, to serve

1 Preheat the oven to 180°C (350°F/Gas 4). Lightly grease four 250 ml (9 fl oz/1 cup) ramekins or ovenproof cups (see tip).

2 Combine the flour, half the sugar and half the cocoa in a medium bowl and mix well. In another medium bowl or jug combine the milk, egg and butter and whisk until combined. Add the milk mixture to the flour mixture and use a large metal spoon to mix (pic 1) until combined and a smooth batter forms. Fold in the chopped chocolate.

3 Divide the mixture evenly among the greased ramekins or cups and place on a baking tray. Combine the remaining sugar and cocoa and sprinkle evenly over the top of the batter (pic 2). Gently pour the boiling water over the back of a metal tablespoon evenly onto the batter (pic 3).

4 Bake for 25–30 minutes or until the tops of the puddings have set and a sauce has formed underneath. Serve immediately with cream or ice cream.

TIP Deep ramekins, rather than wide shallow ones, work best for this pudding.

124   Mastering the Basics: Desserts

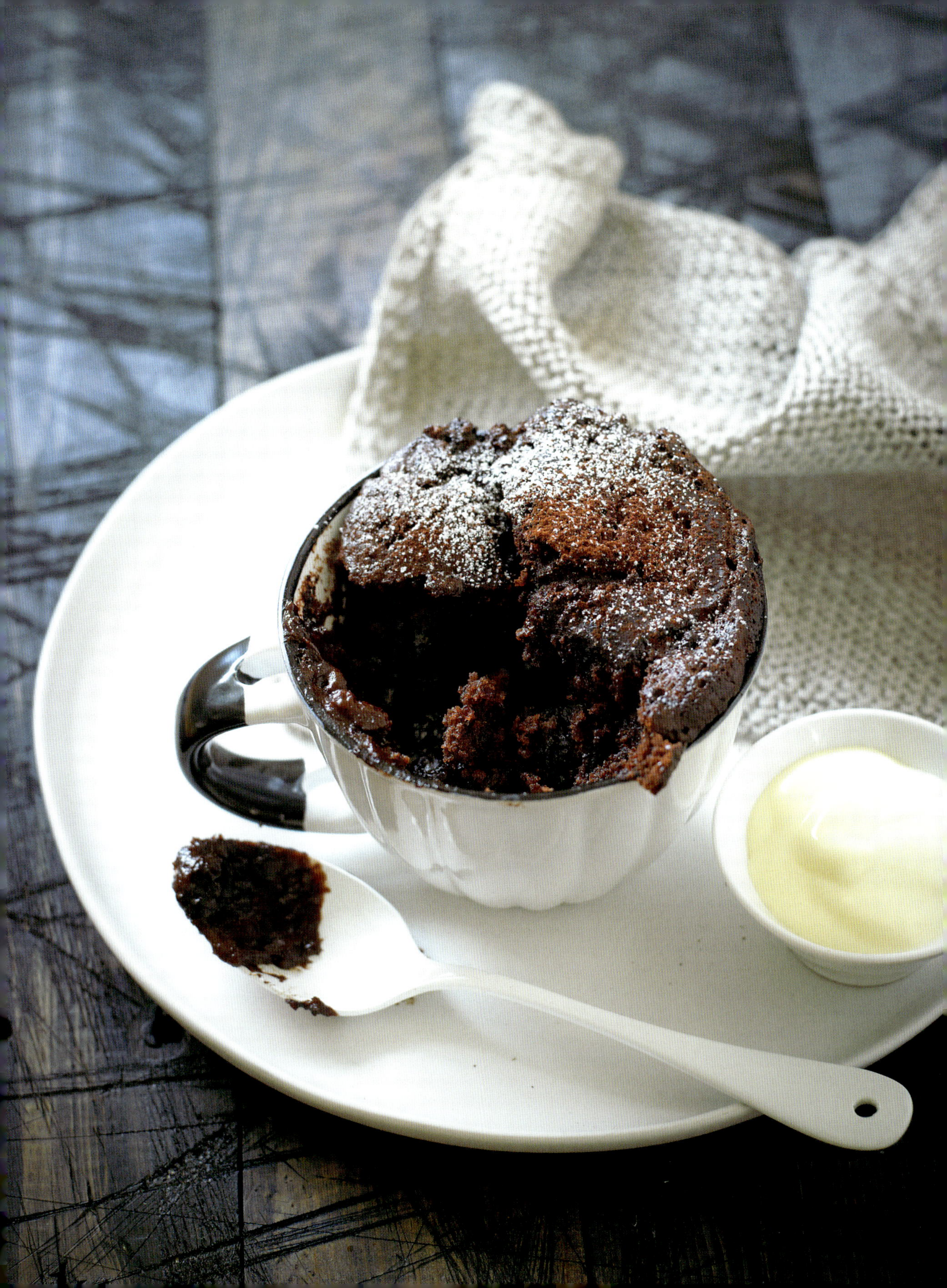

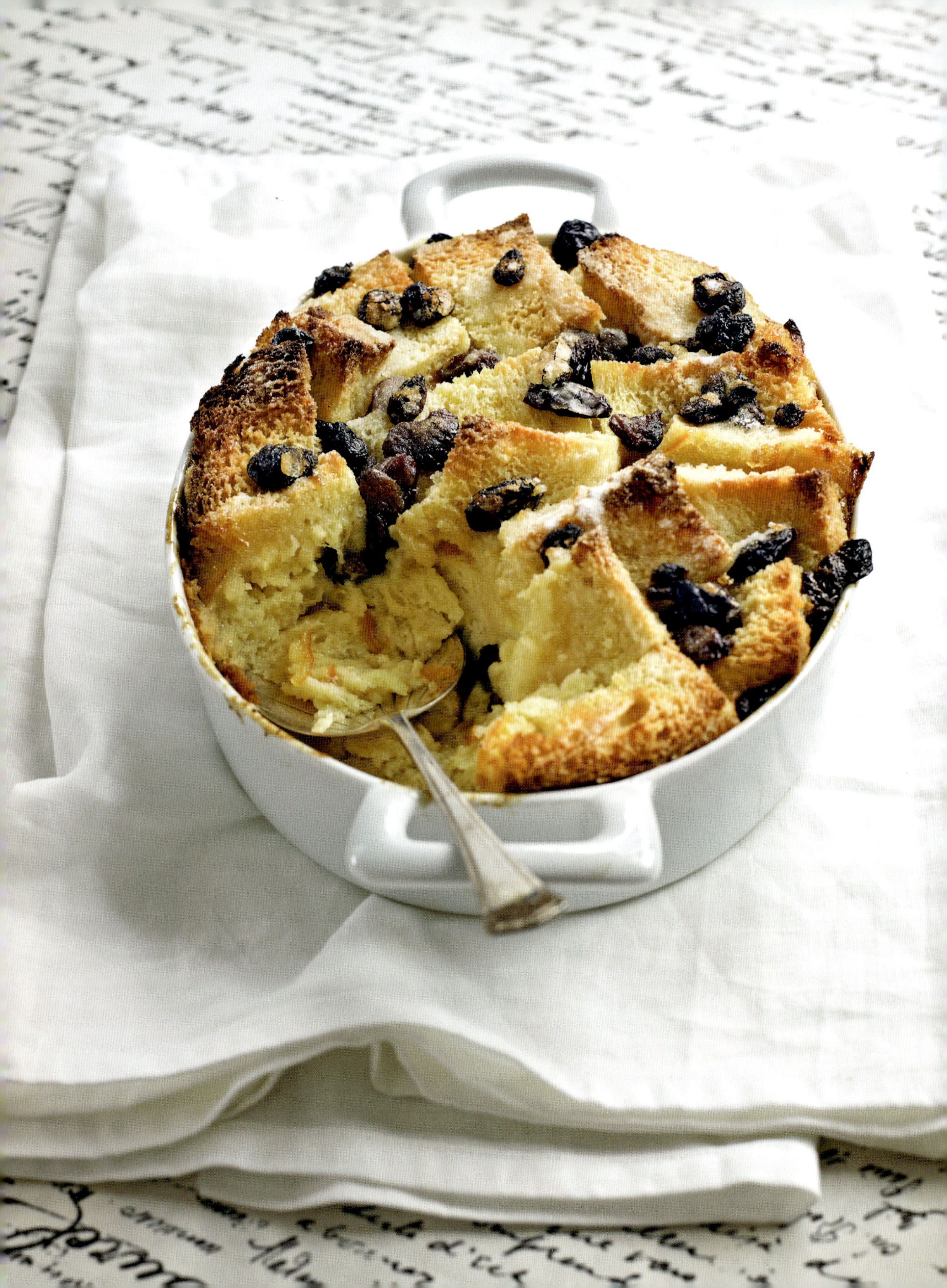

Bread and butter pudding

For this pudding to have the right texture when cooked you need to use the type of bread that will go stale after a day, such as a good rustic white loaf or baguette. Sliced white commercially produced bread lacks the body required to make a good bread and butter pudding.

SERVES 6–8   **PREPARATION TIME** 30 minutes (+ 30 minutes standing)   **COOKING TIME** 1 hour–1 hour 10 minutes

500 g (1 lb 2 oz) day-old crusty bread
75 g (2¾ oz) butter, softened
115 g (4 oz/⅓ cup) sweet orange marmalade
120 g (4¼ oz/⅔ cup) raisins (optional)
4 eggs, whisked
110 g (3¾ oz/½ cup) sugar, plus 2½ tablespoons, for sprinkling
435 ml (15¼ fl oz/1¾ cups) milk
435 ml (15¼ fl oz/1¾ cups) pouring (whipping) cream
2 teaspoons natural vanilla extract
Whipped cream or pouring custard (see pages 22–23), to serve

1 Cut the bread into 1 cm (½ inch) thick slices and trim the crusts. Spread half the slices on one side with butter (you will have some butter left over) and then the marmalade *(pic 1)*, then place the remaining bread slices on the top to make sandwiches. Cut each sandwich into quarters.

2 Use some of the remaining butter to grease a 2 litre (70 fl oz/8 cup) ovenproof dish. Place half of the 'sandwiches' over the base of the dish, trimming as necessary to cover any gaps and form a neat layer *(pic 2)*. Scatter over half the raisins, if using.

3 Use a balloon whisk to whisk together the eggs, sugar, milk, cream and vanilla until well combined. Ladle half the milk mixture over the bread in the dish. Place the remaining sandwiches over the top, unevenly and at angles. Scatter over the remaining raisins. Ladle the remaining milk mixture evenly over the top *(pic 3)*, trying to moisten as much of the bread as possible. Set the pudding aside for 30 minutes to allow the bread to absorb as much of the milk mixture as possible.

4 Preheat the oven to 170°C (325°F/Gas 3).

5 Dot the remaining butter over the top of the pudding and sprinkle with the extra sugar. Bake for 1 hour to 1 hour 10 minutes or until deep golden and the custard is set in the middle. Serve hot, warm or at room temperature with whipped cream or custard.

VARIATION

Banana-toffee bread and butter pudding: Replace the marmalade with 3 ripe bananas, thinly sliced, to make banana sandwiches and scatter any remaining banana slices over the top. Combine 100 g (3½ oz) butter, 145 g (5½ oz) golden syrup and 100 g (3½ oz) caster (superfine) sugar in a saucepan and bring to a simmer. Cook for 2–3 minutes or until smooth and sticky, then pour over the pudding after standing and just before baking.

TIP You can replace the bread with a good-quality fruit bread and omit the raisins.

Steamed Christmas pudding

SERVES 8　**PREPARATION TIME** 40 minutes (+ 20 minutes standing)　**COOKING TIME** 5 hours

110 g (3¾ oz) fresh dates, pitted and chopped
120 g (4¼ oz/⅔ cup) raisins
115 g (4 oz/¾ cup) currants
120 g (4¼ oz/⅔ cup) sultanas (golden raisins)
55 g (2 oz/⅓ cup) mixed peel (mixed candied citrus peel)
115 g (4 oz) coarsely grated carrot
110 g (3¾ oz) coarsely grated, peeled apple
Finely grated zest of 1 orange
35 g (1¼ oz/¼ cup) slivered almonds
100 ml (3½ fl oz) brandy or dark rum
2 eggs, at room temperature, whisked
1 tablespoon treacle
110 g (3¾ oz/½ cup, firmly packed) dark brown sugar, plus 1 tablespoon, extra
120 g (4¼ oz) chilled unsalted butter, grated
110 g (3¾ oz/¾ cup) plain (all-purpose) flour
½ teaspoon mixed (pumpkin pie) spice
½ teaspoon ground nutmeg
½ teaspoon ground cinnamon
100 g (3½ oz) fine breadcrumbs, made from day-old white bread
20 g (¾ oz) unsalted butter, extra
1 tablespoon caster (superfine) sugar
Rich brandy sauce or pouring custard (see pages 22–23), to serve

1 Place the dried fruit, peel, carrot, apple, zest and almonds in a large heatproof bowl. Heat the brandy in a saucepan until warm, then pour over the fruit mixture, mix to combine and set aside for 20 minutes. Add the eggs, treacle and brown sugar to the soaked fruit and mix to combine. Stir through the grated butter. Sift the flour and spices over the mixture and stir to combine. Stir through the breadcrumbs.

3 Trace around the top and base of a 1.375 litre (48 fl oz/5½ cup) pudding basin onto non-stick baking paper, then cut out both rounds. Grease the basin with the extra butter. Put the smaller round of paper on the base. Spoon the pudding mixture into the basin, smooth the surface and cover with the larger round of paper.

4 Place a double sheet of foil on a work surface and fold the centre to make a pleat. Place on top of the pudding basin and use kitchen string to tie it securely below the rim *(pic 1)*. Use more string to make a long loop across the top, attaching it to the string already tied around the rim *(pic 2)* — this 'handle' will help you remove the basin from the saucepan later.

5 Place a small trivet or heatproof saucer in a saucepan large enough to hold the basin. Place the basin on the trivet, then add enough boiling water to the pan to reach two-thirds of the way up the side of the basin. Cover with a tight-fitting lid and bring to the boil over medium heat. Reduce the heat to low and cook for 5 hours, checking every hour *(pic 3)* and topping up the water as needed.

6 Remove the basin from the pan. Remove the foil and paper and invert the pudding onto a serving plate. Remove the paper. Sprinkle over the combined extra brown sugar and caster sugar. Serve with brandy sauce or custard.

1

2

3

TIP You can make this pudding up to 2 months ahead. Cool it in the basin, cover tightly with plastic wrap and foil, then refrigerate. Remove from the refrigerator the night before serving. Reheat for 1 hour (follow method in step 5).

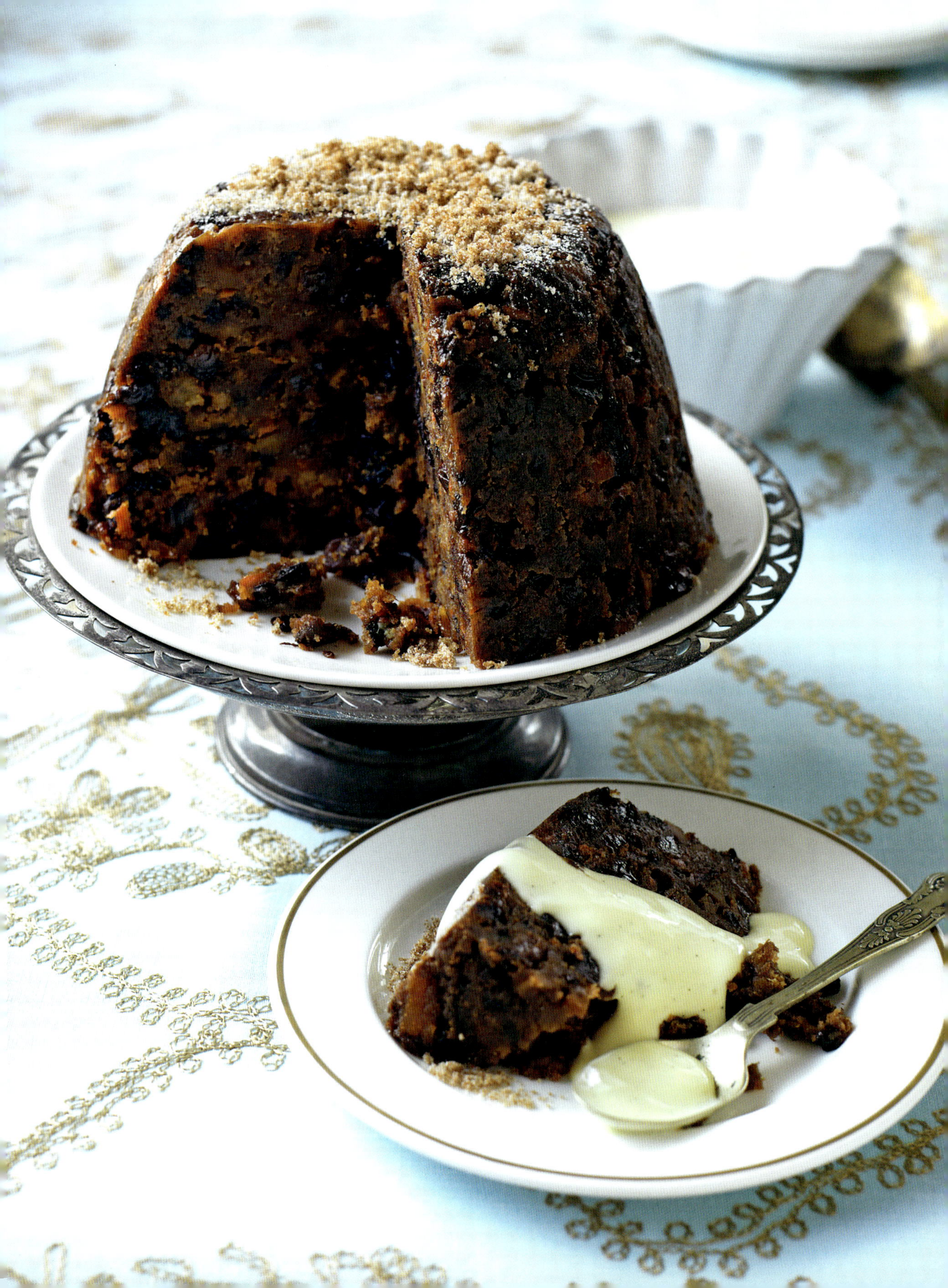

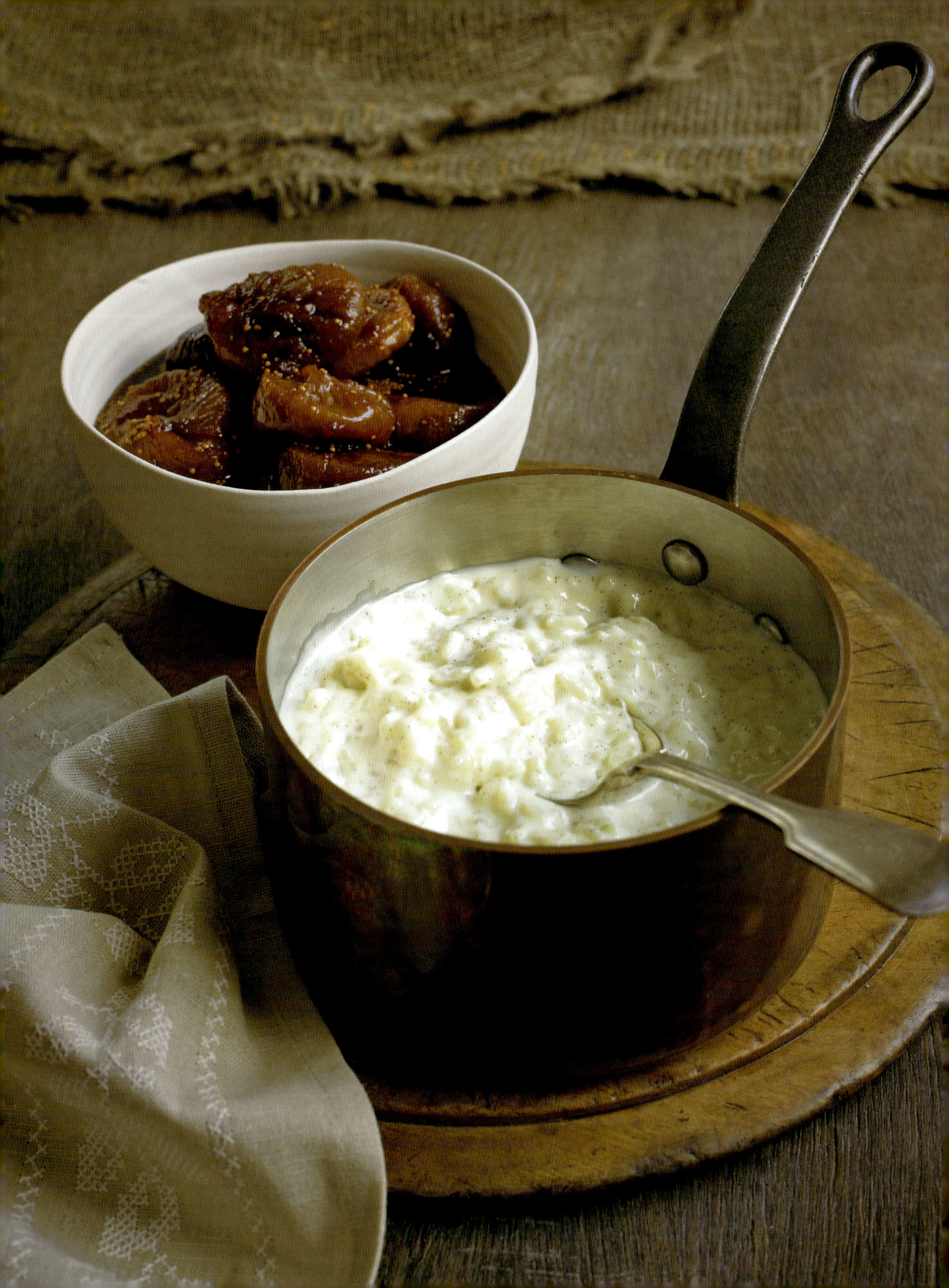

Rice pudding with brandied figs

Rice pudding is the epitome of comfort food. It's creamy, rich and satisfying, plus inexpensive and simple to prepare. Dried figs poached in brandy make a perfect accompaniment and winter warmer.

SERVES 6   **PREPARATION TIME** 10 minutes (+ 2 hours soaking)   **COOKING TIME** 1 hour 30 minutes

- 140 g (5 oz/2/3 cup) uncooked medium-grain white rice
- 110 g (3¾ oz/½ cup) caster (superfine) sugar
- 1 vanilla bean, split lengthways and seeds scraped
- 1 litre (35 fl oz/4 cups) milk
- 200 ml (7 fl oz) pouring (whipping) cream

BRANDIED FIGS
- 375 g (13 oz) dried figs, tough stems trimmed
- 500 ml (17 fl oz/2 cups) boiling water
- 110 g (3¾ oz/½ cup) caster (superfine) sugar
- 125 ml (4 fl oz/½ cup) brandy

1 To make the brandied figs, put the figs in a small heatproof bowl and add the boiling water, or enough water to just cover. Set aside for 2 hours or overnight to soak. Transfer the figs and the liquid to a medium saucepan with the sugar and brandy. Add a little more water to just cover the figs, if necessary. Bring to a simmer and then simmer gently over low heat for 30 minutes or until the figs are tender *(pic 1)*. Remove from the heat and set aside to cool.

2 Combine the rice, sugar, vanilla bean and seeds, and milk in a saucepan and bring slowly to a simmer, stirring often until the sugar dissolves *(pic 2)*. Reduce the heat to very low and cook for about 50 minutes, stirring often, or until the mixture is thick and creamy and the rice is very tender.

3 Stir in the cream *(pic 3)* and cook, stirring, for a further 5 minutes. Remove from the heat and cool slightly. Serve with the brandied figs.

TIP This rice pudding is also delicious served chilled, though you may have to stir a little milk through the pudding to thin it slightly before serving.

Puddings

Golden syrup pudding with custard

This traditional steamed pudding is topped with golden syrup to create an intensely sweet sauce. Pouring custard, either home-made (see pages 22–23) or ready-made, complements it perfectly.

SERVES 6   **PREPARATION TIME** 20 minutes   **COOKING TIME** 1 hour 30 minutes

115 g (4 oz/1/3 cup) golden syrup
2½ tablespoons lemon juice
30 g (1 oz/½ cup, lightly packed) fresh white breadcrumbs
150 g (5½ oz) unsalted butter, softened
150 g (5½ oz/2/3 cup) caster (superfine) sugar
1½ teaspoons natural vanilla extract
2 eggs
1 egg yolk
225 g (8 oz/1½ cups) self-raising flour, sifted
80 ml (2½ fl oz/1/3 cup) milk
1 quantity pouring custard (see pages 22–23), to serve

1 Lightly grease a 1.5 litre (52 fl oz/6 cup) pudding basin, then turn it upside down and trace around it onto a sheet of non-stick baking paper *(pic 1)*. Cut out the round of paper.

2 Put the golden syrup, lemon juice and breadcrumbs in a bowl and mix well to combine. Pour into the greased basin.

3 Use an electric mixer to beat the butter, sugar and vanilla until pale and creamy. Add the eggs and egg yolk one at a time, beating well after each addition. Use a large metal spoon to stir in the flour and milk until just combined. Spoon the mixture carefully into the pudding basin and smooth the surface with the back of the spoon.

4 Cover the pudding mixture with the round of non-stick baking paper *(pic 2)*. Cover the basin tightly with a lid or several layers of foil secured around the top of the basin with kitchen string.

5 Place the basin in a large saucepan filled with enough boiling water to come halfway up the side of the basin. Cook the pudding for 1 hour 30 minutes, topping up the water as necessary to keep it at the halfway point and making sure the water is kept at a boil *(pic 3)*, or until the pudding is cooked through.

6 Carefully remove the basin from the pan and remove the lid or cover. Invert the pudding onto a serving plate and serve with the custard.

1

2

3

> **TIP** This pudding can easily be transformed into a jam pudding by replacing the golden syrup with 165 g (5¾ oz/½ cup) jam of your choice.

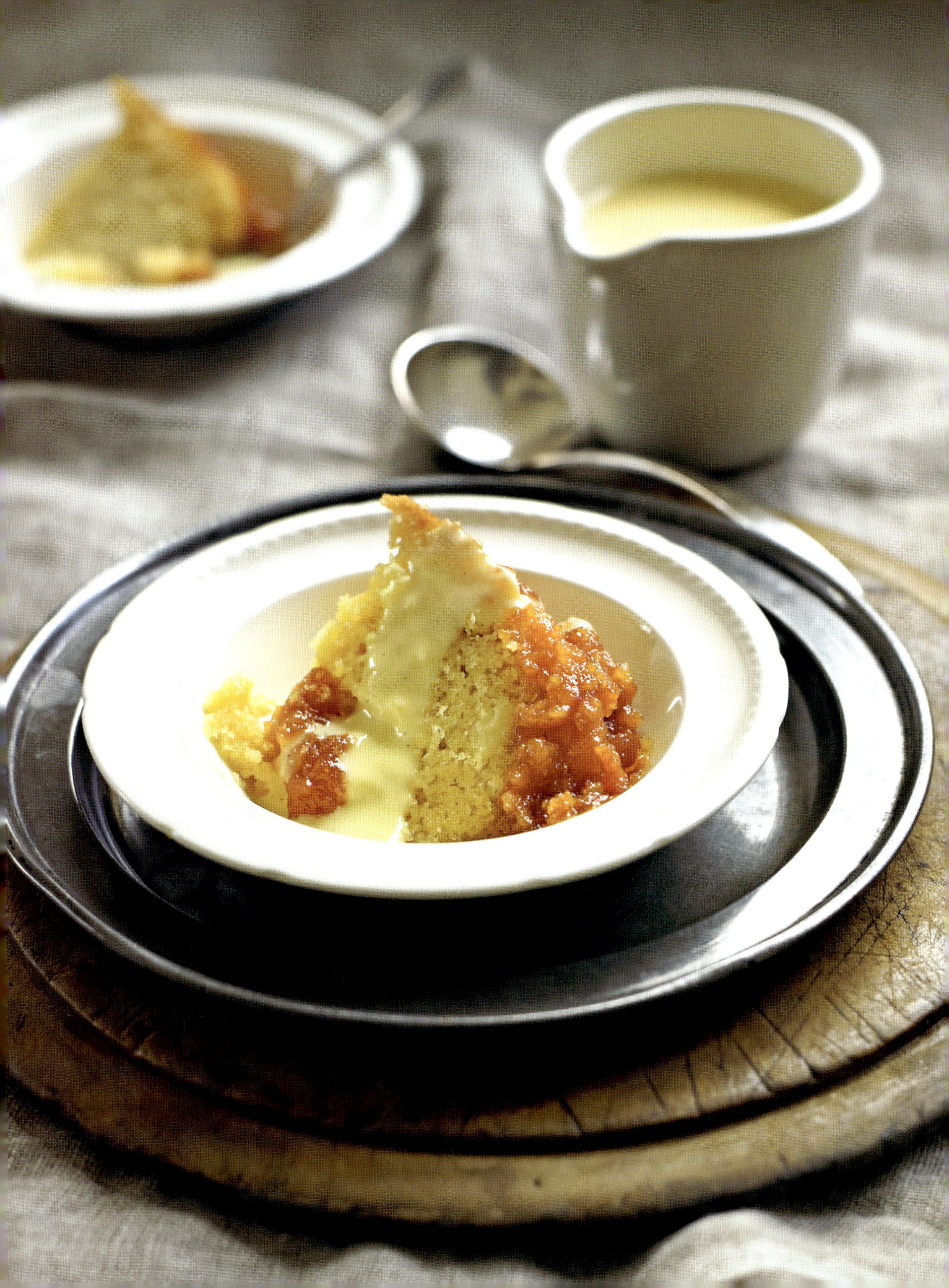

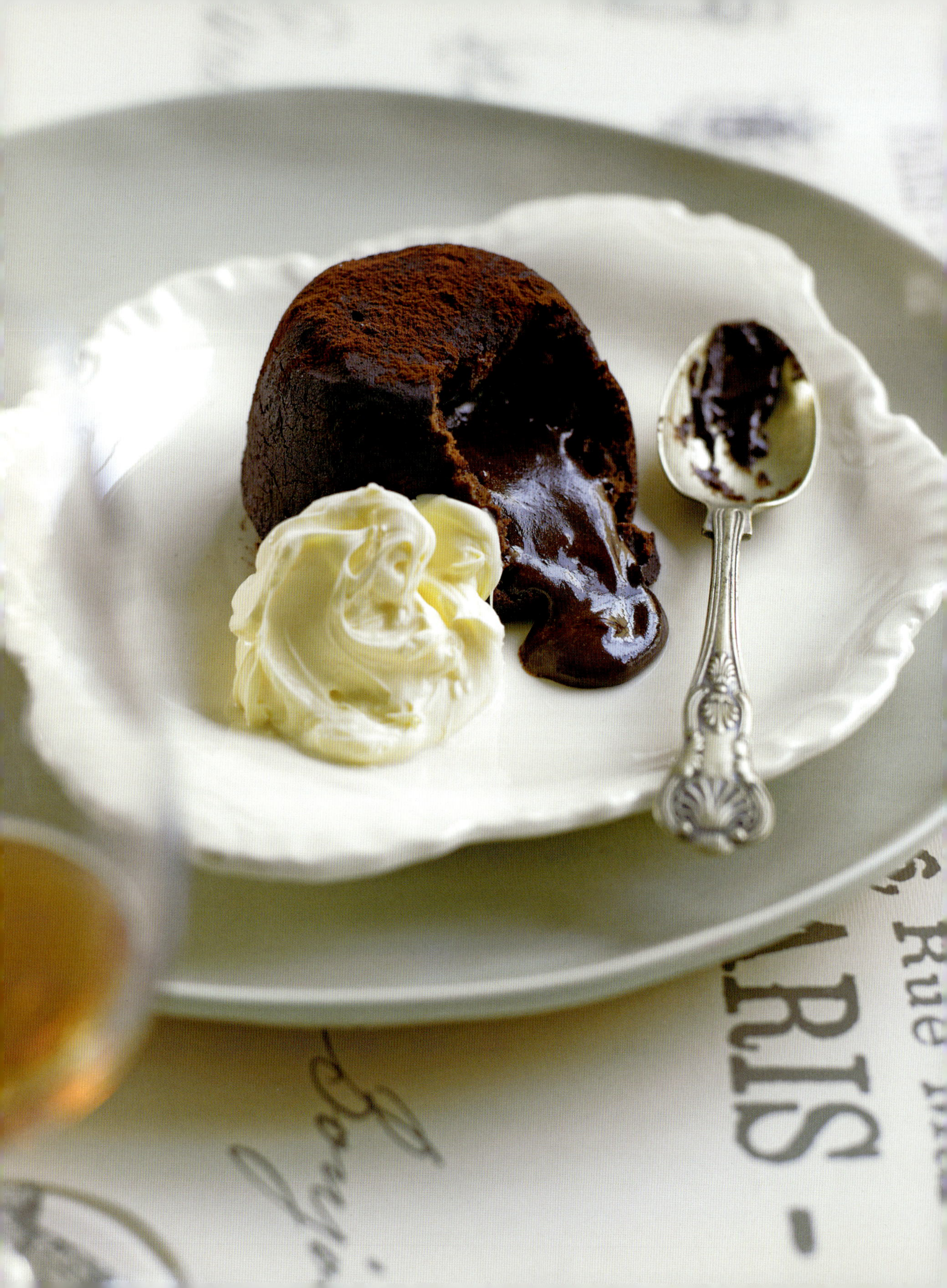
Rue

Chocolate fondant puddings

You may need to make these puddings a few times to get the feel for when they are perfectly cooked, as the timing will vary slightly depending on your oven. Be ready to serve them straight from the oven — if you leave them to stand in their moulds, the gorgeous gooey centre will disappear.

MAKES 10   **PREPARATION TIME** 20 minutes   **COOKING TIME** 12 minutes

Unsalted butter, melted, to grease
Unsweetened cocoa powder, to dust
250 g (9 oz) dark chocolate (70% cocoa solids), chopped
170 g (5²⁄₃ oz) unsalted butter, chopped
4 eggs, at room temperature
6 egg yolks, at room temperature
150 g (5½ oz/²⁄₃ cup) caster (superfine) sugar
2 tablespoons pouring (whipping) cream or orange liqueur (such as Grand Marnier)
150 g (5½ oz/1 cup) plain (all-purpose) flour
Thick (double/heavy) cream or vanilla ice cream, to serve

1 Preheat the oven to 200°C (400°F/Gas 6). Brush ten 125 ml (4 fl oz/½ cup) dariole moulds or ramekins well with melted butter and dust with cocoa, turning the ramekins to lightly coat and discarding any excess.

2 Put the chocolate and butter in a heatproof bowl over a saucepan of simmering water (make sure the base of the bowl doesn't touch the water) and stir occasionally until melted and smooth. Remove the bowl from the pan, and set aside.

3 Use an electric mixer with a whisk attachment to whisk the eggs, egg yolks and sugar in a medium bowl for 4 minutes or until very thick and pale *(pic 1)*. Add the chocolate mixture and use a balloon whisk to stir until combined. Add the cream or liqueur and whisk to combine. Sift the flour over the mixture and use a large metal spoon or spatula to fold together until just combined *(pic 2)*.

4 Spoon the mixture into the prepared moulds or ramekins *(pic 3)*, place on a baking tray and bake for 10–12 minutes or until set on top but still with some give if you gently press the centre of a pudding. Remove from the oven and turn out onto serving plates. Serve immediately, accompanied by thick cream or vanilla ice cream.

Puddings   **135**

Raspberry and lemon soufflés

There's no reason to be daunted by a hot soufflé. Soufflés rise because air incorporated into egg whites expands in the heat of the oven. So the trick is to use a light hand when folding the whisked egg whites through the raspberry mixture, and then serve them without delay.

SERVES 10   **PREPARATION TIME** 20 minutes (+ cooling and chilling)   **COOKING TIME** 18 minutes

300 g (10½ oz) fresh or thawed frozen raspberries
Finely grated zest and juice of 1 lemon
110 g (3¾ oz/½ cup) caster (superfine) sugar, plus 150 g (5½ oz/⅔ cup), extra
3 teaspoons cornflour (cornstarch)
30 g (1 oz) butter, softened
5 egg whites, at room temperature
Icing (confectioners') sugar, to dust
150 g (5½ oz) fresh raspberries, extra, to serve

1 Put the raspberries in a food processor bowl and process until puréed. Push the purée through a fine sieve set over a bowl. Discard the pips. Measure 125 ml (4 fl oz/½ cup) sieved raspberry purée.

2 Place the measured raspberry purée in a small saucepan with 1 tablespoon strained lemon juice, the caster sugar and 2 tablespoons water and stir over low heat until the sugar dissolves. Increase the heat to medium and bring to the boil. Remove from the heat. Combine the cornflour with 3 teaspoons water and add to the raspberry mixture while whisking constantly. Return to a medium heat and cook for 1 minute whisking continuously. Remove from the heat, transfer to a large heatproof bowl and allow to cool slightly, then refrigerate until well chilled.

3 Preheat the oven to 200°C (400°F/Gas 6). Grease ten 185 ml (6 fl oz/¾ cup) soufflé dishes with the softened butter — use a pastry brush to brush the base, then make upward strokes around the side *(pic 1)*. Dust with 75 g (2¾ oz/⅓ cup) of the extra sugar, turning the dishes to lightly coat and discarding any excess. Place the dishes on a baking tray.

4 Put the egg whites in a clean, dry large mixing bowl and use an electric mixer with a whisk attachment to whisk until soft peaks form. Gradually add the remaining sugar, whisking well after each addition, until thick and glossy. Remove the raspberry and lemon mixture from the refrigerator. Add one-third of the egg white mixture and use a large metal spoon or spatula to gently fold together *(pic 2)* until almost combined. Add the remaining egg white mixture and the lemon zest and gently fold through until just combined.

5 Spoon the mixture into the prepared soufflé dishes and use a large palette knife to level off the tops. Lightly tap each dish on the bench to expel any air pockets. Run the tip of your thumb around the inside of each dish to create an edge *(pic 3)* — this will help the soufflé rise evenly.

6 Place the dishes on a baking tray and bake for 12 minutes or until the soufflés have risen and are golden. Remove from the oven, dust with icing sugar and serve immediately with fresh raspberries.

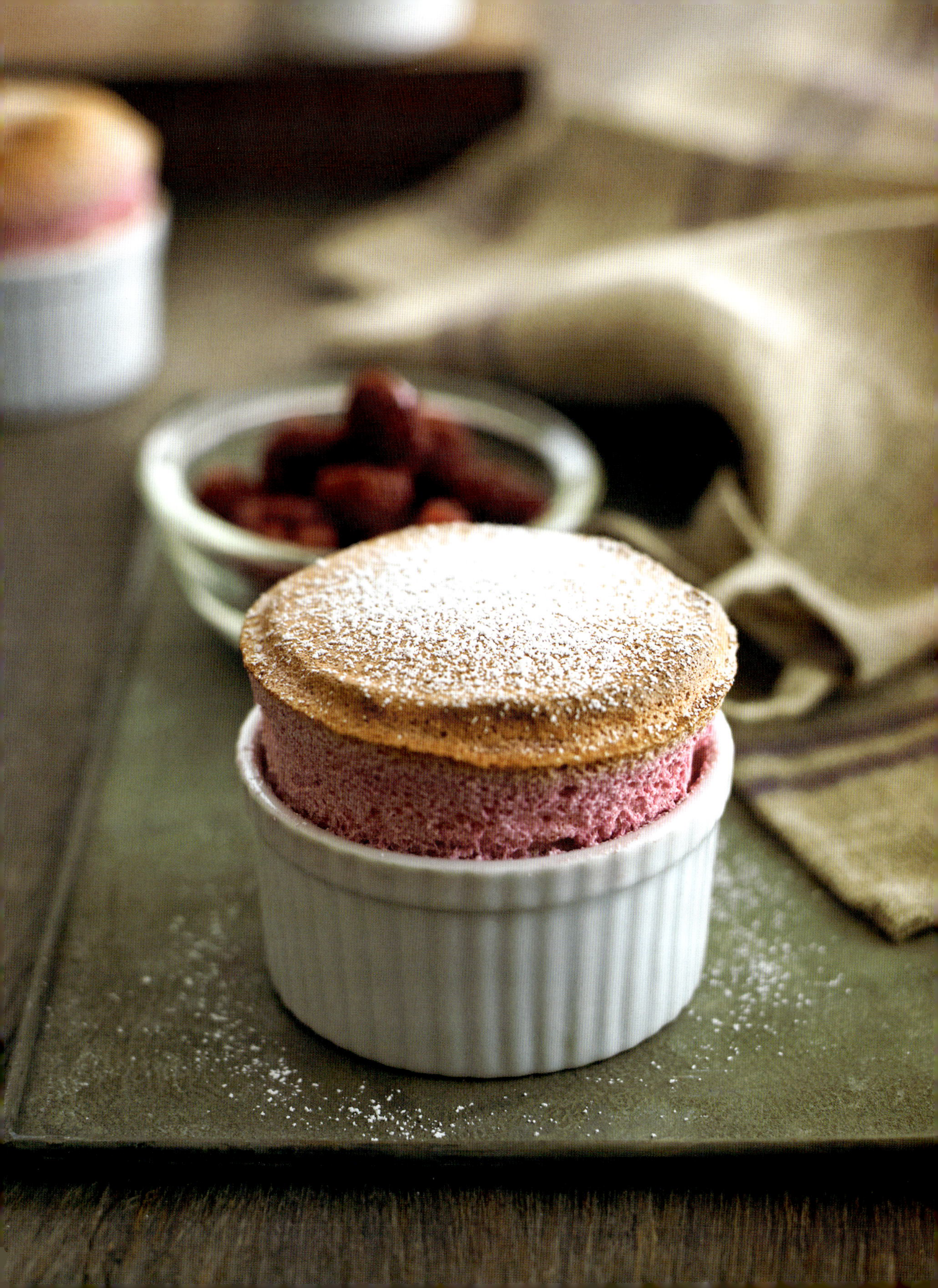

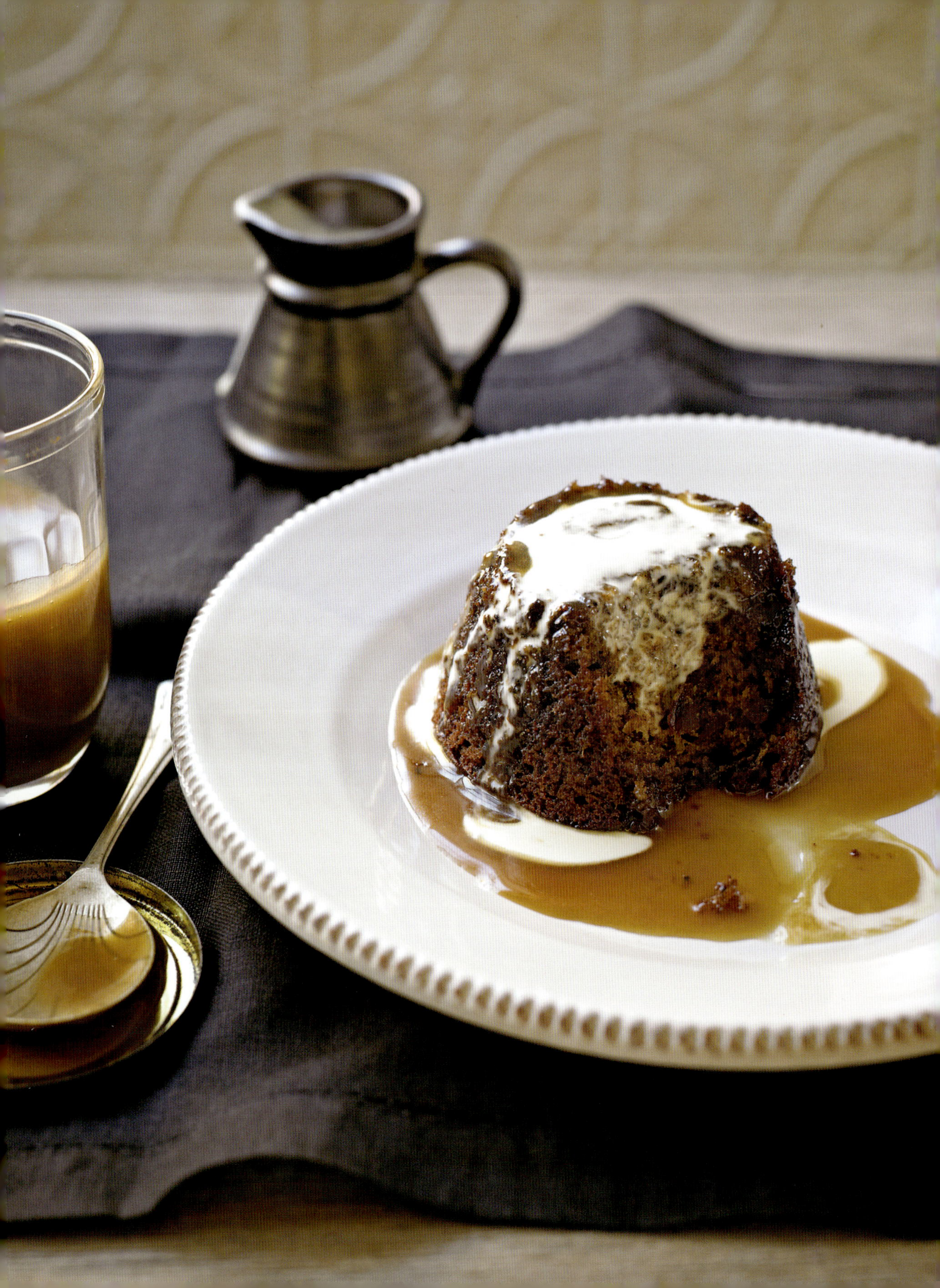

Sticky date puddings

This popular dessert became famous in restaurants and cafes before people began making it in their own kitchens. Homely and decadently sweet, it's also low on fuss and requires only a few ingredients that aren't pantry staples (fresh dates and cream).

SERVES 6   **PREPARATION TIME** 20 minutes (+ cooling)   **COOKING TIME** 40 minutes

200 g (7 oz/1¼ cups) chopped pitted fresh dates
1 teaspoon bicarbonate of soda (baking soda)
80 g (2¾ oz) butter, softened
150 g (5½ oz/¾ cup, lightly packed) light brown sugar
2 eggs
150 g (5½ oz/1 cup) self-raising flour
Thickened (whipping) cream, to serve

BUTTERSCOTCH SAUCE
75 g (2¾ oz) butter
185 g (6½ oz/1 cup, lightly packed) light brown sugar
185 ml (6 fl oz/¾ cup) pouring (whipping) cream

1 Preheat the oven to 180°C (350°F/Gas 4). Lightly grease a 6-hole 185 ml (6 fl oz/¾ cup) large muffin tin and line the bases with small rounds of non-stick baking paper.

2 Put the dates and 250 ml (9 fl oz/ 1 cup) water in a small saucepan over medium–high heat. Bring to the boil, then reduce the heat to medium–low and cook for 5 minutes *(pic 1)*. Remove from the heat, stir in the bicarbonate of soda and then set aside to cool to room temperature.

3 Use an electric mixer to beat the butter and sugar in a medium bowl until pale and creamy. Add the eggs and beat well. Use a large metal spoon or spatula to gently stir in the flour and the date mixture until just combined. Divide the mixture evenly among the muffin holes *(pic 2)*. Bake for 30 minutes or until the puddings are risen and just firm to the touch (they will still be slightly sticky in the middle). Immediately run a palette knife around the side of each pudding to loosen it from the tin and then turn them out onto a wire rack.

4 Meanwhile, to make the butterscotch sauce, stir the butter, sugar and cream in a small saucepan over low heat until the butter melts and the sugar dissolves *(pic 3)*. Bring to the boil, then reduce the heat and simmer for 2 minutes.

5 Place the warm puddings on serving plates. Drizzle with the hot butterscotch sauce and serve immediately, accompanied by the cream.

TIP These puddings can also be cooked in 6 greased and lined 185 ml (6 fl oz/ ¾ cup) ramekins.

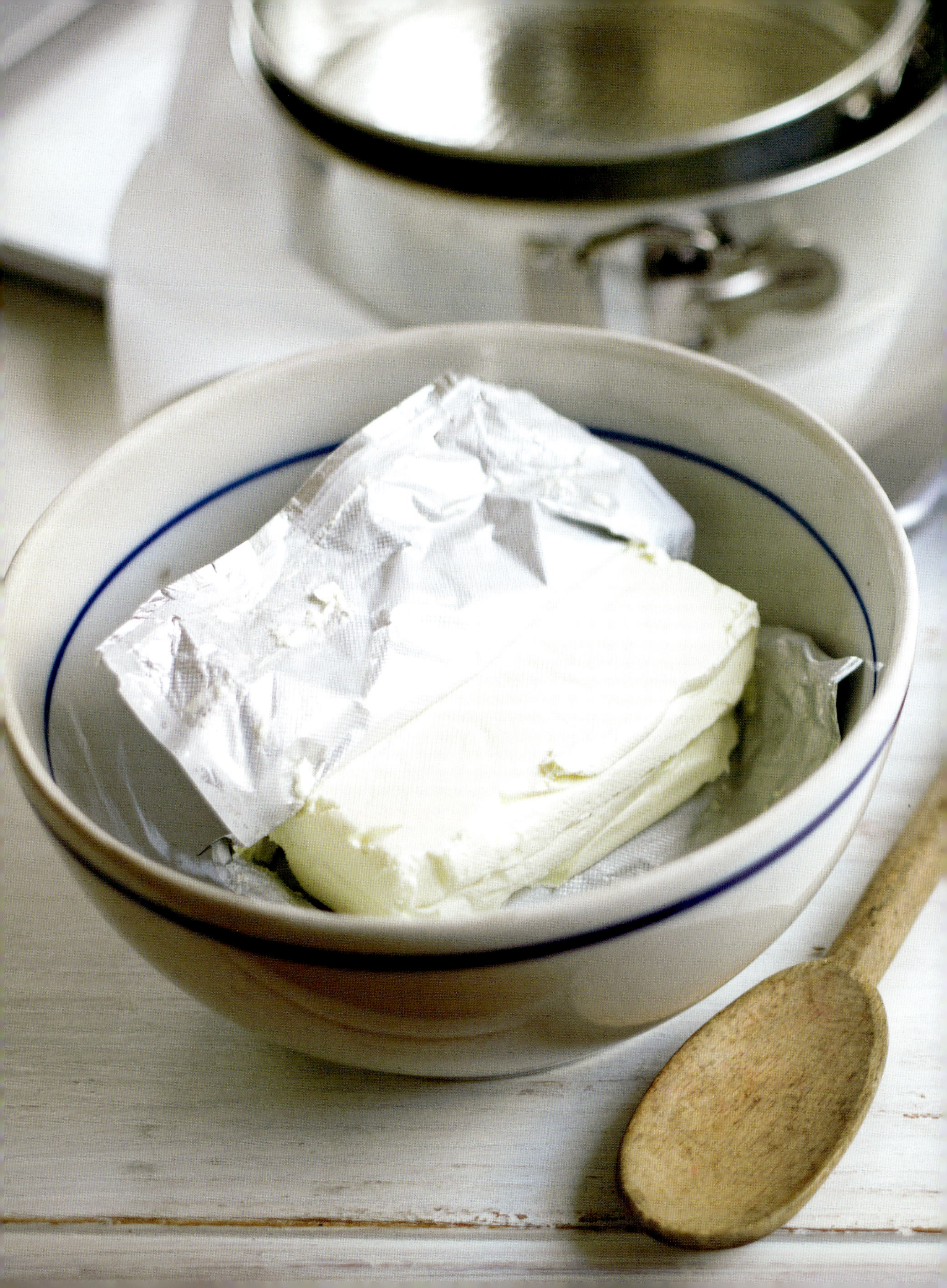

Dessert Cakes and Cheesecakes

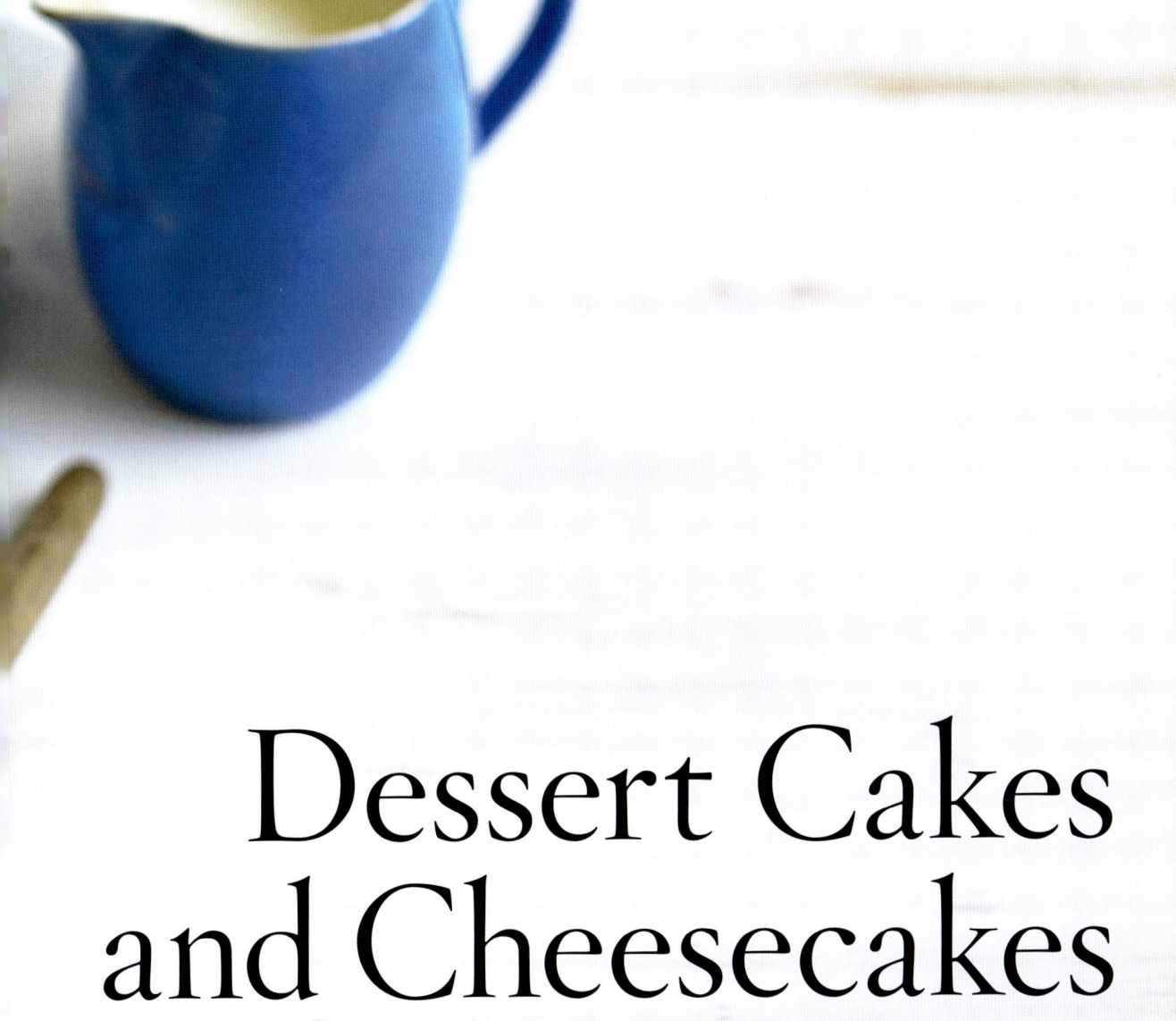

Double ginger cake with lime frosting

This cake has a double hit of ginger, both fresh and crystallised, which produces a strong flavour that becomes surprisingly addictive when teamed with the creamy lime frosting.

SERVES 8–10 **PREPARATION TIME** 30 minutes (+ cooling) **COOKING TIME** 1 hour 5 minutes – 1 hour 15 minutes

- 250 g (9 oz) butter, chopped
- 110 g (3¾ oz/½ cup, firmly packed) light brown sugar
- 175 g (6 oz/½ cup) golden syrup
- 1 tablespoon finely grated fresh ginger
- 150 g (5½ oz/1 cup) plain (all-purpose) flour
- 150 g (5½ oz/1 cup) self-raising flour
- ½ teaspoon bicarbonate of soda (baking soda)
- 185 ml (6 fl oz/¾ cup) milk
- 2 eggs, lightly whisked, at room temperature
- 2 tablespoons finely chopped crystallised ginger, plus extra, sliced, to serve

LIME FROSTING
- 250 g (9 oz) cream cheese, at room temperature
- 60 g (2¼ oz) butter, softened
- 185 g (6½ oz/1½ cups) icing (confectioners') sugar
- 2 teaspoons finely grated lime zest, plus extra, to serve
- 1 tablespoon lime juice

1 Preheat the oven to 180°C (350°F/Gas 4). Grease a round 20 cm (8 inch) cake tin with melted butter, then line with non-stick baking paper.

2 Combine the butter, sugar and golden syrup in a small heavy-based saucepan and stir over medium heat until the butter melts and the sugar dissolves. Stir in the grated ginger.

3 Sift together the flours and bicarbonate of soda into a large bowl. Add the butter mixture, milk, eggs and crystallised ginger and use a large metal spoon or spatula to mix until just combined. Pour into the prepared tin. Bake for 1 hour– 1 hour 10 minutes or until firm to touch and a skewer comes out clean when inserted into the centre. Cool in the tin for 10 minutes, then turn out onto a plate and invert, right way up, onto a wire rack to cool.

4 To make the lime frosting, use an electric mixer to beat the cream cheese, butter and icing sugar in a medium bowl until smooth and well combined. Add the lime zest and juice and beat until combined (pic 1).

5 Insert toothpicks into the cooled cake as a guide for where to cut to produce 3 even cake layers. Use a long serrated knife to cut the cake horizontally into the 3 layers (pic 2). Place the bottom layer on a serving plate and spread with one-third of the lime frosting (pic 3). Repeat the layering process with the remaining cake layers and frosting, finishing with frosting. Top with extra lime zest and sliced crystallised ginger, and serve cut into wedges.

TIP This cake will keep in an airtight container in the refrigerator for up to 4 days. Serve at room temperature.

Mastering the Basics: Desserts

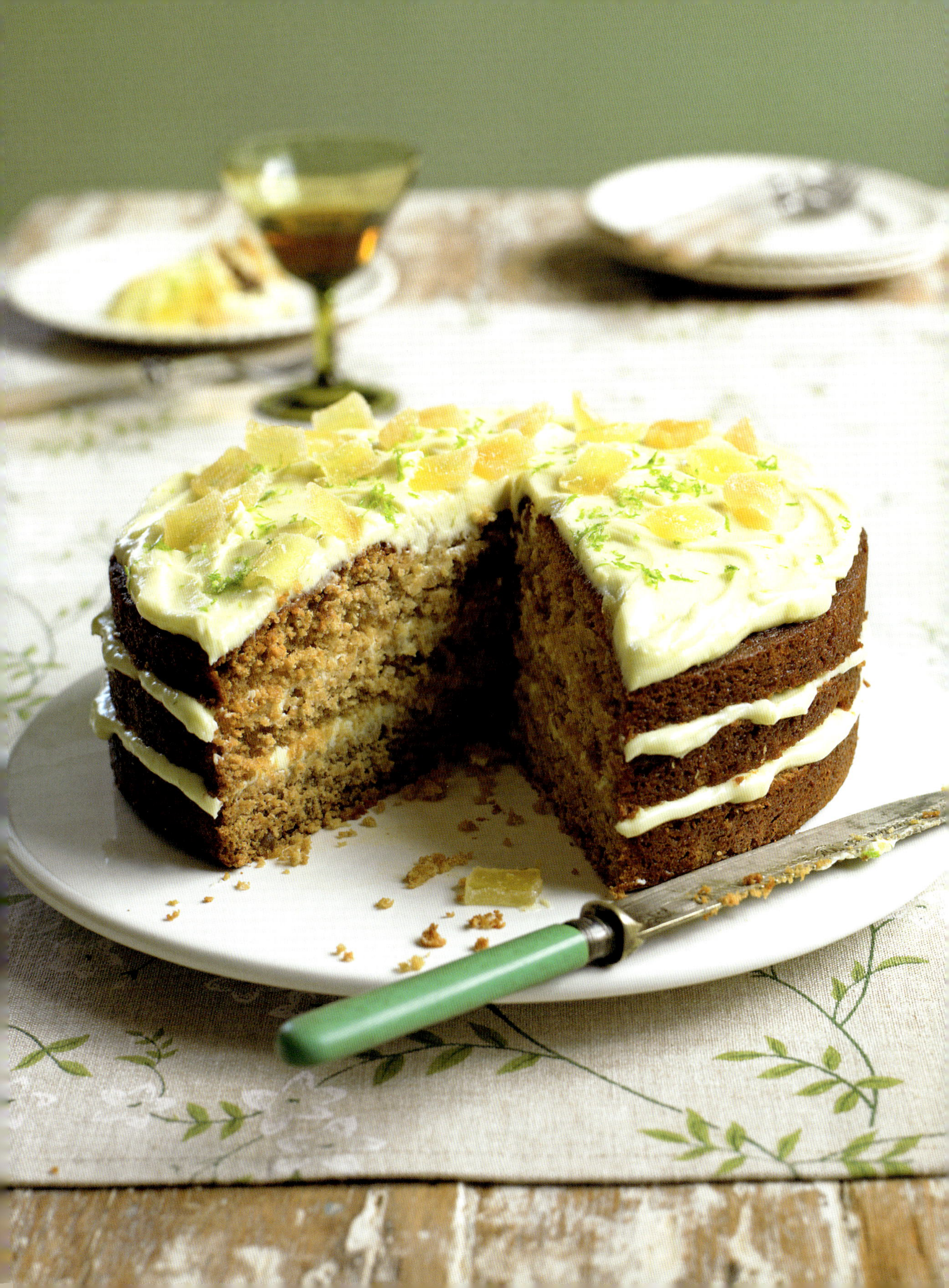

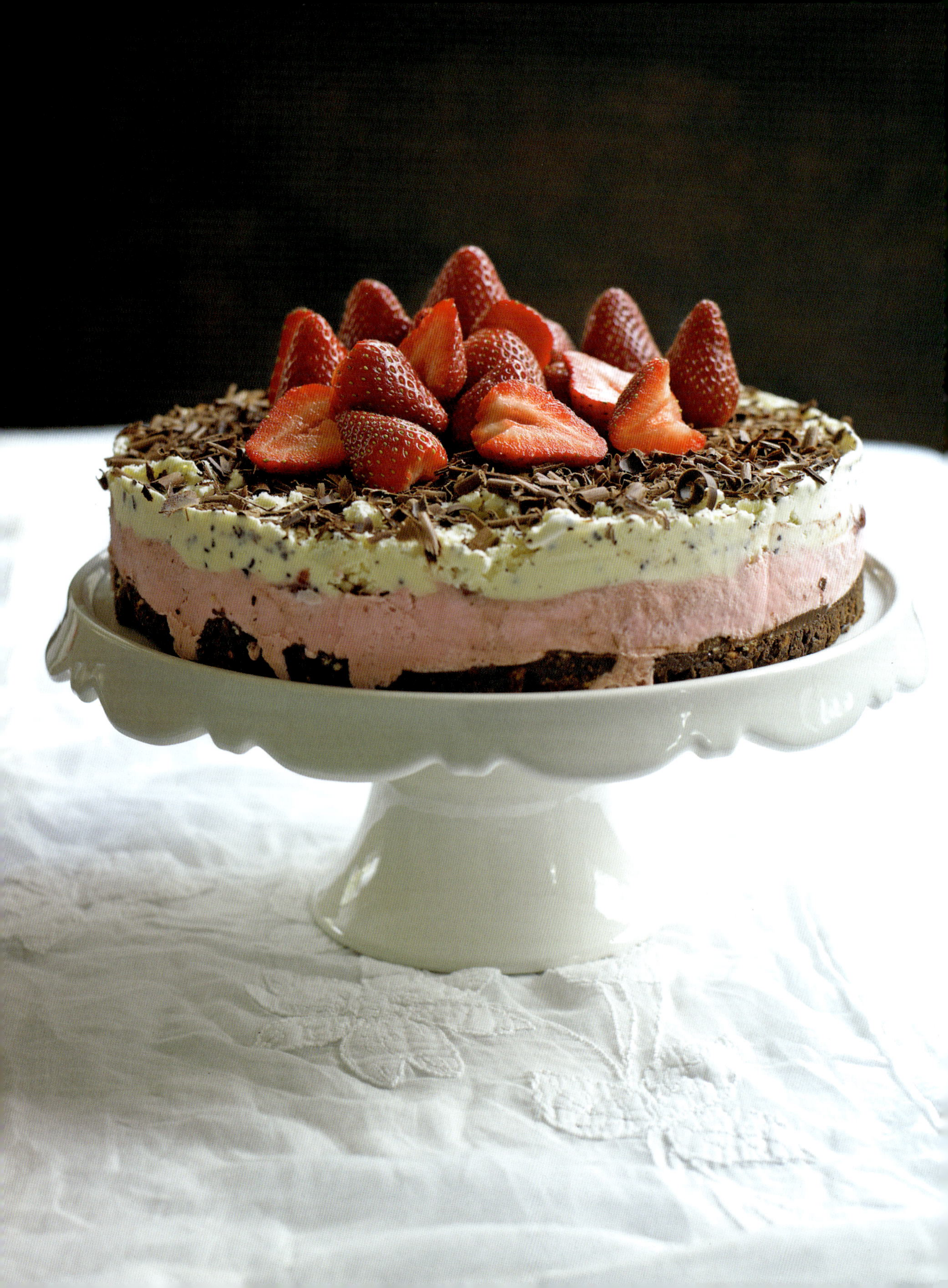

Chocolate and strawberry ice-cream cake

This is the ultimate cheat's dessert. It looks so impressive that nobody will guess you've simply layered a quick-to-prepare biscuit base with ready-made ice cream. It's an excellent option for kids' birthdays, particularly when the weather's warm, and can be customised to cater for individual tastes.

SERVES 8–10   **PREPARATION TIME** 30 minutes (+ 1 hour chilling, 15 minutes cooling and 15 minutes standing)
COOKING TIME 5 minutes   **FREEZING TIME** 5 hours

200 g (7 oz) dark chocolate, finely chopped
125 ml (4 fl oz/½ cup) thickened (whipping) cream
200 g (7 oz) shortbread biscuits, coarsely chopped
1 litre (35 fl oz/4 cups) strawberry ice cream
500 ml (17 fl oz/2 cups) chocolate-chip ice cream
80 g (2¾ oz/¼ cup) strawberry jam
375 g (13 oz) small strawberries
30 g (1 oz) dark chocolate, extra, shaved

1 Grease a round 24 cm (9½ inch) spring-form cake tin and line the base with non-stick baking paper. Place the chocolate in a heatproof bowl. Place the cream in a saucepan, bring to the boil, then remove from the heat and pour over the chocolate. Stand for 30 seconds, then stir gently until the chocolate melts. Set aside for 15 minutes or until cooled to room temperature.

2 Place the biscuits in a large bowl. Add the chocolate mixture and stir to combine. Press the mixture evenly over the base of the lined tin (pic 1). Refrigerate for 1 hour.

3 Remove the strawberry ice cream from the freezer. Set aside for about 10 minutes or until starting to soften. Spread over the chocolate mixture, then use a large spoon to press it down evenly and smooth the surface (pic 2). Freeze for 1 hour or until the ice cream is firm.

4 Remove the chocolate-chip ice cream from the freezer. Set aside for about 5 minutes or until starting to soften. Spread the jam evenly over the strawberry ice cream. Spread the chocolate-chip ice cream over the jam, then use a large spoon to press it down evenly and smooth the surface. Cover with plastic wrap and freeze for 4 hours or overnight, until completely frozen.

5 To serve, remove the cake from the tin and use two egg flips to transfer it to a serving platter or cake stand. Serve sprinkled with dark chocolate shavings and topped with strawberries.

Cakes

Italian ricotta cheesecake with red wine figs

This cheesecake has a lighter texture than most, thanks to the ricotta. Use the fresh one that is sold in rounds. The orange, pine nuts and figs create a sublime combination of flavours and textures.

SERVES 8   **PREPARATION TIME** 40 minutes (+ 2 hours standing, 2 hours cooling and 3 hours chilling)
COOKING TIME 1 hour 20 minutes

1 kg (2 lb 4 oz) firm, fresh ricotta
115 g (4 oz/⅓ cup) honey
75 g (2¾ oz/⅓ cup) caster (superfine) sugar
2½ teaspoons finely grated orange zest
60 ml (2 fl oz/¼ cup) strained freshly squeezed orange juice
4 eggs, at room temperature, lightly whisked
35 g (1¼ oz/¼ cup) plain (all-purpose) flour, sifted
65 g (2¼ oz) pine nuts

RED WINE FIGS
375 g (13 oz) dried figs, stems trimmed
250 ml (9 fl oz/1 cup) boiling water
250 ml (9 fl oz/1 cup) red wine
2 tablespoons Marsala
75 g (2¾ oz/⅓ cup) caster (superfine) sugar
Large pinch of ground cloves

1 To make the red wine figs, put the figs in a small heatproof bowl and pour over the boiling water, then stand for 1 hour or until softened.

2 Combine the undrained figs, wine, Marsala, sugar and cloves in a medium saucepan and bring to a simmer over medium heat. Cook, uncovered, for 20 minutes or until the figs are very tender *(pic 1)*. Remove from the heat and cool to room temperature.

3 Preheat the oven to 170°C (325°F/Gas 3). Lightly grease and flour a round 18 cm (7 inch) spring-form cake tin.

4 Combine the ricotta, honey, sugar, orange zest and juice in the bowl of a food processor *(pic 2)* and process until smooth and well combined. Add the eggs and process to combine. With the motor running add the flour and process briefly until just combined. Pour the mixture into the prepared tin *(pic 3)* and smooth the surface with the back of a spoon. Sprinkle with the pine nuts.

5 Bake for 1 hour or until light golden and the cheesecake wobbles just a little in the centre when the tin is shaken lightly. Turn off the oven and cool the cheesecake in the oven with a wooden spoon keeping the door slightly ajar for 2 hours or until cooled to room temperature. Cover and refrigerate for at least 3 hours or until well chilled.

6 Remove the cheesecake from the refrigerator 1 hour before serving to bring to room temperature. Serve in wedges with the figs and some of their syrup spooned over.

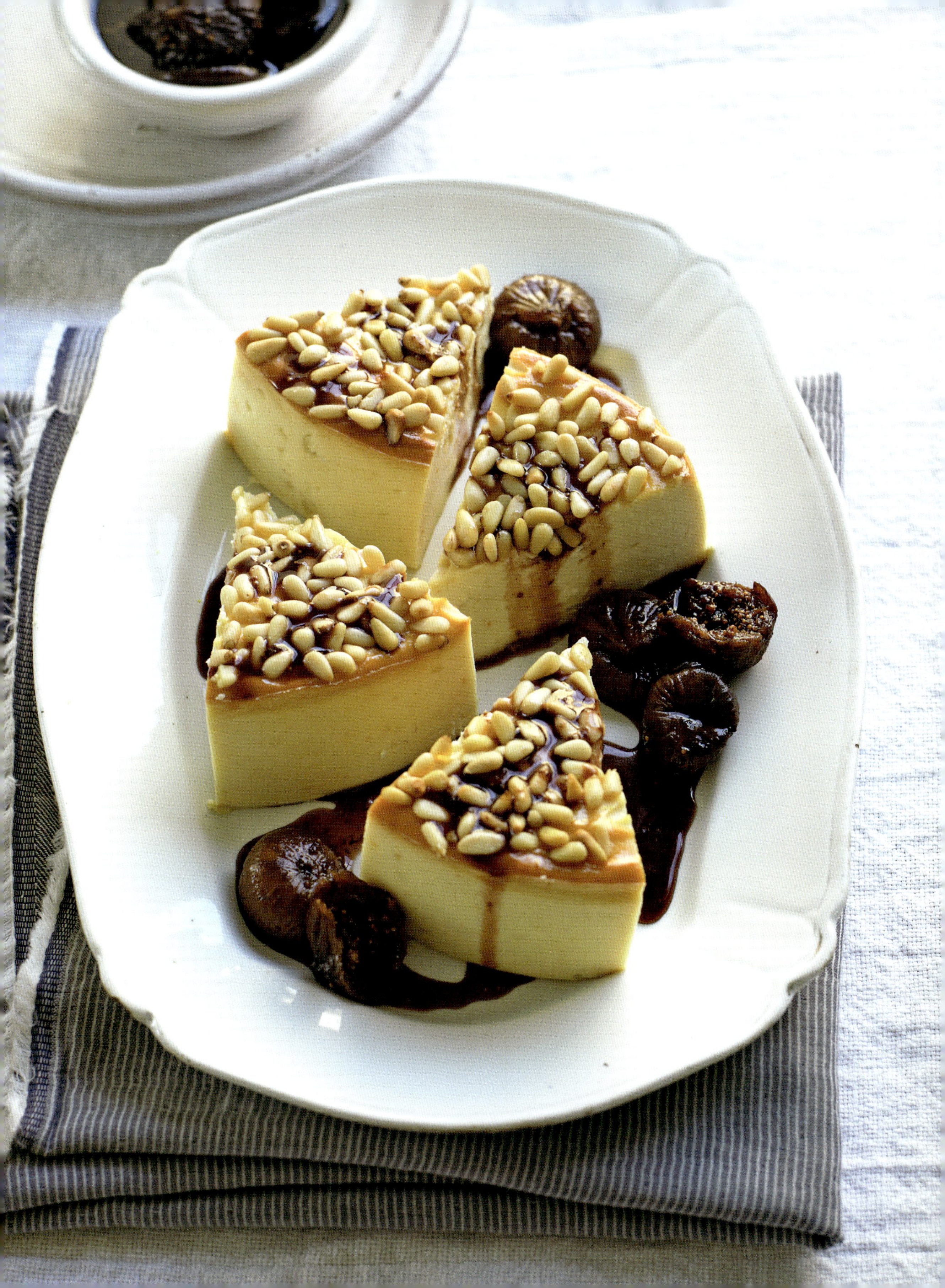

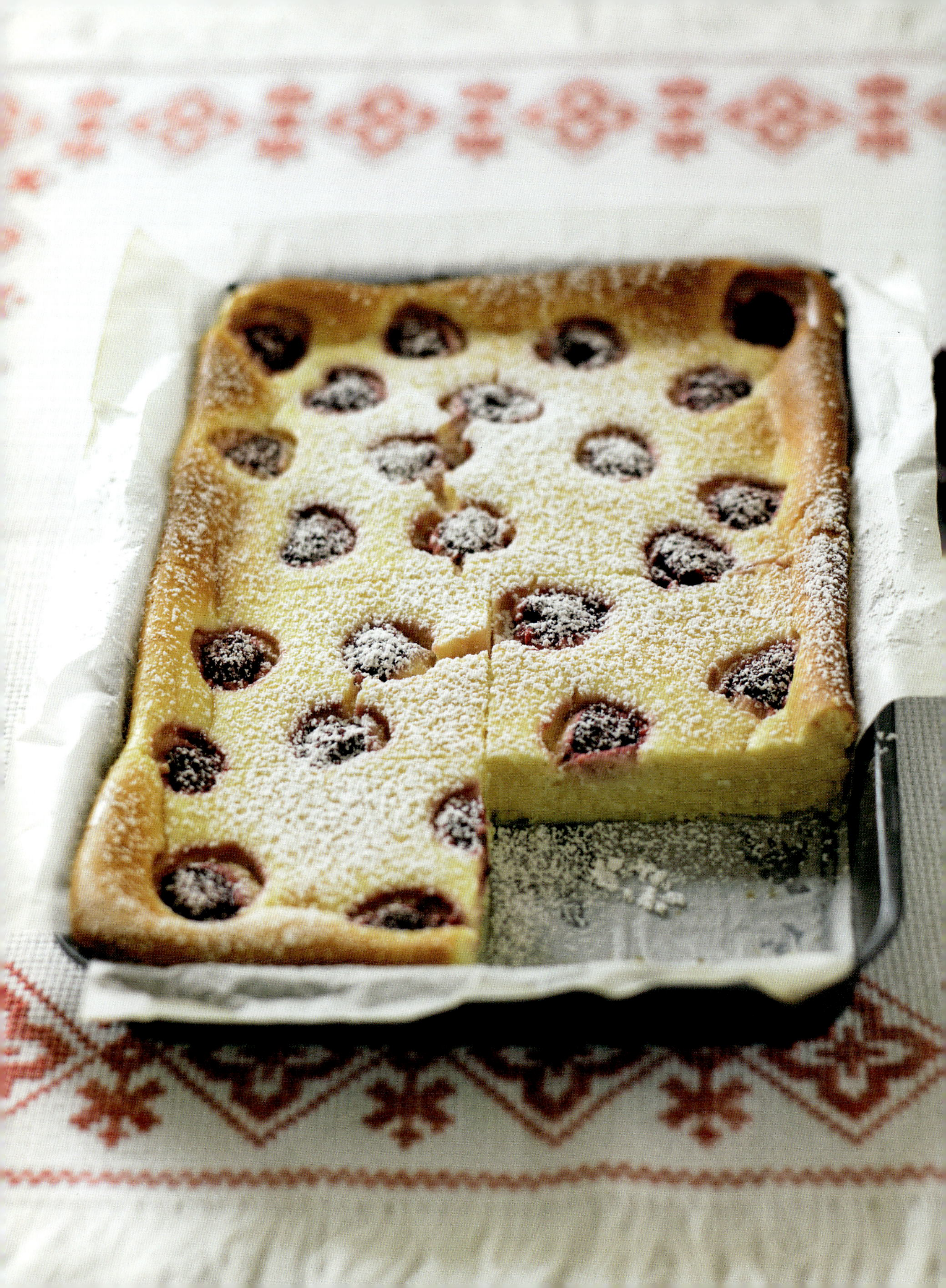

White chocolate and raspberry cheesecake

SERVES 8–10　　**PREPARATION TIME** 20 minutes (+ 10 minutes cooling)　　**COOKING TIME** 1 hour 5 minutes

180 g (6¼ oz) white chocolate, chopped
1 orange
650 g (1 lb 7 oz) cream cheese, at room temperature
220 g (7¾ oz/1 cup) caster (superfine) sugar
1 vanilla bean, split lengthways and seeds scraped
3 eggs, at room temperature, lightly whisked
125 g (4½ oz/1 cup) raspberries
Icing (confectioners') sugar, to dust

1 Preheat the oven to 170°C (325°F/Gas 3). Grease an 18 x 28 cm (7 x 11¼ inch) slice tin and line with non-stick baking paper, extending above the sides.

2 Place the chocolate in a heatproof bowl over a saucepan of simmering water (make sure the base of the bowl doesn't touch the water) and use a metal spoon to stir occasionally *(pic 1)* until melted and smooth. Set aside for 10 minutes to cool.

3 Meanwhile, finely grate the zest from the orange and set aside. Juice the orange and strain. Measure 80 ml (2½ fl oz/⅓ cup) of the juice.

4 Put the cream cheese, caster sugar, vanilla seeds and orange zest in a medium bowl and use an electric mixer to beat for 2 minutes or until smooth. Gradually add the eggs, beating well after each addition *(pic 2)*. Add the orange juice and white chocolate and beat until combined and smooth. Pour into the prepared tin and smooth the surface with the back of a spoon. Place the raspberries on top *(pic 3)*.

5 Bake for 30 minutes (the cheesecake is quite puffed at this stage but it will collapse after cooking), then carefully turn the tin and cook for a further 30 minutes or until light golden and just set in the middle. Place on a wire rack and cool completely in the tin.

6 Dust with icing sugar and serve at room temperature (it is very delicate and soft, so slice it with a sharp knife) or refrigerate before serving for a firmer texture.

TIP You can melt the chocolate in the microwave. Place in a microwave-safe bowl and heat on 50% (medium) for 1 minute bursts, stirring in between each burst, until melted and smooth.

Cakes

Chilled lime and mango cheesecakes

MAKES 12   **PREPARATION TIME** 30 minutes (+ 6 hours chilling)   **COOKING TIME** 2 minutes

2 firm ripe mangoes, to serve

FILLING
2 teaspoons powdered gelatine (see tip)
125 ml (4 fl oz/½ cup) pouring (whipping) cream
450 g (1 lb) cream cheese, at room temperature
300 g (10½ oz) sour cream
110 g (3¾ oz/½ cup) caster (superfine) sugar
½ vanilla bean, split lengthways and seeds scraped
Finely grated zest of 1 lime

BASE
150 g (5½ oz) plain sweet biscuits
80 g (2¾ oz) butter, melted

1 Lightly grease twelve 80 ml (2½ fl oz/⅓ cup) muffin tin holes and line each with three 1 cm (½ inch) wide strips of non-stick baking paper, all crossing in the centre (see tip) *(pic 1)*.

2 To make the filling, put 1 tablespoon water in a small bowl and sprinkle over the gelatine. Leave for 5 minutes to soften. Heat the cream in a small saucepan over low heat until it comes to the boil. Add the gelatine mixture and stir until the gelatine dissolves completely. Remove from the heat and set aside to cool slightly.

3 Meanwhile, to make the base, put the biscuits in a food processor bowl and process to fine crumbs. Add the butter and process until combined. Divide the crumb mixture evenly among the prepared holes and use the base of a small bottle, glass or egg cup to flatten evenly *(pic 2)*. Refrigerate while making the filling. Clean and dry the food processor bowl and blade.

4 Put the cream cheese, sour cream, sugar, vanilla seeds and lime zest in the food processor bowl and process until smooth. With the motor running, add the cream mixture and process until combined. Transfer to a jug, then pour over the bases in the muffin tin holes. Refrigerate for 6 hours or overnight, until the cheesecakes are set.

5 Remove the cheesecakes from the tin by carefully lifting them out using the strips of paper *(pic 3)*.

6 To serve, peel the mangoes and cut off the cheeks. Place the mango cheeks on a board, cut side down, and cut into thin slices, then fan the slices slightly (see page 30). Arrange on top of the cheesecakes and serve.

TIP The powdered gelatine can be replaced with four 2 g (1/15 oz) sheets (gold grade) gelatine. Remove the cheesecakes from the tin as soon as they are set, as the paper strips will soften and break if left for too long.

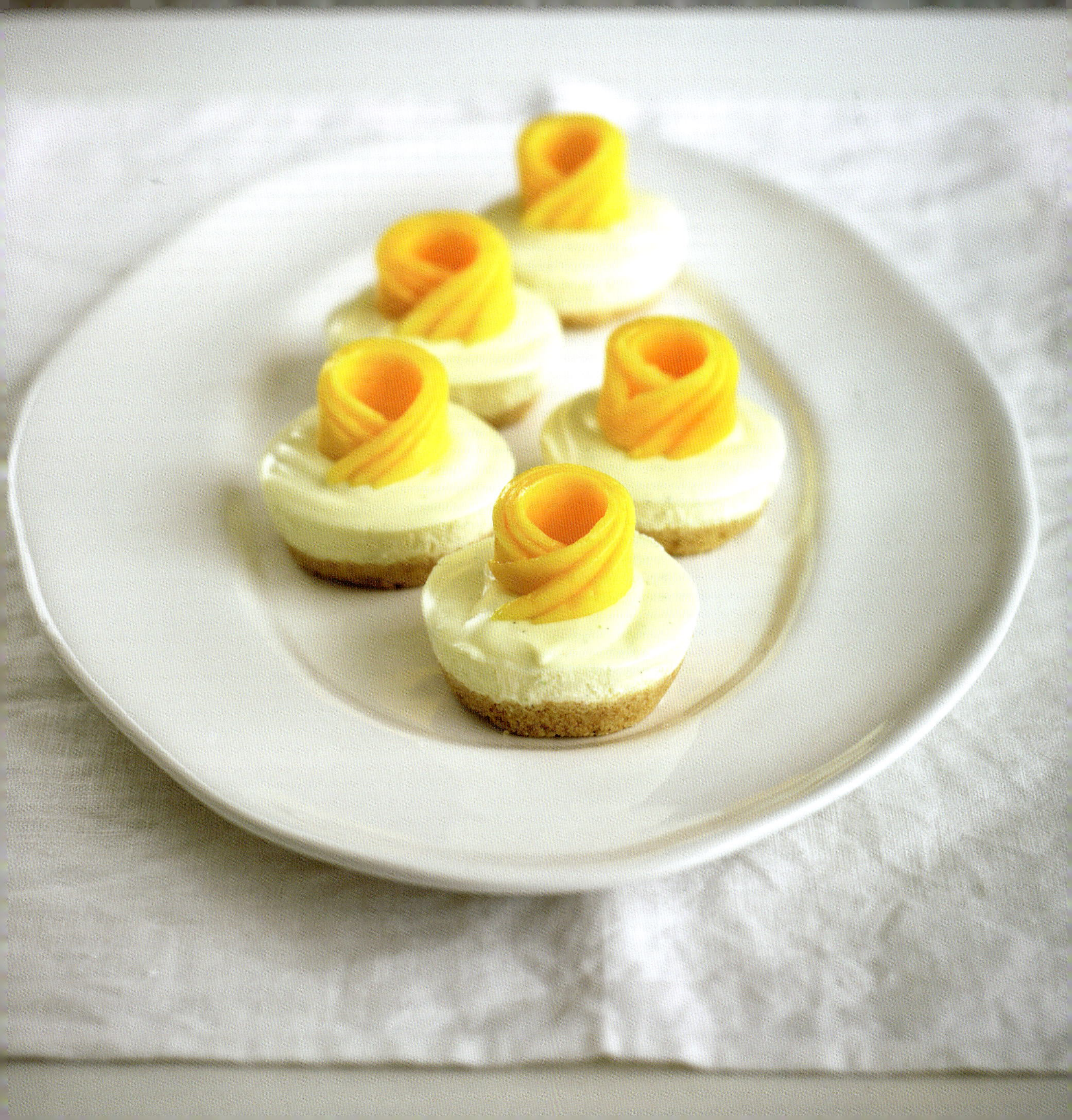

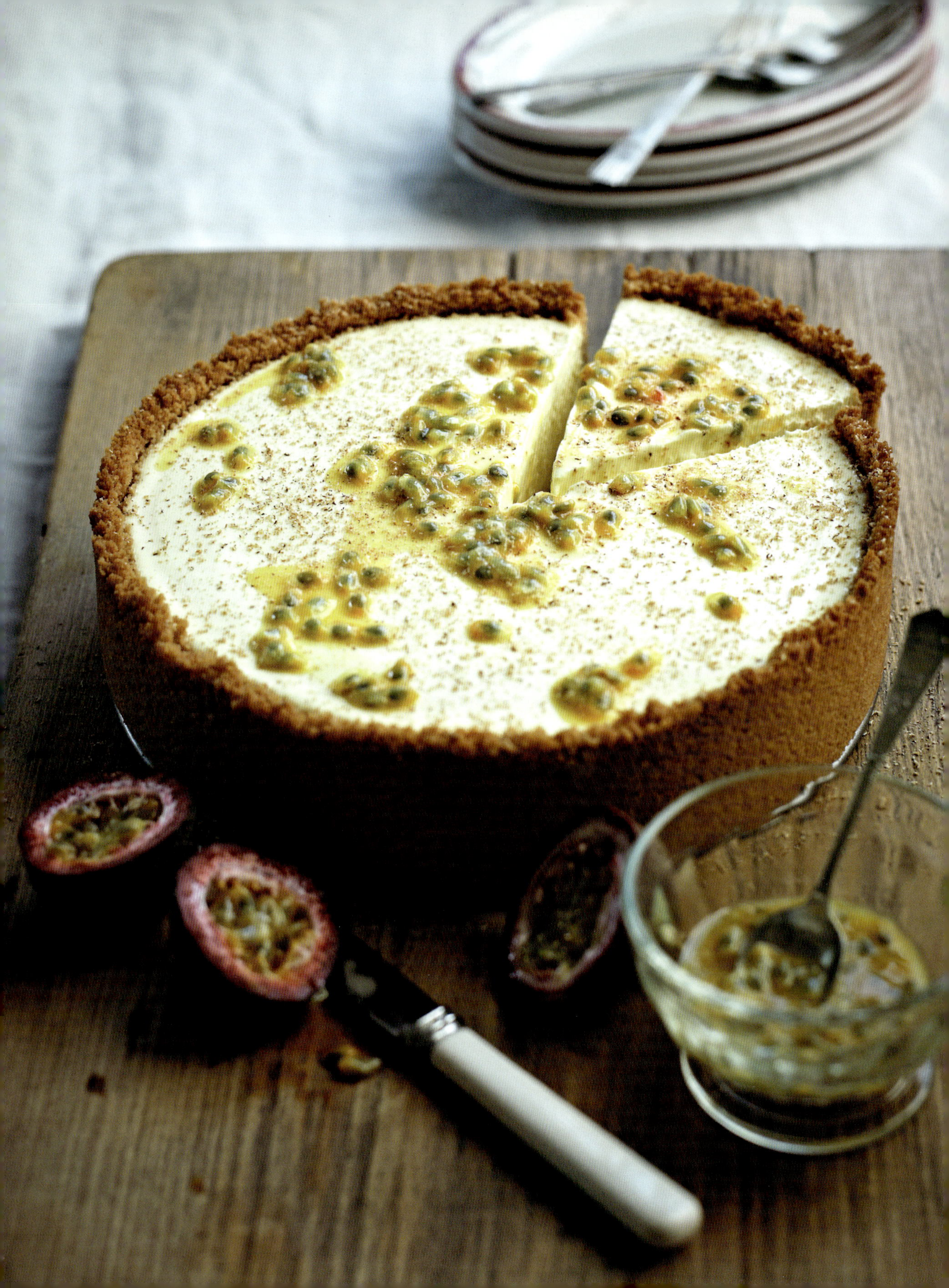

New York cheesecake

Americans adore cheesecakes, especially the version they lay claim to, the New York cheesecake. Creamy, smooth and dense, this style of cheesecake often has a rich sour cream topping.

SERVES 10–12　　**PREPARATION TIME** 30 minutes (+ cooling and overnight chilling)　　**COOKING TIME** 35 minutes

250 g (9 oz) plain sweet biscuits, broken into pieces
100 g (3½ oz) butter, melted
Freshly grated nutmeg, to dust
Passionfruit pulp, to serve

FILLING
750 g (1 lb 10 oz) cream cheese, at room temperature
150 g (5½ oz/⅔ cup) caster (superfine) sugar
2 eggs, at room temperature
1 tablespoon lemon juice

TOPPING
370 g (13 oz/1½ cups) sour cream
2 tablespoons caster (superfine) sugar
¼ teaspoon natural vanilla extract

1 Preheat the oven to 190°C (375°F/Gas 5). Lightly grease a round 23 cm (9 inch) spring-form cake tin.

2 Place the biscuits in a food processor bowl and process to fine crumbs. Add the butter and process until combined. Use a flat-based glass to press the crumb mixture evenly over the base and side of the greased tin, coming 5 cm (2 inches) up the side *(pic 1)*. Refrigerate while making the filling.

3 To make the filling, use an electric mixer to beat the cream cheese and sugar until smooth. Add the eggs, one at a time, beating well after each addition *(pic 2)*. Beat in the lemon juice. Pour the cream cheese mixture over the biscuit base and use a spatula to spread evenly. Bake for 30 minutes or until just set. Remove from the oven and set aside to cool to room temperature.

4 Increase the oven to 220°C (425°F/Gas 7). To make the topping, use an electric mixer to beat the sour cream, sugar and vanilla until smooth *(pic 3)*. Pour over the cooled cheesecake and use a small spatula to spread evenly. Bake for 3 minutes or until glazed and shiny. Transfer to a wire rack and cool completely in the tin. Cover and refrigerate overnight.

5 Dust the top of the cheesecake lightly with nutmeg and spoon over some passionfruit pulp. Serve immediately.

TIP This cheesecake also pairs well with strawberries, sliced banana, thin wedges of plum or a drizzle of honey.

Conversion charts

OVEN TEMPERATURE		
°C	°F	Gas
70	150	¼
100	200	½
110	225	½
120	235	½
130	250	1
140	275	1
150	300	2
160	315	2–3
170	325	3
180	350	4
190	375	5
200	400	6
210	415	6–7
220	425	7
230	450	8
240	475	8
250	500	9

LENGTH	
cm	inches
2 mm	¹⁄₁₆
3 mm	⅛
5 mm	¼
8 mm	⅜
1	½
1.5	⅝
2	¾
2.5	1
3	1¼
4	1½
5	2
6	2½
7	2¾
7.5	3
8	3¼
9	3½
10	4
11	4¼
12	4½
13	5
14	5½
15	6
16	6¼
17	6½
18	7
19	7½
20	8
21	8¼
22	8½
23	9
24	9½
25	10
30	12
35	14
40	16
45	17¾
50	20

WEIGHT	
g	oz
5	⅛
10	¼
15	½
20	¾
30	1
35	1¼
40	1½
50	1¾
55	2
60	2¼
70	2½
80	2¾
85	3
90	3¼
100	3½
115	4
120	4¼
125	4½
140	5
150	5½
175	6
200	7
225	8
250	9
280	10
300	10½
350	12
375	13
400	14
450	1 lb
500	1 lb 2 oz
550	1 lb 4 oz
600	1 lb 5 oz
700	1 lb 9 oz
800	1 lb 12 oz
900	2 lb
1 kg	2 lb 3 oz

LIQUID	
ml	fl oz
30	1
60	2
80	2½
100	3½
125	4
160	5½
185	6
200	7
250	9
300	10½
350	12
375	13
400	14
500	17
600	21
650	22½
700	24
750	26
800	28
1 L	35
1.25 L	44
1.5 L	52

Mastering the Basics: Desserts

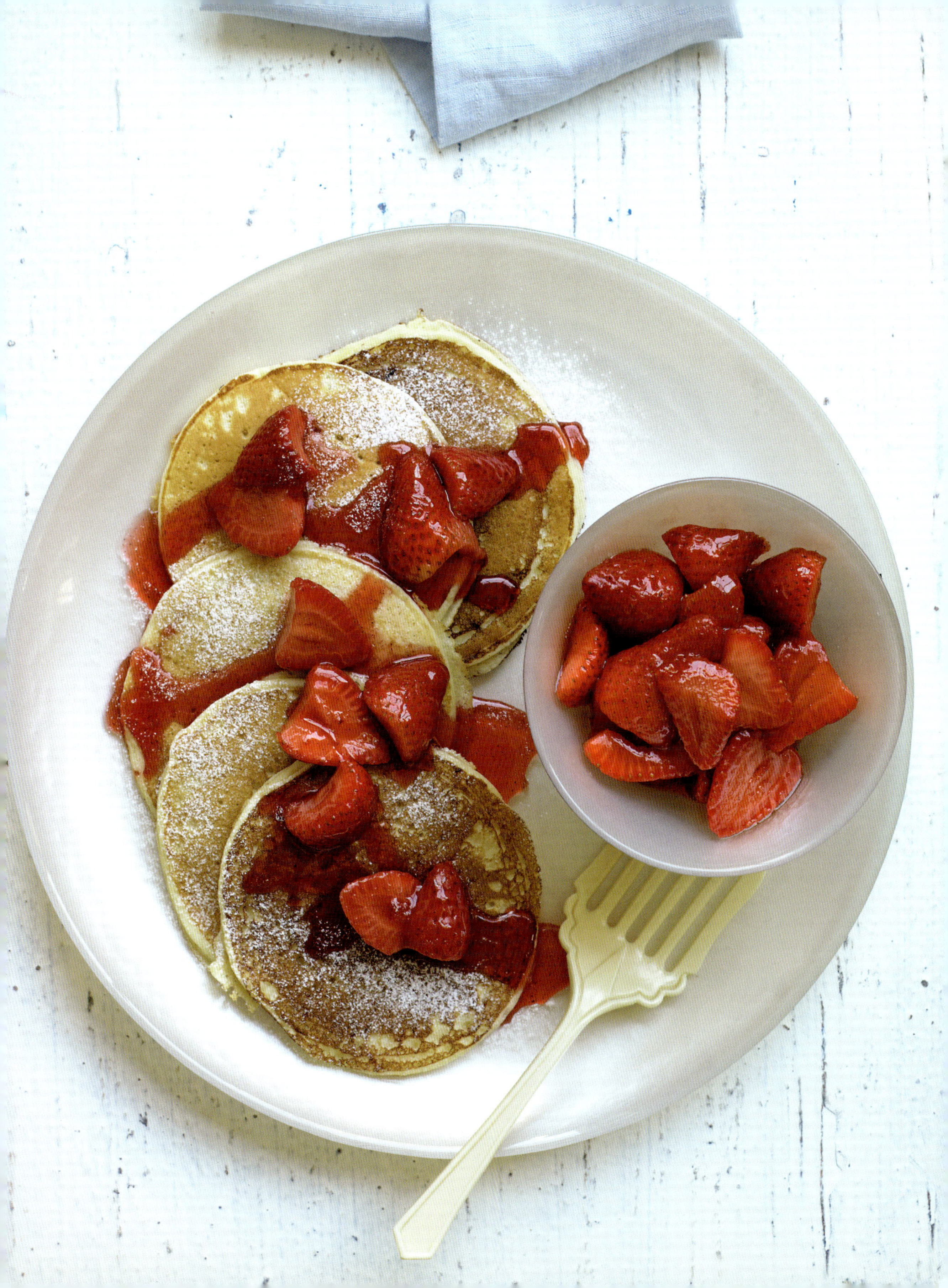

Index

A

almonds
    almond meal, 28
    almond praline, 27
    almond shortcrust pastry, 17
apples
    apple crepes, 42–3
    coring, 76
    rhubarb, apple and strawberry crumble, 64–5
apricot clafoutis, 40–1

B

baked custard, with drunken muscatels, 38–9
bakers' friends, 13
bakeware, 14–15
baking beads, 13
baking trays, 14
banana fritters with lime syrup, 52–3
batters
    apricot clafoutis, 40–1
    banana fritters with lime syrup, 52–3
    ricotta fritters, 46–7
    waffles with chocolate fudge sauce and walnuts, 50–1
    see also crepes; custards
berries
    berry and passionfruit pavlova, 66–7
    berry sundae, 96–7
    crepe cake with berries, 48–9
    freezing and storing, 33
    frosted, 33
    mixed berry fool, 68–9
    see also blueberries; raspberries; strawberries
blind baking, 20–1
blueberries
    crepe cake with, 48–9
    frosted, 33
    mixed berry fool, 68–9
bowls, 12
brandy
    brandied figs, 131
    brandy syrup, 112
    rich brandy sauce, 23
bread and butter pudding, 126–7
brown sugar shortcrust pastry, 17
butter, 10
buttermilk pancakes with strawberry and vanilla compote, 56–7
butterscotch sauce, 22, 139

C

cake testers, 13
cake tins, 14
cakes
    chocolate and strawberry ice-cream, 144–5
    crepe cake with berries, 48–9
    double ginger cake with lime frosting, 142–3
    lemon macaroon and strawberry mousse, 118–19
    see also cheesecakes
candied citrus zest, 34
caramel
    caramel-coated fruits, 27
    créme caramel, 54–5
    making, 26
    pavlovas with caramelised figs, 70–1
    zabaglione with caramelised figs, 80–1
chantilly cream, 22
charlotte
    charlotte moulds, 14
    pear charlotte, 112–13
cheesecakes
    chilled lime and mango, 150–1
    Italian ricotta, with red wine figs, 146–7
    New York, 152–3
    white chocolate and raspberry, 148–9
cherries
    cherry and pistachio parfait, 86–7
    pitting, 76
    syrup, 86
chocolate
    choc-orange mousse, 94
    chocolate and ricotta fritters, 46–7
    chocolate and strawberry ice-cream cake, 144–5
    chocolate cream, 22
    chocolate fondant puddings, 134–5
    chocolate fudge sauce, 22, 51
    chocolate ice cream, 110–11
    chocolate mousse, 94–5
    chocolate self-saucing puddings, 124–5
    dark chocolate mousse, 94–5
    dark chocolate sauce, 22
    decorations, 29
    fudge sauce and walnuts on waffles, 50–1
    making curls and scrolls, 29
    tiramisu, 88–9
    white chocolate and raspberry cheesecake, 148–9
Christmas pudding, steamed, 128–9
cinnamon & vanilla syrup, with poached fruits, 62–3
citrus
    candied citrus zest, 34
    removing zest, 35
    segmenting, 35
    see also lemons; oranges
cocoa powder, 10
coffee
    espresso chocolate mousse, 94
    espresso créme caramel, 55
    tiramisu, 88–9
cold desserts *see* frozen desserts
compote, vanilla and strawberry, 56–7

cream
- chantilly, 22
- chocolate, 22
- crème pâtissière, 23
- fat content, 10
- orange, 22
- passionfruit mousse, 118–19
- rosewater, 22
- vanilla panna cotta with poached plums, 120–1

créme brulée, 58–9
créme caramel, 54–5
créme pâtissière, 23
crepe pans, 13, 44
crepes
- apple, 42–3
- buttermilk pancakes with strawberry and vanilla compote, 56–7
- crepe cake with berries, 48–9
- secrets for success, 44–5

crumble topping, 65
curls, in chocolate, 29
custards
- créme brulée, 58–9
- créme caramel, 54–5
- pouring custard, 22–3
- vanilla baked custard with drunken muscatels, 38–9
- *see also* batters

D

dariole moulds, 14
date puddings, sticky, 138–9
decorations, in chocolate, 29

E

eggs, 10, 80
electric mixers, 12
equipment
- bakeware, 14–15
- cutting and grating, 14–15
- measuring, 12
- mixing, 12
- ovens, 15

espresso *see* coffee

F

figs
- brandied, 131
- mini pavlovas with caramelised figs, 70–1
- red wine, 146
- rice pudding with brandied figs, 130–1
- zabaglione with caramelised figs, 80–1

flambéd pineapple, 82–3
flan tins, 14–15
flour, 10
food processors, 12, 18
fool, mixed berry, 68–9
fritters *see* batters
frosted fruits, 33
frozen desserts
- berry sundae, 96–7
- cherry and pistachio parfait, 86–7
- lemon gelato, 90–1
- making, by hand, 99
- mango sorbet, 104–5
- names of, 98
- peach ripple semifreddo, 100–1
- raspberry and vanilla vacherin, 102–3
- storing, 99
- strawberry frozen yoghurt, 106–7
- watermelon and rosewater granita, 92–3
- *see also* ice cream

frozen yoghurt, 98, 106–7
fruits
- caramel-coated, 27
- frosted, 33
- pan-fried stone fruit, 74–5
- peeling stone fruit, 32
- poached fruits, 62–3, 78–9, 120–1
- preparing, 30–1, 32–3, 35, 76–7
- tropical fruit salad, 72–3
- *see also* names of specific fruits

frying pans, 13
fudge sauce, chocolate, 22, 51

G

gelatine
- characteristics of, 10
- powdered versus leaf, 116
- softening and melting, 116
- unmoulding desserts, 117

gelato, lemon, 90–1
ginger cake, double, with lime frosting, 142–3
golden syrup
- golden syrup pudding with custard, 132–3
- uses of, 10

granita
- characteristics, 98
- watermelon and rosewater, 92–3

graters, 14

H

hazelnuts
- hazelnut meal, 28
- praline, 27
- skinning, 28

honey, 10

I

ice cream
- chocolate, 110–11
- chocolate and strawberry ice-cream cake, 144–5
- ice-cream machines, 12–13, 98
- making, by hand, 98
- *see also* frozen desserts

ice desserts *see* frozen desserts
ingredients, common, 10–11
Italian ricotta cheesecake with red wine figs, 146–7

K

kitchen blowtorch, 13
knives, 14

L

lemongrass and lime syrup, 73
lemons
- lemon gelato, 90–1

Index **157**

lemon macaroon and strawberry
    mousse cake, 118–19
making zest, 34–5
raspberry and lemon soufflés, 136–7
removing zest, 35
limes
    chilled lime and mango
        cheesecakes, 150–1
    lemongrass and lime syrup, 73
    lime frosting, 142
    lime syrup, 52
loose-based tins, 14

M

mangoes
    chilled lime and mango
        cheesecakes, 150–1
    mango sorbet, 104–5
    preparing, 30–1
measuring cups, 12
measuring equipment, 12
measuring jugs, 12
measuring spoons, 12
meringue
    berry and passionfruit pavlova,
        66–7
    lemon macaroon and strawberry
        mousse cake, 118–19
    mini pavlovas with caramelised figs,
        70–1
    raspberry and vanilla vacherin,
        102–3
    secrets for success, 24
milk, 10
mixed berry fool, 68–9
mixing equipment, 12–13
moulds
    charlotte, 14
    dariole, 14
mousse
    chocolate, 94–5
    dark chocolate, 94–5
    lemon macaroon and strawberry
        mousse cake, 118–19
    passionfruit, 118–19
    strawberry, 118

muffin tins, 14
muscatels, drunken, 38–9

N

nectarines, 74
New York cheesecake, 152–3
nuts
    making nut meal, 28
    toasting, 28
    see also hazelnuts; pistachios

O

oil, 10
oranges
    candied zest, 34
    choc-orange mousse, 94
    orange cream, 22
    orange crème caramel, 55
    segmenting, 35
oven temperature, 15
oven thermometers, 13
ovenproof dishes, 14
ovens, 15

P

palette knives, 13
pan-fried stone fruit, 74–5
    pancakes see crepes
panna cotta, vanilla, with poached
    plums, 120–1
parfait, 86–7, 98
passionfruit
    berry and passionfruit pavlova,
        66–7
    passionfruit mousse, 118–19
pastry brushes, 13
pastry cream, 23
pastry making
    basics, 16–17
    blind baking, 20–1
    in a food processor, 18
    pâte sucrée, 16–17
    rolling out, 18–19
    sweet shortcrust, 16–17
pâte sucrée, 16–17
    pavlova see meringue

peaches
    pan-fried stone fruit, 74–5
    peach ripple semifreddo, 100–1
pears
    coring, 76
    pear charlotte, 112–13
    poached in red wine, 78–9
pie tins, 14–15
pineapple
    flambéd, 82–3
    preparing, 77
pistachios
    berry sundae, 96–7
    cherry and pistachio parfait, 86–7
plums
    pan-fried, 74
    poached, with vanilla panna cotta,
        120–1
poached fruits
    pears poached in red wine, 78–9
    poached summer fruits in vanilla
        cinnamon syrup, 62–3
    vanilla panna cotta with poached
        plums, 120–1
pomegranate, removing seeds, 77
praline
    hazelnut, 27
    making, 27
pudding basins, 15
puddings
    bread and butter, 126–7
    chocolate fondant, 134–5
    chocolate self-saucing, 124–5
    golden syrup, with custard, 132–3
    rice, with brandied figs, 130–1
    steamed Christmas, 128–9
    sticky date, 138–9

Q

quinces, coring, 76

R

ramekins, 14
raspberries
    berry sundae, 96–7
    crepe cake with, 48–9

frosted, 33
mixed berry fool, 68–9
raspberry and lemon soufflés, 136–7
raspberry and vanilla vacherin, 102–3
white chocolate and raspberry cheesecake, 148–9
redcurrants, frosted, 33
rhubarb, apple and strawberry crumble, 64–5
rice pudding with brandied figs, 130–1
ricotta
    Italian ricotta cheesecake with red wine figs, 146–7
    ricotta fritters, 46–7
rolling pins, 13
rosewater
    rosewater cream, 22
    watermelon and rosewater granita, 92–3
rum crème caramel, 55

S

saucepans, 13
sauces
    butterscotch, 22, 139
    chocolate fudge, 22
    dark chocolate, 22
    raspberry, 97
    rich brandy, 23
scales, 12
scrolls, in chocolate, 29
self-saucing puddings, 124–5
semifreddo
    characteristics, 98
    peach ripple semifreddo, 100–1
shards, in chocolate, 29
shortcrust pastry
    almond, 17
    brown sugar, 17
    making in a food processor, 18
    sweet, 16–17, 18
sieves, 13
sorbets
    characteristics, 98
    mango sorbet, 104–5

soufflé, raspberry and lemon, 136–7
sour cream, 10
spatulas, 13
spoons
    large metal, 13
    measuring, 12
    wooden, 13
spring-form tins, 15
stand mixers, 12
sticky date puddings, 138–9
stone fruit
    pan-fried, 74–5
    peeling, 32
strawberries
    chocolate and strawberry ice-cream cake, 144–5
    crepe cake with, 48–9
    frosted, 33
    lemon macaroon and strawberry mousse cake, 118–19
    mixed berry fool, 68–9
    rhubarb, apple and strawberry crumble, 64–5
    strawberry and vanilla compote, 56–7
    strawberry frozen yoghurt, 106–7
    strawberry mousse, 118
sugar, 10
sweet shortcrust pastry, 16–17, 18
syrups
    brandy, 112
    cherry, 86
    golden, 10
    lemongrass and lime, 73
    lime, 52–3
    vanilla cinnamon syrup, 62–3

T

thickened cream, 10
tins
    pie and tart (flan), 14–15
    spring-form, 15
tiramisu, 88–9
trifle, tipsy, 108–9
tropical fruit salad, 72–3

V

vacherin, raspberry and vanilla, 102–3
vanilla
    forms of, 10
    poached summer fruits in vanilla cinnamon syrup, 62–3
    raspberry and vanilla vacherin, 102–3
    strawberry and vanilla compote, 56–7
    vanilla baked custard with drunken muscatels, 38–9
    vanilla panna cotta with poached plums, 120–1

W

waffles with chocolate fudge sauce and walnuts, 50–1
walnuts and fudge sauce, on waffles, 50–1
watermelon and rosewater granita, 92–3
whipping cream, 10
whisks, 13, 44
white chocolate and raspberry cheesecake, 148–9
wine
    pears poached in red wine, 78–9
    red wine figs, 146
wooden spoons, 13

Y

yoghurt, frozen, strawberry, 106–7

Z

zabaglione with caramelised figs, 80–1
zest, citrus, 34, 35

Published in 2013 by Murdoch Books, an imprint of Allen & Unwin.

Murdoch Books Australia
83 Alexander Street
Crows Nest NSW 2065
Phone: +61 (0) 2 8425 0100
Fax: +61 (0) 2 9906 2218
www.murdochbooks.com.au
info@murdochbooks.com.au

Murdoch Books UK
Erico House, 6th Floor
93–99 Upper Richmond Road
Putney, London SW15 2TG
Phone: +44 (0) 20 8785 5995
Fax: +44 (0) 20 8785 5985
www.murdochbooks.co.uk
info@murdochbooks.co.uk

For Corporate Orders & Custom Publishing contact
Noel Hammond, National Business Development Manager,
Murdoch Books Australia

Publisher: Anneka Manning
Designers: Susanne Geppert and Robert Polmear
Photographers: Louise Lister, Julie Renouf, George Seper, Jared Fowler
Stylists: Kate Nixon, Marie-Hélénè Clauzon, Jane Hann, Cherise Koch
Recipe Development: Sonia Greig, Leanne Kitchen, Cathie Lonnie, Anneka Manning, Lucy Nunes
Home Economists: Grace Campbell, Dixie Elliot, Joanne Glynn, Caroline Jones, Sharon Kennedy, Lucy Lewis, Sabine Spindler Allan Wilson
Production Manager: Karen Small

Text and Design © Murdoch Books 2013
Photography © Louise Lister and Murdoch Books 2013

All rights reserved. No part of this publication may be reproduced, stored in a retrieval system or transmitted in any form or by any means, electronic, mechanical, photocopying, recording or otherwise, without the prior written permission of the publisher.

A cataloguing-in-publication entry is available from the catalogue of the National Library of Australia at www.nla.gov.au.

A catalogue record for this book is available from the British Library.

Printed by 1010 Printing International Limited, China

The Publisher and stylist would like to thank Breville (www.breville.com.au) for lending equipment for use and photography.

IMPORTANT: Those who might be at risk from the effects of salmonella poisoning (the elderly, pregnant women, young children and those suffering from immune deficiency diseases) should consult their doctor with any concerns about eating raw eggs.

OVEN GUIDE: You may find cooking times vary depending on the oven you are using. For fan-forced ovens, as a general rule, set the oven temperature to 20°C (35°F) lower than indicated in the recipe.

MEASURES GUIDE: We have used 20 ml (4 teaspoon) tablespoon measures. If you are using a 15 ml (3 teaspoon) tablespoon add an extra teaspoon of the ingredient for each tablespoon specified.